THEATRE  AND EVERYDAY LIFE

THEATRE AND EVERYDAY LIFE

An ethics of performance

Alan Read

London and New York

First published 1993
by Routledge
11 New Fetter Lane, London EC4P 4EE

Simultaneously published in the USA and Canada
by Routledge
29 West 35th Street, New York, NY 10001

© 1993 Alan Read

First published in paperback
by Routledge, 1995

Phototypeset in 10 on 12 point Garamond by
Intype, London
Printed in Great Britain by
T.J. Press (Padstow) Ltd., Padstow, Cornwall

British Library Cataloguing in Publication Data
Read, Alan
Theatre and Everyday Life: An Ethics of
Performance
I. Title
792.01

Library of Congress Cataloguing in Publication Data
Read, Alan
Theatre and everyday life: an ethics of performance / Alan Read.
p.   cm.
Includes bibliographical references and index.
1. Theater—Philosophy.   2. Theater and society.   I. Title.
PN2039.R38   1992
792'.01—dc20   92–11913

ISBN 0–415–06941–6 (pbk)

For Beryl Robinson
and our daughter
Florence Ruby Read

CONTENTS

PREFACE

Theatre and everyday life cannot be taken for granted. The one depends on the other for what it can do. This book is about the possibilities of both and the recreation of one through the other.

Theatre is not one thing it is many, and its practice demands the reinvention of criticism that grows in and around it. For example, the empty space in which theatre was said to happen always had a population. *There* is the quotidian from which theatre might learn new stories and ways of speaking surprisingly close to home.

I consider theatre to be an almost infinitely redefinable arrangement of human expressions which are conscious, physical, verbal and witnessed. Each of these operations, this book aims to show, are contingent upon what is culturally perceived as 'everyday life'. Theatre, by definition, is not this daily domain but an extra-daily dimension, beyond the everyday but ironically dependent on the everyday realm. It is the continual negotiation between theatre and its ground, performance and the quotidian, that critical theory has considerable problems in evaluating, if not explaining. This is damaging to a theatre which seeks new audiences among old acquaintances.

This book examines a problem and a hypothesis which derive from this starting point. The theatre is a heterogeneous practice and lacks a critical language which can deal with such variety. An experiential and conceptual understanding of everyday life reintroduces the contexts of theatre in more subtle and varied ways than theatre thinking currently allows.

The idea that theory and practice, common sense and judgement are interdependent underlies this argument. To understand everyday life not just as lived daily experience, that is talking, walking, dwelling, cooking and reading, but as a critical concept which derives from these quotidian practices, provides a perspective from which to understand theatre. Everyday life is after all the habitual world which would appear to differ most greatly from theatre. And yet it provides the context in all cultures from which theatre arises and distinguishes itself.

Regarding theatre from within the perspective of everyday life allows for the formulation of concepts to interpret and judge theatre without seeing it as separate from other daily activities with which it always shares certain relations. This relation between theatre and its everyday context is important to maintain if theory is to have any credibility or meaning for theatre and the places in which it occurs.

This book aims to make the critical discussion of theatre and everyday life possible. The Introduction reconsiders a number of common arguments about theatre and challenges theories applied to theatre which conceal the everyday. 'Lay Theatre' describes some practices of theatre undertaken in a neighbourhood and the ways in which they derived from the everyday life of that locality. 'Regarding Theatre' is an attempt to move beyond a critical theory dominated by vision and questions how what one experiences in theatre is related to knowledge and belief. 'Everyday Life' places these questions of ethics, poetics and politics within the context of the quotidian and traces some examples of practices and writings of the everyday. The second part of the book, 'Nature Theatre Culture', leads theatre back through its recent history to the commonplaces from which it emerged and articulates how this history has made theatre what it is today.

ACKNOWLEDGEMENTS

I am grateful to Helena Reckitt who commissioned this book for Rout-ledge and to Talia Rodgers who has brought it to publication. David Slater introduced me to the theatre and everyday life of south-east London and I valued working alongside him, also Ann Cleary, Fiona Graham and Teresa Watkins who worked with me there. Peter Hulton at Dartington College of Arts gave me the opportunity to work on three projects which influenced my thinking about theatre: editing the monographs *Theatre Papers*, coordinating a European Workshop on theatre and communities and directing Rotherhithe Theatre Workshop. Robert Egan at the University of Washington expected critical theory to be part of theatre practice, and Barry Witham and Jack Wolcott supported my post-graduate research. Dorinda Hulton and John Rudlin at Exeter University asked me to rethink what theatre could be, and Roger Collinson and Jeff Winslow first intro-duced me to theatre. Ernst Behler, Paul Feyerabend, Joseph Roach and Beryl Robinson each made critical contributions to the writing of this book though none is responsible for its limitations.

I value the discussions I have had with: Ric Allsopp, Ellen Donkin, Tony Dunn, Paul Greenhalgh, Mine Kaylan, Lois Keidan, Colette King, Hayo Krombach, Deborah Levy, John Lutterbie, Claire MacDonald, John Munford, Andrea Phillips, Joanna Scanlan, Chris Shore, Mara de Wit; the friendship of: Oriana Baddeley, Ramsay Cameron, Eduard Delgado, Mary Dodwell, Kevin Finnan, Graham Fitkin, Michael and Bairbre Ford, Ewan Forster, Ronnie Goodman, David Graver, Sadie Hennessy, Tony Humphreys, Mary and Stephen Keynes, Stephen Lowe, Anthony Malinowski, Hans Man In't Veld, Ciaran McIntyre, Nienke Meeter, Tania Myers, Chris Polatch, Debra Reay, Kathleen Reedy, Heather and Chris Stevens, Sally Weale; the assistance of: the Ateneu Barcelonès, the Trustees of the Mass Observation Archive, Nina Evans at The British Library, Montserrat Alvarez at the Theatre Institute Barcelona, Liz Fugate at the University of Washington Library, and Lucy Neal and Rose de Wend Fenton at the London International Festival of Theatre; the contribution of: Simon Josebury, Markéta Luskačová, Virginia Myers; and the support of my family especially my grandparents Bernard and Florence Cody; Claire, Jenny, Teresa and Mark Critcher; and my mother Veronica Read.

Every day, which gave rise to this work, was shared with Beryl Robinson to whom this book is dedicated. Every day is now shared with our daughter, Florence.

INTRODUCTION

Is the theatre good? A reply is likely to come back: 'That is not the point, the question is what does it mean?' But here I want to reassert the value of theatre in order not to leave it to those who least care for it. Anyone who has made theatre will point to a difficult truism that appears to diffuse the possibility of criticism: that theatre is always as good as it can be, given what is available to it at any one time or place. But though theatre might be said to be beyond good and evil, theoretical relativism is an inadequate response to its practices. Irrespective of the postponement of value judgements by those who make theatre, responsibility for its future is assumed by those who least often make it, have least competence in it and most authority over it. The question I begin with is therefore an ethical one. Can theatre have value divorced from everyday life? Everyday life is the meeting ground for all activities associated with being human – work, play, friendship and the need to communicate, which includes the expressions of theatre. Everyday life is thus full of potential – it is the 'everyday' which habitually dulls sense of life's possibilities. Theatre, when it is good, enables us to know the everyday in order better to live everyday life.

Theatre is worthwhile because it is antagonistic to official views of reality. It derives equal sustenance from theory and practice, common sense and judgement, everyday life and the specialisms and techniques of expression. In the absence of an aesthetics and ethics which take account of these peculiarities from within theatre, political demands are imposed from outside. These impositions become the common focus of debate in and around theatre and often reflect back on the theatre in cyclical hyperbole: 'Theatre in Crisis' is a common call to arms. But the terms of the debate are set from without by a complex of assumptions concerning theatre's relations to other cultural practices, let alone everyday life. If theatre is critical of life, everyday life is critical of theatre. Critical disciplines removed from the everyday to establish their authority over this problematic domain cannot accept this simple dialectic. Outmoded forms of reference such as 'political theatre' and 'community arts' limit thought

1

to partitioned realms which have very little to do with the complexity of real contexts. These partitions not only patronise practitioners who well understand the ambivalent nature of their work, but worse, dictate boundaries to users of theatre, audiences, which are quite puerile in their simplifications. The reason for placing theatre and everyday life in a single title lies here. While the two might appear to suggest a binary opposition, examining both more closely reasserts the need to think not of an inside or outside of theatre but the way theatre is in dialectical relation to the quotidian. It is not sufficient to address the 'politics of theatre' alone, the structures of funding, arts policies and jurisdictions, but in a remedial act, a practice which combines poetics and ethics, rethink what the theatre and its politics might be. Regarding theatre then means to look at its practice and history to ascertain what warrants criticism before that responsibility is assumed elsewhere. There are sufficient purveyors of official views of reality to make this a worthwhile act. Criticism is critical because good theatre has an invaluable role to play in disarming the tyrannies of the everyday.

An evaluation of performance and the quotidian takes as its object the neglected and the undocumented, reviewing the unwritten theatre in a local network of work and recreation. There seems little need of more writing about already well documented theatres and exhaustively profiled personnel. Between the neighbourhood and its daily life the practices to be articulated are ones which have escaped the professional and the prominent. This is a profane theatre, a discreet and little documented domain of operations which circulate between the most habitual daily activity and the most overt theatrical manifestations distanced but never fatally removed from that everyday world. The problem immediately emerges as to how I can address the ethics and poetics of this theatre within the parameters of a secular and political criticism. What I write is secular in the sense that it does not aim to mystify the origins and effects of practices which themselves already have more or less logic. Both theatre and everyday life can be made to seem mysterious and it has been the prerogative of professionals to sustain this mystery while apparently deconstructing it. Professionalism after all depends on mystery for its role as translator and interpreter of all that is hidden from the unqualified. At the same time the simple is only ever the complex simplified and not to take seriously the mysteries of theatre and everyday life is to consign both to a habitual domain beyond the capacity for change and improvement.

If theatre does not happen in an empty space, what does? Everyday life – the demands of which pose ethical, poetic and political questions to theatre on its arrival. Ethics is relevant because I have to ask the question how people can live and work together, while valuing the difference between people and accounting for justice in society. A poetics is necessary to ascertain the internal mechanics of theatre, what I mean by theatre and

2

how it produces its effects. Politics are already imbued in these positions because theatre and its thought are possible only within a *polis*, different cultures have different politics that give rise to different theatres with more or less freedom, and theatre's relevance and innovation are contingent upon such variable political perspectives. A philosophy of theatre worth its salt starts from these premises and that debate takes up the first part of this book. A philosophy of theatre is not 'the philosophy of theatre'. It is proposed as one contribution to an enquiry which is in progress on many fronts simultaneously, embracing theoretical fields as widespread as aesthetics and anthropology and practical operations as diverse as musicals and marriages.

Questioning dogmatic positions does not unthinkingly embrace every possible alternative. There is a responsibility to revise and renew those sources from which theatre thinking has historically arisen and to imagine new sources from which it might yet come. This is the project I undertake in the second part of the book, and although it could be read first it is as well to know what I consider theatre to be before approaching new ways to think its history. Here it is the practice of theatre that most interests me and the ways in which criticism of texts can provide ways of regarding theatre within its historical context. Criticism is not explanation, though explanation sometimes precedes it. Criticism is a systematic evaluation which requires judgement and implies the existence of standards. Judgement is a word which carries threatening overtones. But everyday life is the domain where the power associated with the term is finally reckoned with and everyday life would simply not exist if action consequent upon judgement were not undertaken every moment of the day. Play, no less than work, requires continual judgement and it is not adequate to trivialise its importance to theatre. The relevance, or even existence, of standards has been radically questioned, yet today they reimpose themselves just as commonly as always, and with even less involvement from the practitioners whom they most affect. From the pedagogy of theatre to the performer's obituary, via the critic and the arts mandarin, there is a continual negotiation of what constitutes an 'acceptable standard'. What follows reiterates the importance of excellence, the need for theatre to be good, but questions the traditional foundation of these conditions of recognition and the way such traditions determine public opinion outside their own limited domain. Criticism and history are thus bound as the latter dictates the parameters and effects of the former.

But why write about theatre in this way, now? There are clearly both opportunities for radical development and conservative retrenchment in the arts. It is rare for there to be simply one or the other, despite the inevitable quarrels between generations, and now there is evidence of as complex a combination of these forces as in other times. The words used to describe 'now' give an indication of this cultural complexity. Industrial cultures have been described as living through a 'post-industrial' age, 'the end of the mechanical age', while the term post-Fordism has been used to describe the prevalence of flexible production systems themselves. The 'society of the spectacle', and 'postmodernism' describe associated states from a cultural perspective where confidence in progress has dissolved and the industrial has given way to the ephemeral: to services, tourism, communications proliferation and invisible earnings and finance. If 'All that is solid melts into air' what is left for a theatre that trades on the transience of images, the passing of actors from the presence of an audience? Is not the impermanence of theatre destined to dematerialise along with other information codes on the air, be subsumed within communications in general and television in particular? There is after all no *a priori* value that theatre holds over television, not even its ability to stimulate group response, and neither does it have any generic right to the power and effects of the live medium, as the diversity and physicality of contemporary music has demonstrated.

While the architectural solidity of certain theatre buildings steadfastly refuses the impermanence of their trade, in the shadow of these theatres there continues to be innovation and experiment. It is this theatre I take as my object in this book. I am reluctant to name this theatre mistrusting the connotations preordained categories bring and the innovative possibilities they exclude. It is not fringe theatre, community theatre or educational theatre. It can incorporate the characteristics of all, or none, of these generic forms at any one time. Because it is a theatre resistant to official views of reality it is not possible to describe it with the language of that officialdom. This theatre is peopled, in its performers and audiences, by those with a deep resistance to theatre traditions as academic, who reinterpret and return these traditions to the theatre where they belonged, to the frontiers of everyday life. This theatre has drawn voraciously on the urban experience, the televisual and filmic, the fine art tradition and cabaret, the novel and pedestrian experience, the quotidian. The place this theatre has traded its wares is the street, the factory, the school, the prison, the farm: in fact almost anywhere including the most solid of theatre buildings I have described. As though it was never genetically suited to the architecture on offer this theatre has spawned a rash of 'new' theatre architecture to house its aspirations. In this act it follows the theatre in the round, the community centre, the black box, the experimental space, all of which had been thrown up by previous 'revolutions' in reaction both to the architecture of the past and the theatre contained therein. The 'fringe' was not named as such at the beginning of these developments in Britain but soon became both a home for the alternative and a margin to the centre, confirming the geographical and economic status of the mainstream which commanded the central pedestrian axes of the city. Currently there is renewed experiment internationally with 'non-theatre' spaces, significantly the architecture of the industrial period, reconditioned for a 'new theatre to meet a new public'. New theatre there may well be, but the identity of the audience continues to confirm the suspicion that the 'old public' is simply willing to travel further to see what it has always wanted – good theatre. Nevertheless the Old Museum of Transport in Glasgow, the Gaswerk in Copenhagen, the Cartoucherie in Paris, the Mercat de les Flors in Barcelona mark a shift from the attempt to purpose build for the future, rather, in the spirit of bricolage, resiting from the past. Ironically theatre comes home to roost in places where the transport, technology, munitions and decoration of the everyday, trams, power, arms and flowers, were once fashioned. Where something was once made, serviced, detonated and sold, the simulacrum has taken hold.

So, theatre may be many things but it is not for my purposes a building. By the end of the book I will return to places of performance and how they pre-empt what theatre can be. But for now I consider theatre to be a process of building between performers and their constituencies which employs the medium of images to convey feeling and meaning. While traditional theatre buildings might provide heat and light for this exchange, they also serve to solidify this process as institution and representation. Institution because of the stratified and organised nature of the process of witness that entering buildings inevitably entails, particularly where such buildings are recognised as conventional theatre spaces. Representation because of the expectation that entry to such buildings brings with it: one of Classical mimesis, truth to life, the fourth and invisible wall and the myriad conventions of the theatre that permeate its identity. This serves to remind us that theatre is a public act and one which is unlikely to relieve itself of the institutional conditioning that fashions all such societal formations. These are also precisely the features which attract many to the theatre as a 'good night out'. And why not?

It would be churlish to deny these features, yet irresponsible to accept them uncritically as determinants of theatre in general, or somehow essential to theatre or its future. It is after all these expectations which have been addressed already and enduringly by theatre practitioners. From the proliferation of dance forms to physical theatres, environmental work drawing on the site-specific tradition of sculpture, to carnival forms derived from localised calendar events, the inadequacy of the categories describing the work underestimates the imperative they share to move beyond the 'mimetic', to the 'cathartic'. And this continuing provocation to tradition occurs at the end of a century which has already seen a succession of transformations in theatre forms and contents. There is a veritable explosion of expressive forms developing in and around the rubric of theatre in direct reciprocation to their apparent loss from the everyday. This proliferation of performance stretches theatre's limits of definition and does nothing to deny the possibility that theatre continues to be 'a good night out'.

It is the dialectic between these traditions and conventions and the challenges of contemporary work that characterise theatre's dynamic. Each of these traditions and conventions has given rise to the radical experiments that depart from them. Speaking about theatre 'now', as well as using words which at different times have meant the same thing, 'modern', 'contemporary' and 'new', reminds us that innovation is always contingent upon a boundary waiting to be transgressed. There is of course no modernism without an attendant and pre-emptive realism.[1] The whole dynamic of arts practice derives from its evolution and internal coherence set off against former traditions and movements, habits and customs. Without this context criticism would be impossible. The problem now with such an internal dialogue of forms is that it simply fails to communicate anything outside its own codes and significations. Criticism no longer speaks out so much as in. This book asserts that it is no longer an option to be against interpretation and evaluation. It is only through evaluation that the public responsibility of criticism is established. In a period when pastiche in art and architecture gave rise to the term postmodernism, in places where television advertising trades off the internal coherence of its own history with adverts within adverts, the theatre of reaction cannot distinguish itself from the play of images in the street, on the tube, in the home. Theatre answers back but adrift from everyday life, divorced by disciplinary neatness or cultural engineering, fails to reach new audiences beyond the accidental tourist.

The only thing that can distinguish theatre now is an ethical stance. An ethics of performance is an essential feature of any philosophy and practice of theatre. Without it a set of cultural practices which derive from a very specific arrangement of power relations between people are unhinged from responsibility to those people. That might be a fashionable view but one which the following has to contest if only to ask the question which remained a preoccupation to the present century, that is, what is good about theatre? Theatre after all contributes to an idea of social or public good the best organisation of which should be the central debate of a public politics. Theatre's narratives, however disjunct through aesthetic experiment, always offer alternative realities and insights to the everyday, and those who make theatre are for better or worse paid a certain respect and sometimes achieve the status of exemplary figures. Good theatre stands face to face with its audience. Where theatre has been able to do this it has changed lives and histories. Where it hasn't it has imaginatively impoverished itself and its audience. This claim has nothing to do with a 'religious' morality of dogmatic 'oughts', but is derived from a reconsideration of the 'ethical' as a means to locate and interrogate the social determinants of cultural theory and practice. Given the confusions which surround the status of the 'social' in that theory, it is important that the question of ethics should be reassessed. Ethical concerns after all have important things to say about the relations between people that bear more than a passing resemblance to theatre. Yet I am also aware of the ideological problems that such a proposal brings in its wake. An ethics of performance does not validate any arguments for censorship. An ethical theatre cannot be produced in the purpose-built design of another time. It can only be built as a response, and with a responsibility, to its traditions with constant attention to a vocabulary drawn from the frontier disciplines that press upon its borders, new ways of describing the problematics of place, aesthetic value and audience that are central to its continued existence.

These disciplines are ways of thinking about the world that have demonstrated explanatory potential when applied to theatre practices. Anthropology, semiotics and psychoanalytic theory have all provided insights as to the shared characteristics of a diversity of theatre forms, and how and why theatre is a quite distinct activity from other art forms and everyday life. What is *critical* about these approaches is less clear, though each in distinct ways has offered alternatives to current practices, and by implication valued another way of doing things. The problem is that each other way, whether it be the revelation that societies are theatrical, retain ritual, or that personalities dramatise interaction, leaves little imprint on anything but the remotest corners of the theatre's operations, not to mention everyday life. The lack of an ethics of performance, the ethical implications of theatre and its effects, has compounded this effortless marginality. This is an important reservation when wishing to ascertain what is good about the theatre and how judgement of its qualities is to be conducted in anything but the margins. For instance, to take a concrete example, in the case of an anthropology of theatre the critical task might not be to domesticate the exotic but to exoticise the domestic.[2] As Henri Lefebvre said of everyday life: 'the fundamental question would be to grasp a certain quality, difficult to define and yet essential and concrete, something that "just a quarter-of-an-hour alone" with a man from a distant culture would reveal to us.'[3] The ritual enquiries of theatre anthropology have enriched the possibilities of what is considered part of the theatre field, but as field work, have left to some degree, the domestic to the sociologist and the statistician. The nature of the domestic is chameleon in the sense that the theatre maker is often not of the place of performance, knows little about it in a geographical or historical sense and less about its emotional qualities. This 'lack' is an ethical concern with very specific cultural consequences. Ethos after all derives from the sense of 'being at home' and to deny this propensity for the theatre maker would not appear to me to be an encouraging start for a theatre philosophy. The local and particular are as demanding of consideration now as the cosmopolitan. They are closest to the everyday, are less easy to extrapolate from their context and less easy to bring 'home' to be studied. This difficulty does not make them more interesting but demands considerable investment on the part of any theatre concerned enough to look beyond its own imported context. 'Being there' and 'being here' are no longer so easy to define. Being here and critical is as urgent a project as looking elsewhere, though does not deny those who are elsewhere. Obviously 'being here' depends on where 'here' is. If it is a place where cultural capital accumulates it provides a departure point for 'being there'. Travels in the name of theatre, which replicate with heightened political sensitivity the 'grand theatre tours' of the Victorian period, are still only a relatively recent phenomenon, and like the grand tour have inflated the relevance of the exotic over the domestic. Being here for me is London and Barcelona in the 1990s, but there should, if this book touches on first principles of theatre, be a fundamental connection and distinction with what it is like to make theatre there, wherever that might be.

Does theatre make any 'particular' claims to ethical judgement when considered alongside other cultural practices? Should the following, for the sake of polemical strength, speak of an ethics of art rather than performance? Despite the political imperative for solidarity among the arts I will assert that such solidarity cannot be confused with uniformity. The arts are all 'socially produced' yet are so distinct in their operations as to make holistic statements about them meaningless. To betray the specificity of theatre is to betray its value, what many people seek to defend through their own labour of interpretation. That activity stretches between historical study and anthropological field work, and while I take issue with each in the following, both are preferable to the loss of the theatre in vague aesthetics of creativity. Theatre provides what is literally a body of work to those who care for it, a body with specific characteristics which derive from everyday life. The problem with the grouping and generic discussion of the 'arts' is that it leads to an impasse not unlike that described by Arthur Schopenhauer in a parable:

> One freezing winter day, a herd of porcupines huddled together to protect themselves against the cold by their combined warmth. But their spines pricked each other so painfully that they soon drew apart again. Since the cold continued, however, they had to draw together once more, and once more they found the pricking painful. This alternate moving together and apart went on until they discovered just the right distance to preserve them from both evils.[4]

Preservation from evil is not a sufficiently stimulating premiss on which to build a philosophy of theatre, or to conduct a theatre operation. For that reason I am not willing to dissolve any of the strengths of arguments that follow with spurious generalised links between the arts in the name of solidarity, or in an attempt to gain by proxy special credence that is not theatre's due. While other artistic forms are considered later in the book, for instance cinema, it is not to establish elevating hereditary links but to expose the catholic borrowing that already exists between cultural practices as well as intellectual disciplines, and the peculiar relations such borrowings have with the reservoir of everyday life.

While each art protects itself from the outside and preserves itself from within, practitioners and theorists within each cultural field conduct their own interplay worthy of consideration. Why should they cause each other such discomfort? In theatre it is something of an illusory dance around a convenient but tired scapegoat. The practitioner who avowedly thinks and the thinker who ostentatiously practises can still, unfortunately, be ostracised by those who believe specialism demands a choice between the two. But on closer examination there is no 'two', they are one. The idea of thoughtless practice any more than unpractised thought is absurd. My understanding of what theatre is cannot tolerate such separation. I have never subscribed to the old saw: 'That may be right in theory, but it won't work in practice'. Though the everyday offers critical judgement in the form of such commonsense sayings not everything that issues forth from that domain is any more to be trusted than the knowledge of the most abstruse school of thought. Everyday life does however demonstrate the intimate relationship between thought and action. It challenges us to acknowledge that the 'split' between theory and practice masks the understandable fear of the relationship between the possible and the real. But this is true of everyday life and little sympathy extends to those who inflate this conundrum beyond its appropriate dimensions. It is 'artists' and 'intellectuals' who derive professional currency from this inflation, mocking by their play of alienation the involuntary alienation of those whose everyday lives are so oppressed as to deny any real possibilities for change.

If I have just taken away one of theatre's old saws, what is deemed worthy of more attention? If the primary question is no longer how to reconnect practice and theory I propose another axis for discussion. How can one recognise, retrieve and review the unwritten theatre? That is, not just the theatre that never existed as writing, as script, as text, but as with so much of what I have described as theatre, that which is simply never taken note of. Does this unwritten simply vanish? It has become too significant a part of what I consider to be theatre to be allowed to disappear in this way. But it is not just a question of 'notation', for documentation brings with it so many of its own problems. First it is a question of asking what to look for and where. Theatre's relation with everyday life remains a domain of unwritten negotiation, a domain where the licences granted to theatre are implicit rather than explicit and in their apparent absence are all the stronger in their influence over what theatre can do. This is the domain of 'small print', where theatre is just discernible beneath lengthy tomes and all the more significant for its discreetness.

In saying that theatre is antagonistic to official views of reality I have made a first attempt at defining the hopes I have for it, if not its effects. But this begs the question as to what I believe theatre to be. Theatre is an expressive practice that involves an audience through the medium of images at the centre of which is the human body. It is the only arts practice that foregrounds the body in this way, and as such includes performative forms from dance to death rites within its parameters. The presence of the body in the act of theatre presents particular methodological problems and opportunities to theatre analysis. The disciplines which have been directed towards theatre, particularly those with sophisticated conceptual apparatus for describing being human, can categorise and describe its practices, the gestures and meaning of hand and eye movement for instance, but seem unable to explain with sufficient critical flexibility the contexts of its creation. The organs of the body are not organs of theatre before the everyday which gives them meaning. The everyday humanises organs of the body and profoundly affects the meaning ascribed to them. The anthropology of theatre has traced this transformation in the extra-daily domain, but as Henri Lefebvre says: 'This transformation operates in the everyday realm, it flows from the everyday and concludes within it. Otherwise it cannot exist.'[5] In all situations the everyday has to be known before its theatre can be understood. Unfortunately the veracity of analytic disciplines has been established at the expense of their relations with the everyday – objectivity and scientific credibility make demands on their languages which divorce them in unhelpful ways from the complexities of contexts. Divorced by their status of objectivity from everyday life an analytical paradigm is as likely to miss the ruses and tactics which characterise theatrical manifestations as to identify them. It cuts out and turns over aspects of theatre, then examines them, but in so doing alters their conditions of existence so fundamentally as to lose sight of the 'real' the discipline claims to explain and the value judgements that such realities demand. Those who use disciplines with a history of such transformation, particularly anthropology and sociology, do so now with a renewed sensitivity to these issues. Self-reflexive criticism in James Clifford[6] and Pierre Bourdieu, to name just two exponents from these fields, has made the innocence of 'being there' and returning with anything but a haversack of fictions, impossible. This is not an argument for the neglect of these fields – each has provided profound insights into the theatre and revolutionised the nature of writing its history – but neither is it an acceptance of their considerable and increasing cultural capital in the developing arena of theatre studies. The problematic relation between such disciplines within the academy and everyday life are reason enough to approach their adoption with circumspection, if not downright scepticism.

The future of the theatre will rest upon, in small part, the pedagogic questions both institutional and informal that such analytic practices give rise to. The most enduring and disturbing of these, alongside which the sensitivities expressed above pale into insignificance, is teaching which rests upon methods governed by textual analysis alone. Theatre will remain predominantly governed by the forms and contents of textual narratives as long as such literary bias persists. Put bluntly, the idea that theatre, along with dramatic literature, can be subsumed within a department of literature is nonsense. These are not, I hope to show, the only stories of theatre. Such narratives provide the canon of one theatre tradition, a theatre governed by the 'script', and lack the perspectives derived from discursive practices endemic to everyday life. That many of the most formative resources for understanding theatre are inherent within written texts should not disqualify this argument. It is not words that are the problem and I do not seek a mute theatre. It is not writing that is the problem and I do not endorse a witless physicality. It is the existence and promotion of categories derived from literature which simply mean very little to a theatre which values the relationship it has with people's everyday lives and the vastly more complex panorama of the body and its practices that theatre of any worth has to command.

The naming of theatre carries forward implicitly the arguments I am making. Theatre begins from a point of coalescence, not a polarity. The word theatre itself carries with it the suggestion of a theory within practice. Theory comes from the Greek *theorein*, which was derived from two words: *thea* and *horao*. *Thea* describes an 'outward look', the way in which something shows itself.[7] This sense of theory as epiphanal rather than private and obscure is the sense in which theory is valued here. It is to be distinguished from the notion of idea in *ideo* which suggests the 'self' seeing or *contemplio* which removes the outward look completely to a discreet realm of personal conduct. The resonance of these root words for a book about theatre and everyday life dictates the choice of the term over and above drama or performance. Both these latter are contained by the word theatre in much the same way as Joseph Beuys considered the word sculpture as addressing the question of 'human productivity', retaining the traditional term to describe an arts activity concurrently reshaping it to cover a new semantic field. Considering theatre in this way combines analysis of a conceptual entity and a multiplicity of practices with certain common features. Here theatre, like sculpture, is considered part and constitutive of an expanded field.

But why identify in this bountiful multiplicity a conceptual entity? Does this not replicate the removal of theatre from its context by other disciplines afraid of its heterogeneity? The philosophical aspect of this work is one that considers concepts to be 'tools', the conceptual a 'tool box' designed to prise open the nature of theatre.[8] The point is not to create a monolithic system or set of propositions which replicate other disciplines and replace one 'ology' with another, one theatre with another, but to ask questions which are pragmatic ones: not 'is it true?' but rather 'is it good?' 'does it work?' and 'for whom does it work?' Relativism and pluralism at this time make it all the more critical that the conceptual nature of theatre be understood within a thoroughly historic and geographic perspective. Without such an understanding the value of an ethical stance, the ability and motivation to make value judgements on the basis of more than relative terms, will be compromised from the beginning. Theatre is an unstable entity but in its instability shares something with the masses of moments that make up everyday life and the masses that live the everyday unnoticed. Retrieving one implies the retrieval of all three with the aim the recreation of one through the other. Knowledge of all three will not just derive from description or record but the command of conceptual tools with which to ascertain that which is 'life enhancing' in each, and that which is 'alienating'.

Concepts are useful in identifying and discussing transient phenomena and theatre is the transient art *par excellence*. It is theatre's prerogative to exist in a place for a unique, unrepeatable moment and then to perpetuate in the memory, but no more. The advent of recording media such as video invites theatre to believe it perpetuates, for future consideration and appreciation, but has done little or nothing to alter the essential ephemerality of theatre. Indeed the proximity of the root word for video, *ideo* or 'I see', is indicative of the partial view of the lens that denies its claim to theatre. But it remains the stubborn fact that concepts are interpretive tools and require something to work upon however transient. To date it has been the excrescence of theatre, its waste products that have fascinated researchers, rather than the body and its vital organs. What is raised by these issues is the question: what precisely are the 'documents' of theatre? This question of 'documentation' is a key methodological problem in what follows particularly given the status I grant the unwritten theatre. The history of theatre takes as its starting point extant remains, papers, reports and in the modern period photographs. Theatre semioticians have pointed out the contradiction for the theatre historian that threatens an impasse: that the objects one is concerned with literally do not exist at the time of their study, and that one is in danger of producing a history of theatrical documents that are more or less subjective, partial, elusive and incomplete. Without saying they are 'dishonest' as such they constitute a less than definitive source from which to construct a 'history'.[9] This fact theatre history shares with other historiography, though with added poignance given the objects of interest. But to move from history as chronology to the origin of the word *historia* for the Greeks, that which lies behind phenomena, the logic of phenomena, usefully links questions of meaning and documentation which are examined in the latter part of this book. It is in the debate between theatre and its history that the 'meaning' of a theatre is not so much teased out as forced out. This meaning is important, contingent as it is on contemporary perspectives and umbilically linked to practices of theatre now. This is not to say that theatre history has a utilitarian purpose, but divorced from questions of what theatre can do today it will become an irrelevance.

It also happens that history writing, historiography, is one of the prominent ways of 'fixing' theatre and as such constitutes the remainder from which theatre now has to distinguish itself if innovation is an objective. Historiography is just one way of writing the practices of theatre and demands special consideration in the final chapter. The relations between other writings and theatre are inextricable and informative. There are plays, reviews and criticism, autobiographies of actors, biographies of directors, technical manuals, introductions to stagecraft, voice, movement and dance, works which derive from social sciences, literary analyses, genre studies which identify movements, polemical discourse, diaries, and so on. All are fashioned by their nature after the event at more or less distance to the practices concerned, and conform to the features of literacy associated with each form. Like the fieldnotes of the anthropologist they are not the culture they describe. Yet they retain an association with that culture which is problematic. Writing offends the corporeality of theatre by its limited range of representational forms, which, though dependent on manual dexterity, are slight in comparison to the performer's flexibility. Writing up has been removed from its proximity to the practices of theatre, historically on the verge of the stage, to academies and journalism. This secondary estate flourishes while a small but trenchant strain of published writing from within theatre persists, charged by its relations to a body of practice. In the last century it has been writings by Stanislavsky, Meyerhold, Artaud, Copeau, Brecht and Grotowski which have had most enduring influence on innovative theatres in Europe and North America.

There is in the sense of the practitioner as theorist few more suggestive writers about theatre in the English language than Peter Brook. At the beginning of his best-known work, he claims: 'I can take any empty space and call it a bare stage.' This of course is not in question, any more than rulers throughout history have said: 'I can take any empty space and call it my country.' The problem is that those responsible for theatre have rarely acknowledged that there is no such thing as an 'empty space'. They have been surprised, mystified and sometimes dismissive when people who inhabit that space have a point of view concerning the theatre's arrival. As Brook affirms at the end of the book: 'Truth in the theatre is always on the move.' The truth is that the empty space can no longer just be seen as just that.

The Empty Space is a seminal work which deploys a deeply metaphoric quartet comprising: deadly, holy, rough and immediate, to analyse a theatre.[10] The strength of the work did not however lie primarily in this model and very rarely is it heard to describe theatre now. This is not unusual given the significant gap between the critical discourse of theatre from within and the public discussion of theatre from without. The strength of the work grew from a contract between what had been 'done' and what was being 'said'. The saying requires this validation by theatre work conducted elsewhere for its efficacy. The test of theory here remains its performance. This is not unusual and nor should it be so, there being many writers of theatre whose work is legitimised by a practice beyond its theoretical dexterity. In exceptional cases, such as Antonin Artaud, it is precisely the absence of practice which galvanises disciples to a set of writings such as *The Theatre and Its Double*. But the polarities which Brook adopts to describe theatre in *The Empty Space* speak of others which return in his writings in different places: between the passive and the active to be consumed in his early writings and interviews by the 'communal', the 'secret' and the 'open', the 'vulgar' and the 'mystical', and most pertinently for this book the world of the 'imagination' and the world of the 'everyday':

> In the theatre of illusion, the curtain goes up and supposedly there is the world of imagination, and then the curtain goes down and we are all back in the everyday world, as though the everyday world has no imagination and the imaginary world has no everyday. This is both untrue and unhealthy, and must be rejected. The healthy relationship is the co-existing one.[11]

Brook's examples of this coexistence, in the child's play and African society are preoccupations of his later work and travels. But the coexistence of these polarities, and specifically that of the imagination and the everyday, are left on the air with his theatre practices themselves showing why coexistence is in the end a practical affair. But for others without resources and time, people to collaborate with from various cultures, the possibility to experiment with the confidence of continuity, in other words almost all those actively working in theatres today, the coexistence is a fraught one. If there is coexistence between the imagination and the everyday it is time to discuss that dialectic, to talk about what one means for the other and identify some of the ways in which they are important for each other here and now.

It remains in any case that all the above-mentioned writers are producers and the fact is that there is much less known of their theatre from other perspectives than would in most disciplines constitute a fully informed view of a field of enquiry. Audiences and performers whose role, if the nature of theatre is one of exchange, has been no less decisive than producers are simply elided. In this sense the majority of those making theatre are considered, like audiences, to be speechless, until orality has become literacy. This is another important manifestation of the unwritten theatre. All the texts above share both an inner coherence, whether radical or conservative to a tradition, and an outer identity with communities, audiences, constituencies of consumers. While modes of analysis of people as consumers are not nearly as prevalent as analyses of producers, theories of reception introduce us to the active participation of such consumers in the creative process. These enquiries have disturbing implications for theatre beyond the most rigidified structures of production and consumption. The theatre act is one of engagement between performer and audience that makes such dichotomised stratification wholly inadequate. The production/consumption polarity, compounded by cultural theory derived from a vulgar simplification of the Marxist economic model, has been superseded by the complexities of society described earlier, and its cultural formations. It is this complex of relations for theatre, the creation of images and their contexts that has been approached most successfully through the anthropologist's and the sociologist's strategies. Both have their own dogmatic dimension which conceals the lack of a critical perspective. Neither demonstrates nor ·claims an overall explanatory strategy for how theatre occurs. Both have galvanised thinking about theatre as a cultural activity, as practice. But in the absence of a totalising interpretive strategy, it is literary theory which inappropriately retains its force. In places where theatre's traditions still rely so heavily on literary antecedents from which its pedagogy if not its activity still derives there is much to be achieved by drawing on surprising affiliations with other disciplines which might be temporarily, and medicinally, opportune. These are, like medicine, not to deny the importance and relevance of other approaches when the subject is rehabilitated.

In order to poach on the unwritten theatre criticism needs to address the 'aura' of theatre, its unrepeatability, its resistance to mechanical reproduction. The notion of 're-production' that lies at the heart of the textual tradition in performance has already been countered by many groups and individuals working towards a theatre where the aura does, as Walter Benjamin says, most definitely rely on 'presence in time and space, its unique existence at the place where it happens to be.'[12] It is this phenomenon which relates all the theatres I have spoken of above. The point here is not to participate in the wake of theatre, in the wake of television, but to insist on its resilience, to look at the place of the theatre's comings and goings, and to engage those interpretive and critical tactics most suited to the task in hand. The middle chapters of this book take on this task with recourse to one or two perhaps unusual sources. These include well-known texts by familiar writers, such as the work of Walter Benjamin, a critical tactician with feet firmly placed in the everyday as well as a head in the esoteric, but also philosopher of science, Gaston Bachelard, painter and theorist of composition, Paul Klee, film-maker, Humphrey Jennings, novelist, Franz Kafka, film theorist, Yvette Bíró and cultural critic, Raymond Williams.

The problem of thinking theatre, and the reason for invoking such an unholy alliance of critics, is that it has already become common linguistic currency describing so many things it is not. It is a truism to say theatre is used as metaphor so wide is its influence as a vocabulary of pretence. But the recent period has reinforced this contention with alarming generality, and the assumption that 'all the world's a stage' has become part and parcel of political and media analysis. I live in a 'society of the spectacle' and some of us inhabit a 'dramatised society'. If we fail to define what the aura of theatre is, it returns only too quickly as metaphor, literally carrying the will of others to power like the *Metaphorai*, the public transportation of the streets of Athens. Theatre has always had this relationship with the *polis*, it is fundamentally political in its relationship to the subject and the state. Because of its pervasive metaphoric role, as much as its practical ambition to appropriate the powers of belief politics considers its prerogative, it remains subject to censorship and compromise. While the Lord Chamberlain no longer presides over a British theatre his spirit has insinuated itself into the heads of those who make theatre in periods of economic restraint and conservative tendency.

Like my definition of the purpose of theatre, it is the purpose of this book to contribute to a widespread debate and challenge to official views of reality. This purpose derives in my case from a belief in socialist principles. Such principles cannot themselves, by definition, become an official view of reality and I therefore do not use the word socialism. Central to these principles is the understanding that resistance to oppression is a constant aim for people within history and that reading, writing and acting are central to any conscious process of resistance. These people are not the 'monstrous abstraction' that Søren Kierkegaard talked about when he refuted the 'idea of the public', nor the 'silent majorities' that Jean Baudrillard described when he looked for the masses. I start with those in mind who do not expect representation, who are nevertheless the cause of all writing and labour, a lay man and woman whose everyday lives are an infinite improvisation of making do, of making up and making theatre. Such broad statements serve to clarify that an understanding of theatre as 'conduct of life' has always been in tension with the notion of theatre as 'specialised activity'. The latter is of initial interest in this book, technique plays an important part in this conception of theatre and I do not wish to give credence to the negation of skill by introducing the concept of the everyday. Skill and technique after all abound in the quotidian and embarrass the theatre into silence when it betrays this reality of performance. I am not saying that everything is theatre, nor that everyone acts, nor am I 'offering up a hagiographic everydayness for its edifying value'.[13] There remains nevertheless, however fraught and prone to the imaginary, the need to move beyond the domain of the theatre as named and defined into the realm of the quotidian, the everyday, where micro-theatres are in constant states of emergence and disappearance. This I take on as the book proceeds, and in detail in the chapter entitled 'Everyday Life'. For now it is useful to think of the everyday as that which escapes everything which is specialised, the ill-defined remainder to everything in life thought worthy of writing and record. It is habitual but not unchangeable and is therefore worth taking seriously, for it is the reality which we are made aware of when theatre is good and return to when theatre is done. The following insists that it is the mythic relationship between a productive theatre and a passive consumer that is problematic, an artificial model which derives from a faulty premiss that can be countered on ethical, political and poetic grounds. The premiss is that everyday life must be pushed aside for theatre to occur. The opposite is true. Everyday life must be known, and intimately, for good theatre to happen.

Is there not, finally, a contradiction in this writing up of an unwritten theatre? Writing from within the theatre being described cannot, and nor would it wish to, preclude subjectivity. After all, disinterested vision has already been questioned and for theatre to occur always gives way to participation. Participant observation though, as anthropologists have long understood, leaves little room for texts. If I can make any claims to 'objectivity' they aspire to the kind described by Nietzsche:

> 'objectivity' is not meant to stand for 'disinterested contemplation' (which is a rank absurdity) but for an ability to have one's pros and cons within one's command and to use them or not as one chooses ... All seeing is essentially perspective, and so is all knowing. The more emotions we allow to speak in a given matter, the more different eyes we can put on in order to view a given spectacle, the more complete will be our conception of it, the greater our 'objectivity'.[14]

Writing has become caught up in the invention as well as the representation of cultures and the following is very deeply ingrained in the theatre practices from which it derived. I hope to make more apparent how in the next chapter. That said, practices are not a naive domain separate from the writing of texts, but caught up in those texts in a number of significant ways. My journey to the theatre which I talk about in the chapter 'Lay Theatre' took me across London, in a commute that replicated the motion of reading from the left to the right of the page. I see the city, I live in it, but I read about it and others too. Some of these writings are central to this book – the work of Michel de Certeau has been formative in ways which will become apparent in the reading of what follows if they have not already done so. A book of de Certeau's which has been influential throughout is *The Practice of Everyday Life*. Its cover, when seen on the underground, would sometimes draw responses. A common one was 'Live it don't read it!' But the two operations if they were ever separate seem importantly to coincide with certain writers whose work you can literally move into, take up residence, put out your things, have a conversation and then move on out into the everyday which does not deny, or make a mockery with its infinite complexity, of all that has been read. The point surely is to live it, to read it, and to write it, and if the following etches out the possibilities between these operations there may be thought to be certain benefits to have accrued to a theatre. The wise-crack on the train points to an important reminder for those beached on the wilder shores of postmodernism. Despite the propensity of the last decade to 'read' the city like a book, its architecture as an urban alphabet, the city remains what it is – significant for its difficult realities as well as signifying imaginative possibilities.

In what follows informants of ways of doing have to some extent become co-authors. Academic expectations are that published sources be recognised. For that reason notes point to a diversity of sources which it would be well to follow up if only to establish ways in which I have taken others' writing in vain. But these notes do not, unfortunately, take account of that other body of informants who bring the texts to life by the practices and questions they pose. This is not often a visible theatre of the kind that Peter Brook is able to build his metaphors upon, but it nevertheless underwrites what follows and includes the theatre practices, stories, inventions and arguments that I have met in my work. Scholarship, like any social practice, marks out its own place and from this position a criterion of choice as to what is 'worth knowing' comes into effect. The motivation to write comes from making my own theatre but also importantly seeing and participating in theatre which I regard highly, from the work of Pina Bausch, Het Werkteater, Peter Stein, Els Comediants, but also and importantly a myriad individuals and groups in Europe and the United States making their first or second performance whose lineage would seem to have more to do with a poet like William Blake, a philosopher like Gaston Bachelard, a writer like Antonin Artaud, a film-maker like Humphrey Jennings. This 'other' tradition asks how, in Britain at least, modernism was politically submerged in the angry words of a generation whose revolution was to dramatise the everyday rather than to re-vision it. This revolution was timely for an academy that sought security in texts and discourse, in a written theatre that could be linked with the writings of other auspicious wordsmiths of performance. The murmurings of the everyday, just recognisable in these works, were lost again for other literary concerns. I have tried to tilt this lineage somewhat towards film theorists, philosophers of science, mass movements and apparently irrelevant phenomena of the everyday to see what is taken for granted about theatre before the very sophisticated technologies of the social sciences are used to take it apart. It is this ground clearing that I believe a philosophy of theatre should be engaged in, not to clear an empty space for theatre, nor to ordain a ministry of theatre, but to ask how this ordination has previously come about, how and why spaces have been made for it, why it is worthwhile. This requires consideration both of a contemporary theatre in the first part of the book, but importantly, in the second, the perspectives of past theatres which classify what can and cannot be done by those making theatre today.

It is with critical regard that this work takes as its first perspective the shadow of Peter Brook's paradigm for theatre. This is a reminder that theatre propagates its own official views of realities which need constant attention. The empty space must be rethought as a populated place. To start from a premiss that imagines a space into which an actor enters is to endorse a clearing before an occupation by theatre. The following begins from the reality of people in a place, the space which is made by them, and to which the theatre dis-poses itself. The empty space will, on closer inspection, be recognised as the place of the everyday, making it no less attractive to a theatre practice, unless of course that theatre insists on its privileges.

Part I

PRACTICE CRITICISM QUOTIDIAN

1

LAY THEATRE

The theatre I am going to describe in this chapter took place between 1978 and 1991. I write about it because it has a shape that might be recognisable and provides a model of analysis. Transforming an activity of life into a model is only useful when it elucidates theatre in practice. There seems little justification in removing theatre from the places where it occurs simply to establish its existence, like taking from the wild the example of a species you know is rare but cannot resist putting on show in a state of captivity. This operation of separation is central to any academic pursuit of reality, and it is one which often ignores the partial procedures of analysis and in the process loses sight of the complexity of the object under scrutiny. No palaeontologist would remove a fossil without recording its relation to other fossils in the strata, no archaeologist an artefact, and no anthropologist would record a marriage ceremony without mention of the habitation and the terrain. Recognition of a context does not however guarantee that the conditions of identification will persist for very long. The fossil and artefact might appear in a museum, the fieldnotes in a library. This transition from one milieu to another is the precondition for one culture taking note of another. Objects which are removed in this way are reclassified in generic types with their own consistency but separated from the circumstances in which they took their place. Because theatre leaves such confusing traces – the remaining artefacts are not the thing itself but its detritus: architecture, costume, props, prompt-books, photographs, ephemeral and critical writing – it has been to date mainly a question of categorising everything but the theatre itself. In the last chapter of this book I will undertake some of these operations myself and am not averse to them if they have any meaning for theatre now. But here a contemporary theatre presents, through its proximity, an opportunity to ascertain different objects of study which are worth recording for future thought.

The theatre I want to write about was based in a converted Victorian grain warehouse on the River Thames. From there work was undertaken in local estates, on the street, in schools, neighbourhood centres, in factories and city farms, on the river and in halls and buildings designed for theatrical purposes. I joined this work after it had begun, and left eight years later with it continuing in diverse ways. Participants lived in local authority housing within walking distance of this base, and the relationship between local living and theatre making was considered central to the project. The fact that this was a project, a means as well as an end, is important. The process of 'making theatre' was not thought to be immutable but an imaginative arrangement to be negotiated with people and places. This aspect of the work does not differ from other theatres, reaching back to the first Elizabethan age – a set of socially licensed operations with remarkably permeable boundaries. There are many instances of theatre's willingness to remain within these limits of definition through self-regulation and there are now, as I have described, many others which have redefined these limits by seeking to transgress them. In this sense the term theatre describes a variety of operations including those conventionally associated with theatre and those which might seem less so. The plurality of these operations were more important than the assertion of a proper name for the project which in its singularity would have concealed the nature of the work. The time spent in this location was an opportunity to establish, individually and collectively, what the practice of theatre could be. This involved understanding the relations between theatre practice and neighbourhood, questioning received wisdom and formal education, and conducting a critical examination of theatre and the practices of everyday life.

Those who engaged with this work were on a daily basis being tested in unconventional ways; each person was expected to conduct themselves as a thinking artist with sensitivity and scepticism to the context in which they found themselves. Having worked in the area for some years it was impossible to take seriously a purely theoretical objective of describing the community as 'working class' (sociologically incorrect), 'white' (racially unobservant), 'cockney' (topically inaccurate), and even the simplest geographical description of the area was difficult enough. There were very few people within it who would commit themselves to defining where one district ended and another began. It was not theory that was a problem, or what it took to understand practices through thinking and writing, but the shifting and plural nature of theatre activity in a location. This jeopardised the project in that it simply took longer to quantify, if not to see, results which were occurring – and the time of supervision is rarely the time of the everyday. The time of authority excises the casual time that everyday practices punctuate, the lacunae and pauses, the breathing spaces in which local relations are played out. But this was a symptom of the work which derived from a complex relationship between a community of hosts and guests, not a rationale for evading criticism.

Supporting a theatre in such an area for thirteen years eventually gave way to closure. Keeping a theatre open is more or less difficult.[1] Closing a theatre is a provocation to say something else. Where there is interruption in what has been a continuity, questions are asked as to how and why such a situation could have arisen. For 'being there' becomes pattern and habit and is the point at which everyday life begins to incorporate a theatre into itself as though it were somehow natural and given. But this habitual world threatens the fragility of a theatre which demands recognitions and favours that few can afford. There was always something there, but the remains of theatre are less coherent than buildings suggest, and it is these fragments which are testament to what happened and why a theatre rarely sinks without trace. That a building remains, means little in a time when the combustibility of theatre has been so reduced. Like other transformations in the neighbourhood a theatre can become a cinema, a bingo hall and a carpet warehouse within a generation.

For those involved in the project at its closure this was a confusing time, attempting to interpret and act upon fissures between an institution and a neighbourhood which felt itself teased and disappointed in equal measure. The terms of the engagement were never explicit and more was always promised than could be delivered. In and around everything that was argued about, theatre continued to be made with countless different groups and individuals. These included: young people in and out of school, both in the classroom and on local housing estates; older people between sixty and ninety years from the area who met independently in theatre groups or as part of the social life of a neighbourhood centre; young adults with learning difficulties and older adults with physical disabilities; people who were isolated within the neighbourhood for a variety of reasons, be it single mothers, people without housing, or those who were unemployed; social groups who met in certain pubs or through local clubs for sports and computing; other interest groups consolidated through common interest in music, dancing or politics. The term 'community theatre' generally used to describe work with groups other than those of a professional status misses the complex relations between the actuality of such people's lives and the theatre they make. To begin with, the term community is now redolent with implications of 'ministry', or social engineering, and useless when applied to the multiplicity of voices discussed here. Further it underestimates the very forceful role many of these people held within the local neighbourhood. It was they who commanded cultural capital in the local currency of exchange: stories, blahs, advice, tricks, cons, jokes, songs, physical shows of strength or sleights of hand.

Those who had a vested interest in the workings of the project began to make demands upon it which questioned the status of theatre within a set of everyday operations. At one meeting it was decided by people in the neighbourhood that the production budget would be better spent on washing machines to allow those who had children in the area to participate in theatre while the washing was going round. A dilapidated theatre was to become a beautiful launderette, an equation which had considerable logic but little sympathy from those whose own idea of a theatre was in need of resourcing. The theatre van was run into the ground, along with the local mechanic who cared for it, transporting equipment from hither to thither while forays began to take place from the area back to the country to remind the institution that financed the project that it was healthy, belligerent and seeking the independence it warranted. The government of the enterprise became more fulfilling and problematic. Increasingly the demand was made that if the project was 'of' the neighbourhood it should be finally answerable to the people of that locality. The presence of people from outside this domain was resisted in ways which reproduced relations of exclusion that the project had been established to counteract in the first place. Despite such local difficulty it was apparent that the kinds of model for participation and control that this theatre initiated were ones that an institution would be wary of, and indeed there came a point where the institutional expectations were reimposed to obviate the necessity for such subtle and time-consuming structures. It was here that the official view of highly complex realities demanded not a tactical response to real needs but a limitation of damage in an apparently uncontrolled context.

The quietude which followed this period in the final years of the project was deafening. The building was emptied of all but the most persistent groups by a series of decisions, perhaps long overdue and after the event, to clarify the relationship between certain groups using the theatre and the institutionally sanctioned pedagogic aims of the project. Denied a base, the groups who perceived themselves to be no longer welcome in the building, or were told they were not welcome, simply regrouped elsewhere claiming the title of the project as their own, a strategy which all but brought lawyers in to wrest it back. Here theatre deterritorialised and proliferated in diverse ways linking back to the moment before the 'arrival' of a theatre when stories were played out in and around everyday life and common places: under the arches of a tower block, in tenants' association halls, between parked cars. Given that naming had been such a problem for so long it was wholly appropriate that in its most critical phase of friction, a neighbourhood and an institution should argue about who owned a title.

The title was Rotherhithe Theatre Workshop, an unassuming name that nevertheless combined some significant features for those who made claims to it. First it was of Rotherhithe, a specific geographical community in south-east London which stimulated an unusual degree of loyalty from its population. Perhaps because of its apparent isolation from the rest of the city (it was contained by a sharp meander in the river), by its pride in neighbourliness and tradition of work in the docks, all of these features were to some degree threatened by demographic change wrought by urban development. This was perceived for better or worse as one of the last strongholds of mutual solidarity that had long since characterised the East End of London. Second it was a theatre: not an unusual feature of the area, there had stood till relatively recently a grand Hippodrome on the corner of the local park, but now with the exception of the civic hall or church meeting rooms an unusually large single space where people could meet, make theatre and make a mess. Third it was a workshop, or 'the workshop' as it was referred to throughout – linking the traditional workings of a wharf to the newer languages of cultural process as distinct from product.

These anecdotes might seem inconsequential, but reviewing the unwritten depends on them. For all anecdotes establish a peculiar relationship between theory and practice and relate event and context in ways not immediately ascertainable from more distanced 'objective' voices. It was anyway these everyday occurrences that held most interest for the project at its most creative and difficult times and to write about the work as though it were always thought through in classified and distinct categories would be quite erroneous. That is not to say it was not continually being considered, simply that those involved knew that thinking theatre was not the facile operation of other disciplines applied to the activity, it was the activity of theatre making itself throwing light on those disciplines and the everyday lives they claimed to describe. In this sense theatre became its own way of seeing – a shift which would not have surprised many theorists who from the fields of sociology, psychology and anthropology had long valued the symbolic, theatrical and performative qualities of everyday life and its cultural operations.[2] There was understandably the expectation that participants should grasp the alternative models to their own practice, that they should be able to compare and contrast approaches to making theatre in neighbourhoods, near and far, conceptually similar and different, and that they should continually critically address their work. But the development of community arts had been no preparation for the complex and shifting relations on a day to day basis that living and working in the same neighbourhood threw up. It was this lack which distanced the project from the language and prescription which the conjoining of the words 'community' and 'arts' implied. Where these words were considered too general to describe something as distinct as theatre practices and their relation to the everyday lives of people in places, replacing them with alternatives such as 'neighbourhood' or 'celebration' no more accurately described the activity. Nevertheless, left with the split between this group of practices and other theatre forms it seemed critical to define a social space which could accommodate the practices that occurred without irrevocably divorcing them from their contexts.

Central to this social space was the inhabited space, the living places of those involved, the flat on a local estate bringing each participant into direct contact with the locality and its people. These estates included some in close proximity to the river – Swan Buildings and Adams Gardens – but others further afield such as Silwood and Abbeyfield Road with problems of dereliction associated by some with local authority ineptitude and by others with deep poverty. A senior administrator visited, from the distance of the institution which funded the project, to see why it was this accommodation should cause, on such a continual basis, so many seemingly intractable problems – there had been bath floodings from above, frozen pipes and waterfalls in the thaw, radiator collapses, break-ins, lock-outs, squattings and evictions. That this was the life of those dependent on a metropolitan council with mounting debts and a backlog of repairs seemed irrelevant. The administrator arrived at the theatre around the time that a local hospital for women in south London was closing. This was a controversial decision and typically was being resisted by those in the project who often became involved in the most overt political manifestations of power in the area. There were posters at the theatre announcing the closure and appeals for help, and there had been performances in support of the cause. The administrator saw one of these posters on which was depicted a substantial if dilapidated building and suggested that the hospital when empty might make a suitable dormitory for the participants in the project, thus relieving the 'complication' of council houses. The suggestion was met with the incredulity that involvement in different worlds brings and reconfirmed the need for participants in the project to stay living where they were with all the attendant problems that would entail.

Beneath this story is the implication that the very nature of the project lay in the location of its participants within a neighbourhood, dispersed within a geographical area in proximity to a working base. The journey that each person made to and from that base and other centres in the area became a daily mapping of the locality and its theatre possibilities. These daily journeys were at their shortest undertaken for a year, at their longest throughout the thirteen years the project ran. The story also emphasises the relations between the locality and other adjacent areas where political imperatives connected the interests of one group with another. Shopping, health care, swimming and recreation, hair cutting and laundry, all happened in the locality where the newcomer lived alongside those with whom they hoped to work (or wished to avoid). The excision of 'students' from the neighbourhood through accommodation, cut out and separated, has been a conscious architectural and social movement of the campus institutions and one which is particularly deleterious to an education in theatre. It parallels the removal of objects of study from their context to conditions thought most suitable to their comfortable perusal. For those involved in this project there were other more subtle ways of avoidance and negotiation if they wished to remain aloof from the lives of those with whom they lived. This was of course a two-way process for both the neighbourhood and the newcomer. These tactics and ruses were in different people developed to different degrees and some estates would conduct them in quite different ways to others.

In one, a woman who was well known to the project and instrumental in its history watched over and assisted the arrival and departure of each newcomer as though they were her family coming and going. In another, a man would proposition them on a regular basis as though reputation did not travel. In another, children would daily arrive on their doorstep expecting the flat to be a play space for them, a haven from school, which for one year it was and by the following it was not. None of these encounters amounts to an immutable law of relations between a theatre and a neighbourhood but each displayed a certain logic which is definable. Care, desire and utility played their part in sustaining interest between individuals whose motives for being in the same place might have been coincidental but in the end were expressed through a relationship to theatre.

Let me briefly take a concrete example of a process which already sounds too abstract. I was working in a local factory. An elderly woman was working next to me. She knew I was 'not for real', that I had another place to go to after clocking-off, even if she referred to it somewhat dismissively as 'that draughty warehouse'. She was one of a group of women invited back by the factory, annually after retirement, to work part-time when schedules were heavy. Mary was working on the 'extruder', a machine which excreted a small but violently coloured amount of icing onto the top of passing biscuits. She bent my ear with her stories, along with the other woman who worked in this part of the plant. Her task was to check the biscuits as they went by on the conveyor to ensure any imperfections were segregated and disposed of. Occasionally, and without warning, the extruder would disgorge a rogue emission (either a rainbow combination of colours, or an abnormally large quantity of mixture). When either happened Mary would grab the offending article and with a lightness of touch belying arthritis, shape the setting form into the caricature of a head. These 'rogues' were then sent on their way with the others, through the ovens, to be baked and inspected at the end of the line. These heads were not just reminiscent of the factory management, who were treated with ribald affection, but more despised political figures, particularly a woman prime minister who at the time was not held in high esteem. After baking they were retrieved and either pocketed for the children 'indoors', or eaten for dessert after a cook-in-the-bag meal had been heated in the ovens and eaten, perched invisibly between the machines.

This sculpture of the everyday was always accompanied by stories and gestures drawn from as far from the workplace as one could imagine. Sometimes the figures were used to play these out, sometimes others having heard the stories over the years added incidental detail and diverting puns. This 'group', for it was the extruder group, played out the story of a bride who lost her husband-to-be in the factory, the apprentice who was lost in the biscuit-mix, the visit of the princess to see her wedding cake, the fire that burnt all their aprons, the wildlife that lived between the ovens and innumerable 'works outings' to the seaside which resulted in other weddings, lost husbands, disappointed fiancées and more wildlife. I will return to these stories and their theatre later.

Here at work was a trust between people who knew each other well and the infinite possibilities of a good story well told – which usually meant well acted. This all happened for this theatre group in the time of retirement, normally associated with some form of leisure. But for them leisure did not break with everyday life, the normal condition for time to be thought of as leisure time, it was part of work because work had always been part of their leisure. The works outings were a litany of strenuous lifts – crates on and off coaches, friends in and out of deck chairs – which could hardly have been considered uneventful in the sense that leisure is considered an escape from effort. The cultural significance of this break for what we expect theatre to be is debilitating. It is a rare treat to be 'allowed out' to see theatre in work time – more often it is seen in leisure time when all that is expected is a flight from the everyday. Distraction and entertainment have become the expectation of this time, and boredom, never mind education or critical thought, is treated with considerable suspicion. This is a shame and accounts for why the phrase 'A good night out' so often disappoints when it is a 'theatre night out'.

Good theatre cannot be boring theatre – and yet vast tracts of theatre are undeniably boring and more provocative for being so. This is a characteristic theatre shares with religion which Henri Lefebvre described as disguising and transfiguring 'living boredom'. As far as Mary and her friends go they knew only too well the power of boredom and they had developed sophisticated theatrical means to ensure their plight was not an endless wait for the return of a belt. These inventions were a necessity not an existential nicety – the factory 'suggestions box' on the wall above their station had a less than promising sign hanging over it: 'Suggestions Box Suspended'. The negotiations between theatre and everyday life were here constantly underway and replicated a myriad other settings where infiltration was met with a certain wonder. In each case looking was only half the story, the rest came from participation.

The multifarious nature of these negotiations denied not just a name or title to the project but the overarching construction of a single discipline with which to have analysed them. Like a Trojan Horse the newcomer to the situation or workplace smuggled in a panoply of techniques and disciplines deriving from theatre and everyday life which were more or less alien to the locality. Some were expert in practices such as cooking or mechanics, others versed in sociology or anthropology, others were theatre practitioners whose belief systems seemed to deny the validity of any theoretical discipline speaking for the immediacy of their work. The best theatre was always a collage of these approaches used in subtle and undogmatic ways where the situation demanded, and always starting from the congruence of practices and theories within the everyday lives of those with whom contact was sought. Anything smuggled in was of course met with a panoply of techniques and specialisms that those in the area thought constituted a theatre. Here neighbours were more or less ready to resist or incorporate whatever was inside the Trojan Horse; it was for participants to be ready to act and respond.

Each defined a place that was proper to them. Whether that was in a factory, a school, working with people with learning difficulties or disabilities, working on the local city farm, or making events on the river or street, the place taken up was one which had meaning for them and they hoped for others. This was a proper place, not just an empty space into which they moved to make theatre. The place already had its own people with direction and velocities – no site for this work would wait for a visitor, they would observe, participate and lead in equal measure where it was appropriate. The flexibility of a community that might from the outside have appeared somewhat traditional and closed, closeknit and unwelcoming to all but the most familiar outsider, was the precondition for this work to occur. None of these classical descriptions of this community could be borne out for a group, though individuals would of course experience more or less of those feelings of alienation and acceptance. What was important was not just the individual's trajectory but the identity of the institution they represented and reformulated by their actions, in this case not just an educational college with its own title, Dartington College of Arts, which was elusive enough as a concept as it was to the locality, but theatre, which already had a reputation in the area and one which was worth examining by those new entrants to its milieu.

The traditions of theatre here were long and problematic. If you owned a pub in the docks it was likely you played the piano and sang, and if you didn't someone else did for you. Some pubs were known for this, others for their expertise in darts, or the ability to answer the most obscure general knowledge questions. To enter the right pub in the right way was of course as in all neighbourhoods a mundane rite of passage. But to enter a pub and instigate a performance was quite another matter for the anonymous newcomer. This was no conference of the birds, an exotic barter between theatre and cultures, but a conference of words and languages that had a certain proximity and therefore more potential for grave misunderstanding. It was a domestic arrangement and therefore one with the potential for real conflict to occur, with its own logic, not simply the random violence of strangers. Two pubs which sandwiched the theatre on the riverside, The Mayflower and The Ship, told, in their ebb and flow of popularity with participants in the project, something of the rise and fall of aspirations others had for the area. The Ship went through a series of turbulent transformations with furniture and fittings resembling a more and more lush boudoir. The Mayflower, despite its greater popularity with 'city folk', maintained its wood and sawdust look in an inverted display of heritage. Both, like The Neptune across the street, announced their links with the sea, others like The Jolly Gardeners with the pastoral traditions of the area, and China Hall with an exotica that could only disappoint on entry. The Angel, just upriver, announced itself somewhat self-reflexively as 'The Famous Angel' hinting at the growing divide between common knowledge of a pub worth going to and the commercial attraction of a 'riverside lifestyle'. Performances happened in the bars and in rooms above all these places because this was where the participants met most regularly and from where new participants for theatre could be found.

Older people in the area had their own traditions of singing and the presentation of scenes and fictions. Hats were always important, deriving from trips to the seaside, 'when it was worth visiting', and beanos, days out in the company of the works colleagues. All the local stereotypes come into play when words like 'beano', 'down hopping' and 'evacuation', are coined, but in the years of the project these were very real memories in physical and emotional form for the older people of the area with whom theatre was made. If we did not work with these people, and to evade older people was the stated aim of some, there would be little opportunity not to be involved in some way, whether as an audience to their countless performances, on coach trips, when the television came to film them, when they needed a hand on and off the coach (for reasons of physical infirmity or, more pleasurably, one too many drinks), or to be dropped off by car to their homes in the area.[3] There was none of the passivity here associated with growing years and the trenchant critique of everyone else's theatre work by these people, as well as their own, was encouraging and withering in equal measure.

Where older people met younger people might in other circumstances have caused friction, but the purpose of this work was, as well as having a good time and something to say, to assert the possibility that generations were not inherently bounded. Rather the boundaries between young and old had material, mental and ideological origins each of which demanded revisioning through theatre. Working with older people, in groups with modest names like The Rotherhithe Gems or The Toynbee Players, did not mean casting older people in plays or devising reminiscence events. The rhythm and modes of expression that many older people have at their disposal destabilise the conventions of a theatre which thinks it knows itself. With people on both sides of the Thames, and further afield, it was apparent that the accumulation of expressive vocabulary, both gestural and verbal, was a process of reciprocation with age. Often what was lost in terms of physical agility was replaced by a cunning and improvisation to circumstance. In this process theatricality and credibility were heightened to the literally incredible levels that one might associate in more mundane times with the most consummate performers. But then this is generally known and nervously tolerated by a professional theatre which relies on the belief that it is special and separate from such behaviour and ability in all but its most apologetic and hagiographic fawning to ageing stars. Theatre panders to their dotage because it has excised the activity of older age from its practices and possibilities. The theatre sits uneasily between ideas of 'the people' and hagiography which celebrate equally and debilitatingly the power of the mass and the individuality of those who rise from it.

On the other side of a nonexistent divide there were many young people in the area whose obsession with all forms of rapping and scratch demonstrated a sophistication born from knowing that appropriation and repetition was not just the darling device of the avant-garde. These were, starting from different premises to older people, still the arts of accretion and accumulation, often pastiching and ironically commenting on tradition and expectation. Gaining entrance to such groups was more difficult than others unless of course you came, as some did, with required musical skills or equipment which could be stripped down and reassembled for the purposes in hand. The question of improvisation was here central. Forms which allowed for improvisation were often treated with considerable suspicion, and in this way choreographers and musicians found themselves in a strange defensive alliance of spontaneity. On one occasion, as was often the barter system in the theatre, the visit of a Belgian theatre company of international notoriety was traded off with workshops with people from the local area with their own celebrity. In return for performing a collage of Shakespeare, interspersed with video and violent physicality, the company agreed to an informal evening of musical improvisation with local musicians. The event was like other such occasions a mix of the surreal and the pragmatic, the improvising expectations and affected bongo primitivism of the avant-garde company clashing with the electronic complexity of the music group. The 'ownership' of the 'fragmentary aesthetic' by those with cultural capital is contested by groups as diverse as Kids of Survival in New York and the 'homeless' inspecting Los Angeles. Their own lives, like those here, were already a constellation of the unforeseen, and to them documentary or factual theatre would have appeared a mite dogmatic.

Improvisation was challenging not only because it was not fixed and demanded an ability to listen and respond, it was also deemed to be something, ironically, that was institutionally sanctioned and often thought to be fey. This view came, at different times, from those whose lives depended for survival on a range of improvisation and negotiation skills that few outsiders could draw upon. The conventions and codes of the artistic activity would present to these same people a split between what was natural and what was cultural. The ruses of fishes and plants, 'now you see me, now you don't', the tricks and jokes that made up the everyday life of the area were used here to challenge the institution of theatre to step up or stop its pretence. They announced that, within the restraint of acknowledged forms, all structures were open for reformulation. Of course they were not, and what was more there was nothing, monetarily at least, to be made from improvisation and this was still for many, with or without a job, the bottom line.

Where technology held pride of place in the daily life of the local musician there was the need for constant logistical support to move gear from place to place. Hundreds of miles would be driven each week in the theatre van moving items of gadgetry as though avoiding a raid by the bailiffs. This technology was something alien to many of those training whose understanding of technology was closer to the root of the word *techne*, a revealing of themselves through a discipline such as choreography or dance, writing for performance or acting. The connection between technique and technology was not as innocent as it might have appeared. For the gadgetry that kept aliens at bay from the music was not dissimilar to the technique flourished by the person training to be 'expert', 'specialist', over the locality. The fact that one was purchasable and the other learnt was little relief for those who lay outside both. Those who lay outside this circle of technique and technology were 'lay' by their very nature. They by their presence sanctioned theatre's occurrence by presenting the producers with participants as well as a community, an audience, a neighbourhood and on occasions a market. In other words a definable user whose interest might be in hearing, seeing, and making sense of this activity. The point here, and the purpose of discussing the work at all, was not to reproduce this economy of exchange but to revision it at every turn, to consider nothing about theatre or everyday life unchangeable. The means to this end is what I call a lay theatre. A 'lay theatre' was one which defined itself in relation to and distinction from a profession or a religious conception of belief. It was pragmatic, secular and critical. That it was not professional did not mean that it lacked expertise – it just did not propagate experts. After all, those who were recognised and respected in the area were known for being able to turn their hand to more than one thing. It would have been pointless to facilitate a specialism which would not allow the recipient to continue their relations with what they knew and had chosen to live within.

Most theatre would appear to accept as a precondition for getting started that it produces while someone else consumes. Who produces, and who consumes, has rightly been a question worth asking for it divines the flow of cultural authority which inflects other power relations in society between those who have and those who lack. But this set of polarities misses the 'real' that the theatre hoped to capture in its work. For any long-term experience of working with theatre in a particular place demonstrates in surprising ways each day, and most often on a Sunday, the variety of expressive practices, some which could be considered theatrical or performative, that are central to the life of groups and individuals. The economic model of base and superstructure, like other antipodes which assert themselves as a rationale when no other more subtle explanation is forthcoming, required casting in new and more rigorous ways. It was for the lay theatre, and the places it occurred, less a binary opposition and more like a process of accretion with the transition between one stratum and the next difficult to discern to the uninitiated. Programmes of education propagate rationalities which can as easily cover and conceal these features as illuminate them, and the lay theatre demanded new tactics of criticism for the evaluation of the coincidental creativity of everyday life.

It is only in the most clearly stratified cultural situations such as those places where theatre is named, staged, curtained and bankrupted, that these questions of consumption and production are replicated on anything like the polar models that analysis would have us believe are the stuff of theatre. Everywhere else and continually, negotiations between performers and audiences, producers and consumers are taking place, at this minute with emphasis one way, the next minute the other. There is nothing immutable about these relations and it is these liminal states which are what define theatre beyond its most obvious forms.

As I said in the Introduction, to understand these processes requires a repertoire of analytical procedures that in some way makes claims to being more subtle than those of the statistical analysis of sociology or the fieldwork of anthropology, that might derive as much from the subtleties of taste in cooking or the pragmatics of mechanics. There are strategies available in specialist disciplines which are essential to this work yet none can claim full explanatory felicity to the complex situation that the theatre maker meets and certainly none alone provides the critical basis from which to make the daily value judgements that are necessary to theatre making in those circumstances. Anthropology, psychoanalytic theory and sociology share certain problems in their employment of concepts which have a double articulation. On the one hand they are held to be findings from empirical evidence; on the other they become diffused, as Raymond Williams has shown, in forms of discourse dependent on concepts of a limited and specialised pedigree.[4] Like all truly educational activity, work like the lay theatre does not happen here at the behest of such disciplines, incarnated in the institution, as though practices were there as the justification of theorists and bureaucrats, though it undoubtedly challenges and advances interpretive disciplines to greater hermeneutic subtlety. Rather, given the well-being of people is at stake as well as the understanding of their lives, it is practices which are fostered, and the arts of theory derived from these activities in and on the world are always contingent upon these practices.

This suggests there is an ethical aspect to the activity, and of course there is. It is impossible not to engage with ethical concerns in a process involving people in places coming together for the purposes of pleasure, education and excitement. These concerns, as I have already explained, are nothing to do with a religious idea of morality but are the recognition that the audience is the predisposition of the performer and that the one cannot do without the other. This goes for the simplest most local theatrical exchange as it does for the broadest and most international of issues concerning the entry of one to the place of the other. There has been much written via the developments of critical theory and postmodernism about the status of 'the other' and the need for regional and local specificities to be considered, not from the imperialism of a centralist perspective but from within those communities themselves. This would appear to transfer to the global level the understanding that one does not speak for the other but with them and that this dialogical principle is central to democracy. This is not a case for self-renunciation, Nietzsche has well and truly taken such romanticisms to task, and there remains residue of what he called 'sugar and sorcery' in claiming the predisposition to feeling for others. But these seductions urge me to caution, rather than inaction, and hence the case for an ethical perspective. Theatre by its nature speaks to the other and often for the other. It has the benefit however over other arts of not casting this moment of ventriloquism in stone, in writing, or paint, but in the process of image creation between a performer and audience. The theatre, whenever it works, is a forum, but to resist the definition of that capacity as a finite aesthetic form seems as important as resisting the conception of theatre as any other single thing. This continually transformative project does not freeze life in an eternal interval, a duration, but suggests a beyond, a 'movement' to something better, that is always possible but often difficult to achieve. As Paul Klee said of the arrow, a bit farther than customary! – than possible? The lay theatre was a movement through the imagination and images to a domain beyond everyday tyrannies to take better notice of the real pleasures of everyday life.

This movement was grounded in particular places beyond the empty space. The building which provided the base for this project was a Victorian grain warehouse, converted in the first wave of docklands redevelopment. It lay on the south bank of the river, downstream from Tower

Bridge, at one end of a long winding perimeter road connecting a major local trunk road to what had historically, though now it seemed euphemistically, been described as Downtown. Sandwiched by the graveyard of an early eighteenth-century church, St Mary's, and the river, this was one of the first conservation areas to be subjected to developers' attention in the era of water-centred urban regeneration.

The residue of the building's former use was apparent in a crane which remained adjoined to its riverside rear wall and which in its immobility stood for the seizure in the trade which had given the warehouse its purpose. The building had once been used to store grain, swung through its riverside openings and disgorged onto horse-drawn carriages on the adjacent street. To say that the building was now a theatre, or that its conversion had somehow eclipsed its history, was forcefully challenged by those who were directly related to its other pasts. The name of the wharf in which the building stood, 'Hope-Sufferance', conveyed something of this history. The apparent dichotomy of the words was in fact an ironic compound – Sufferance referred to the special dispensation afforded a landing place for cargo when the London Port was strictly licensed and centred upriver of Tower Bridge. It was once a place of danger and oppression and the theatre taking its place was part of a lineage which was forgotten at your own risk. It was these demands which prompted serious thoughts about the health and safety of a contemporary theatre and on what terms this safety had been brought about. Something more was at stake for those in the area whose uncle, grandfather or brother had worked and died in the building. The meaning of heritage here takes on a quite different hue – what is inherited by the theatre is the accumulated losses of capital's gain, gain achieved at the behest of a locality which could not necessarily be expected to return anew to the building as though nothing had happened.

A lay theatre occurs through this accumulation of credit and debt. It is a form of continual accretion in a place where the strata slowly build towards something with meaning and relevance. A theatre which is not attuned to these historical traces is one which denies the purpose of its presence in a place, and one which depends on anonymity for its well-being. It is literally 'fly by night'. People are known in places for their style, their wit, their accumulation of credibility and they, like the best theatre, are looked towards for how they will express and perform this accumulation of wisdom, in the process making it incredible. It is often with irony and self-deprecation, the false modesty of the home-made instrument of the street musician played off against the mock formality of their evening wear. But it is worn with dignity no less. The best places, like people, in any locality are ones where accretion has taken place, a steady accumulation of identity and caring authority derived from the ability to surprise and provoke pleasure.

The origin of the local name, Reder Heia, suggests like all names its own history of accretion – Heia, a place, Reder, where cattle were landed. It is suggestive of two traditions of the area, before the seventeenth century, the grazing grounds of the city, and more recently the heart of its docklands. This derivation evokes Walter Benjamin's archaic representatives of the storyteller: the resident tiller of the soil and the trading seaman, the dweller and the traveller, in the pasture and from the port of a city. This side of the river had once been densely populated, the tidal wash of the bank protecting the area from disease and plague in the seventeenth century. Where industry, net making and boat building gave way to commerce in the nineteenth century, the Pool, as this stretch of river was known, became central to the livelihood of the region. Widespread damage during the Blitz, containerisation, restrictive labour practices and silting of the river channel each contributed to the movement of trade downriver and the running down of the docks.

The theatre took its place here before the boom and outlived the bust. For a Conservative decade the area represented one of the cornerstones of government policy and in its architectural eclecticism played out the dreams of the postmodernists. For others, closer to home, it represented a process of decivilisation. Here a new city was being reclaimed from the docks stretching from the financial centre eastwards and combining advanced electronic capability decked with neo-classical facades and interwoven with rural thematic rides and walks. The theatre project was, as with other institutions and individuals in the area, caught up in the opposition to the most avaricious aspects of this development, not merely as a statement about the return and inflow of capital to a city it had left some years before, but on historic grounds supporting those whose lives had in the simplest and most profound ways been affected by the changing nature of the area. There were those who had been moved inland from housing close to the river during the war, who wished to return to a river rapidly being blocked by luxury development. Streets with evocative names like Elephant Lane, Paradise Street and Dockhead were being subsumed into a thematised 'dockland trail' for the curious visitor. There were those who regularly met to play, to hide, to think, on the wasteland near to the theatre building. When this was penned for development into housing, scenes were made to establish the different and more imaginative uses it had always been put to by the young people in the area. A processional event involving those who stood to lose most by development moved from the site along the river to play out resistance in the theatre itself. Here the doors of the warehouse were seen as dispensable, they were a threshold to be crossed when the picturesque detritus of the environment threatened to overwhelm the critical nature of the theatre being made. In the street older people sat up at night telling stories and singing to protect a children's play site from levelling, and, in the years of city-wide government and subsidised public carnival, decorated boats plied the river declaring the need for local democracy over land use. Throughout this process there was the claim from the authorities that fair rent or first-chance purchase plans for local residents would protect the housing from an exclusively City market, thus preserving the local character of the area. But the reality evident from the cars which began to appear was of course quite the opposite. Where it was local people buying into property it was the same local people who controlled other areas of local life for better or worse. To call this group a mafia would be an ill-definition, but there was an interplay of capital and honour associated with such description that was evident in many local transactions, including those which allowed the theatre to occur. For theatre to take its place here it was expected to negotiate with other interests and demands on a day to day level. One day those of us who could be found in the warehouse would be offered offcuts of carpet, the next a crate of Penrose's biography of Picasso. It rather depended which lorry was where and who was driving. In this the underside of an area reflected the surface patterns of commerce and negotiation that were being celebrated in a widening radius of entrepreneurial greed from the square mile.

If development was leaving its mark on the area, the building in which the project was based did not escape the attentions of the graffiti writers. There had been short-lived and unsuccessful attempts to start a variety of creative projects in the building previously and its relationship to anything but drugs and the arts of hallucination was unclear to many whose scepticism of the arts was deepest. But a small and committed group, not uncommonly for the area financially supported by an institution 'elsewhere', knew that a long-term project made up of theatre makers housed in the area could begin to make contact over many years with a locality and its people, if at every turn this process avoided any hint of philanthropy or cultural do-gooding.[5] This was of course not an easy conception to lay to rest and throughout the years of the work there were those in the area who claimed this was all, in essence, the project entailed. But the practices undertaken, the commitment to the detail of people's everyday lives, and the curious association between everyday lives and creativity which marked the theatre denied this suspicion in all but its most antagonistic opponents.

What happened was central to this resistance to philanthropy. It was always expected that approaches to work would belie the expectations or boundaries of what was considered natural or somehow immutable in the local culture. Contrary to expectations, deeply rooted and prejudicial, that the antipode of experience in the country might be found in the city, it was discovered by those who worked in this theatre that the landscape of the area and its communal solidarities shared as many connections with the most intimate village life as it did with ideas of the alienation of the inner city. There are of course alienating aspects to village life and the level of psychological disturbance in such areas is well known to be as prevalent as in certain cities. But here the sense of alienation derived from a widening gulf between the grandiose achievements of the locality, its docks, ships and international horizons, now past, and its impoverished future expectations. The best prospects for a river navigator lay in the malfunctioning oddity of an 'expense account' river bus beyond the pocket of most who lived, as distinct from worked, in the area. Country/city polarities were also belied by the buildings in the locality. Opposite the theatre, for instance, stood St Mary's church with its chaotic graveyard unfashionably close to the local inhabitants, a phenomenon which after the plague had forced the removal of burial areas to the outskirts of conurbations. The church was surrounded on one side by Victorian ware-houses which had been in places renovated and repaired, like the theatre itself, and in others allowed to deteriorate into a jungle of inquisitive and acquisitive opportunities. The streets were narrow and winding, at places along the riverside, cutting sharply inland to avoid the riverside warehouses and in other places curious anomalies such as a city farm. Here the city reconfirmed itself as an antipode with the country: in the background to the farm animals, there emerged the postmodern frame of oblique angled high rise luxury apartments. The name of the dwelling, 'Cascades', returned as quickly as possible to the wilderness which the authors of this vision of a city on water wished to return its customers.

Introducing the idea of the area as the country in the city began to undermine the idea that monolithic definitions need prevail. My preference was to work with the situationist idea that the emotional states of an area might be as useful for living and practising in an area as sociological surveys.[6] Both empirical evidence and phenomenological surveys are important in a place where the categories of assessment have long been rooted in a prejudicial separation between one life and another. The situationists had a well known exercise of reading off the landmarks of one city with reference to the map of another. In this way, map in hand, they would seek out the Eiffel Tower in Berlin, the Statue of Liberty in London. Revisioning the locality in this way and its relationship to the more problematic nature of the financial City, with which it had had a long and troubled association, demanded that the contexts of analysis used did not simplify the social context to the charming but idiotic finality of statistical sociology. Rather the social space in which theatre occurred, the place it took up, was understood to be a shifting set of relations and negotiations that in each and every case needed analysis and continual renewal through theatre.

This went for work with people who had become labelled and contained by institutional niceties, as it did for the landscape, the street and the river. Where there was divide between social groups, the young and the old being the most obvious, the intention was to break down these categorisations and explore through theatre the ways in which creativity arose from difference and similitude. Communities defined by interest and geography have their symbolic dimension, which was central to the operation of the project. Symbolic in the sense that terms like community are understood only as something when used, and in use it is the relations between communities that gives need and cause for understanding. Where boundaries are perceived, and this differs for those involved, they are perceived symbolically in that people ascribe meaning to the boundary and the relations it implies.[7] This is an important definition as it resists the dogmatic fixing of location as somehow wholly determinant on the work as distinct from a contingent and negotiable set of relations. It was this symbolic relationship between people and their perceptions that was the day to day theatre-making milieu, not an external decree as to the identity of the area drawn from this or that study. Communities were here as imagined as realised, and it was this deeper structure to behaviour that was the focus and interest of the work.

'Being there' for the theatre maker in this milieu was different to 'being here'. It was this movement to a place which was not of origin that was the distinctive preliminary to work. This journey, beloved of anthropologists, for students and neighbours in different ways, carried with it dangers as well as promises of illumination. Inverting the exotic for the domestic the theatre maker makes strange the familiar world of the presumed and habitual patterns of everyday life. In this process of making strange a transformation takes place which cuts out the material and turns it over into the cultural context of theatre, removing it in the process from the fabric of which it was once a seamless part. The journey involved in 'being there' imposes upon the theatre maker the necessity to look twice, consciously to ascribe value to something which 'being here' simply incorporates into the background. As Walter Benjamin says in describing a common experience, the relation between foreground and distance is never retrievable in quite the same way after that first glimpse of a new place. It was in recovering this first look that the theatre maker could be reminded of where imagination worked upon the material of life, and where habit and stasis could tyrannise everyday pleasures.

It is questionable what responsibility an institution might have to an area of this kind and its 'becoming' theatre makers. It was not after all a Mission which promised a life elsewhere, in the next world, and it certainly made no claims to serve up its participants to the nirvana of professional theatre. But the utopian aspects of the project did not help stringently enough to question the romantic gestures at the root of the work. A dystopia was the inevitable outcome when parameters could not be set for what literally might have been, and was for some, a life's work. It was difficult for those outside the project to understand the subjective nature of this enterprise and its continual need to be personalised. But unlike areas of neat disciplinary distinction between well-founded areas of work, favoured playwrights or methodologies of performance, for instance, which are always more or less personalised by those who work one way and those who work another, there was very good cause for such an approach in this context. Here it was not schools of work, nor models which led the way, but daily experiences in which were grounded arguments as to ways of making theatre. It was precisely schools and their allegiances, neat divisions and their inadequacies, cosy presumptions about this or that genre that were being countered by a project which in seeking out its historical context discovered somewhat nervously it was already a small and partial part of that historical context.

An institution which chooses to separate itself from the lay curriculum, from the social space, from communities, however one wishes to describe the precondition of institutional education, is in an ethically weak position to arbitrate over a project, combining students, staff and a neighbourhood, which seeks to return to that formation to work critically and creatively within it, however problematic or romantic that might be. Politically, if not financially, the external authority remained strong however, and when confronted with the rationalisation that economies demanded chose to close the project which had given rise to a lay theatre. The separation and objectivity of institutions has few instruments which can persuade those involved in such work to give up and go home. Because going home is precisely the experience closest to the activity of 'being there' rather than 'being here'. All theatre makers have something they call a home and it is the provocative divorce of education to entice them from that context to allow for the development of new and progressive perspectives and techniques. But importantly the imagination works both on difference and equivalence. There has to be somewhere for the imagination to work a connection between these two environments. Being there is no use unless it is seen to be part of being here. Here and there in this respect become everywhere. If they are irrevocably split by the regime of education, a nowhere, answerable only to the academy and its specialist disciplines, will be the impoverished outcome. The lay theatre provided one such 'in-between', a 'meantime' for those involved to get their bearings. The gains were always jeopardised by insecurities and a lay theatre is not by definition for everyone. But representing as it did a minor proportion of what constitutes theatre pedagogy today it could not be regarded as greedy.

This process is particularly important for the theatre maker who wishes to do more than service an industry which is intellectually and emotionally discredited in many people's eyes. This state of dissatisfaction with theatre is described in the apocalyptic language of ending and beginning: there is a crisis in theatre, a dearth of 'new writers', a demand for a return to the classics. But the underlying causes of these seasonal tribulations and misinformed categories are not attended to, simply the symptoms. Once theatre's principles, management structures and practices have been challenged what is left for a future generation who wish to make theatre with and for people who to the innocent eye appear not to be touched by theatre? This lay at the heart of the project and as the description of local theatrical tradition suggests, there is always a danger in ascribing the category of theatrical ignorance to any community however seemingly reserved. The minutest gestures in certain relations form a micro-theatre which could challenge the most assertive forms considered under that title. These micro-theatres are in constant stages of emergence and disappearance and it is only because the economy of exchange in theatre is so brutally incompetent and unsubtle that these workings are not recognised in the same social space at all.

Consider the school play which occurs in multifarious venues and settings day in day out, not to mention the cacophony at seasonal festivals. Here often in the most unsubtle ways the panoply of what is considered innovative in the avant-garde is played out with more or less consciousness. It is no longer sufficient simply to point out the parallels in fine art between the coincidence of child creativity and the ability of adults to replicate this behaviour, but to place this work alongside and within the world of the theatre 'proper'. In the child's wave the theatrical deceit is pulled down, the parent waves back and instils confidence in the child that they are being seen. They have been told not to wave but they always do. They know who is there and watching with regard for them, and it is only professional training which stops actors doing the same on nights they know who is in. The theatre logic of the child in the play, searching out their own audience, suggests a personal theatre is underway in the depths of theatrical convention and in the most institutionalised settings.

Theatre work in schools does not necessarily mean working on school plays, the most overt and perhaps least superficially interesting manifestation of theatre in such places, but participating in the life of an institution which has always valued symbolic systems of communication and heightened gestures of restraint and control. Where these disciplines prevail, from the architecture to the staff room there is visible a microcosm of other relations between peoples and generations. The site for theatre here is not a service to the staff, a support system of those who are already expert or for those who have missed the relevant courses, but one which inaugurates an exchange between presence and absence. The newcomer brings their concerns, the sheath of arrows of the outsider, and takes away a sheaf of papers, notes, drawings, reflections and gestures from an 'inside' which inscribes their work from then on. The separation between educational theatre work and other theatre forms, the exceptional theoretical rectitude and energy of the movements that protect and endorse these areas as radical, suggests that something is endangered and frightened by pluralism of approach. Dogmatism asserts itself where the theatre thinks it can play the single discipline game of other more conceptually efficient and dominant systems of practice and thought. The theatre cannot defend itself in schools as a worthy subject, worthwhile for core study, as long as it attempts this on the ground of other discredited rationalities. It is precisely because it is unreasonable and critical that it is a form for education where the installation of one value will only be as successful as its acquaintance with another possibility, a reference point. Theatre here, despite its craving for security and intellectual acceptance has to say: farewell to reason. That is not to say: goodbye to thought.

Theatre within schools in the area is one of the most overt and less subtle activities a theatre in a locality might participate in. The school is a corral where, to a greater or lesser extent, in the present system the possibilities often diminish with age, the imagination is still fostered as a part of the human disposition. Confronting the locality and responding to the neighbourhood has long been central to the curriculum of all but the least progressive schools. But this need simply indicates the extent to which institutions must go to bridge a divide that their constitution depends upon for credibility. Where the intention is integrated work across age and race, gender and interest, an object is required sufficiently broad in scope to integrate the variety of groups and individuals who might wish to participate and sufficiently localised to allow for common interests and obsessions.

It is worth briefly considering how this occurred in the theatre I am describing. In one case it was thought that a grave in the churchyard outside the door of the theatre might suffice as an object of attention. It provided a text, a location and an interred body worthy of theatrical resurrection. The grave was that of a Palauan Prince, Lee Boo, whose story was known to many in the area but little known outside. In 1783 a mail boat crewed by local men had run aground off a group of Pacific islands. The crew were met by islanders, whose chief organised the reconstruction of their shattered boat. In reciprocation the chief asked whether the crew would return to England with his son, Lee Boo, in order that he might know another life. On arrival back in the docks Lee Boo became familiar in the area and within months had succumbed to smallpox, died, and was buried.

The locus of issues and surprises surrounding this story were ones which could not be ignored by a theatre, particularly one which treated with great scepticism the idea of documentary or local history dramatisations, and rejected all forms of social realism and simplistic ideas of community plays. The gravestone which initiated the activity carried a part of the fable which had taunted novelists and film-makers with its elliptical message. The involvement of a television series added a veneer of technology to the 200th anniversary of this prince's death, and the theatre event which moved from church, to street, to theatre building included the participation of hundreds of young and older people from the vicinity which was to be enveloped by the processional event. The event logistically could only happen once and a sense of uniqueness characterised its construction.

The event began in the local church with a ceremony of reburial. The vicar had agreed to participate in what might have appeared a somewhat pagan mix of ritual and celebration. But then the same vicar was known for conducting a regular hog-roast that had its own bacchanalian dimension and happily harboured within his boundary walls the spirit of 'Ma Rachel', the subject of local ghost mythology. A cortège of sea creatures, incongruously built around the vehicles available to the project, ferried the adorned coffin through the streets in an unintentional parody of the most spectacular local funeral. These events were notorious for their splendour and extravagance with countless limousines decked with a riot of floral tributes spelling out the identity of the beloved and messages of sympathy. In Lee Boo's case it was a forlorn rewriting of history, a long overdue acknowledgement that his end was not quite up to his beginnings. It was a post-colonial gesture to a small island whose status as an independent nation has been continually at the mercy of the strategic interests of Pacific superpowers. To close, having thronged the streets, inundated the theatre workshop and eaten bananas sponsored somewhat ironically by Fyffes, the beflowered coffin was to be lowered to the river, and rowed out into the Thames. But currents of nature are notoriously unhelpful to theatre culture and the top-hatted oarsman was last seen disappearing the wrong way and apparently out of control, towards Greenwich. This same oarsman, a local entrepreneur and cultural fixer, later unhitched his houseboat from a set of adjacent warehouses suffering financial embarrassment, and disappeared in the same direction, downstream, not to return.

The need to work inside and out, with trained and untrained people from the locality and visitors to the area, was typical of other projects undertaken during the years of the theatre. None of these ambitions would be a surprise to those whose work has centred on environmental, site-specific or educational work. The purpose here though was at all times to link that work back and across generations through the participation of older people in the area whose own time was more flexible than it had been in their working lives. The event would be recognised by the participation of the schools but would also expect to challenge the limits of those schools to incorporate within their strictures and structures an anarchistic enterprise. This kind of licensed carnival is understandably the object of derision for those who believe that revolutions occur by confronting, not casting, employees of state institutions such as the law and education. Yet the distinct psychological merit of the work for each participant is at odds with its diffuse sociological meaning in broader political terms. It is the individual's relations to the collective that is provoked by this work on small and discreet levels and in ways which have done more to alter everyday lives than the most abstruse theoretical endeavours could conceive of. While the revolution is delayed the theatre continues to revision the present, by turning its face to past and future. In that sense it will always be the meanwhile theatre.

If this reaching between young and old was one site of activity, the project had to answer for why an adult population, young and old, was invisible in the work. It was not visible because it was working or unemployed. Both became the locus for other performances and prompted the question why the defining feature of the area was its characteristic odour. On emergence from the local underground station one could be forgiven on certain days with a north-easterly blowing for thinking that one had stepped into a world of confection. A sweet but sickly air was what there was to breathe and it was a mark of longevity in the area for those who would answer a visitor's query with: 'What smell?' Living directly opposite the source did little in terms of immunisation except foster my interest in how this transformation of a locality could be so regularly achieved with such apparent disregard from any authority. Few other sensual experiences would have been allowed to penetrate the locality and everything it did. Washing left to dry on certain days in June would radiate the aroma of next year's Christmas puddings. Calendars and clocks could be set by the regularity of production: it's bourbon it must be Wednesday, it's marmite it must be the night shift.

Peek Freans, a brand of baked confections, had occupied a ten-acre site in the locale since its previous premises at the dockhead had burnt down in the mid-nineteenth century. It was reported at the time that the dough flowing from the conflagration had run into the streets and been heated by the flames. By the morning the thoroughfare had baked into an enormous delicacy. At that time the biscuits were being provided for ships using the docks and it was with the technological development of aerating dough that the sweet biscuit as it is known today was developed for a domestic market. For this expansion the company had the foresight to establish what was at the time the largest factory of its kind on the border between Rotherhithe and Bermondsey. The site had previously been used as a market garden to produce vegetables for the city and it was predictive of the future of the area that this marginal pastoral role should give way to an industry of appearance rather than substance.

The closing of the factory by the parent company run from North America was in itself an embarrassment for a well known and if not loved, at least tolerated local institution. Generations had worked in the factory and there were few people we worked with in the area who did not have some story to tell of what had happened in there to themselves, this or that aunt, uncle and so on. Working in the factory itself concentrated the mind on both the absurdity of the object being produced as the example of the 'extruder' suggests but always stimulated a sense of awe at the scale on which the operation, in the end a delicacy, was still being run. At the height of production the factory had employed thousands and now, with technology and reduced production, it was hundreds, waiting for closure and redeployment or redundancy. The site itself however had not diminished and the buildings ranged from the Victorian splendour of the pudding rooms to the vast oven rooms of the 1950s and the predominance of savouries over sweets – small bags for behind the bar. It was in the older area of the factory that an event was created for those who worked in the factory and those who wished to see inside before it closed.

Prising open an institution of this size to reveal its theatre was not as difficult as the security suggested. Within the factory at management level were those same imaginative people who often hold positions of power and harbour unwittingly or consciously the desire to see their place of work put in its place. The production manager at the time was one such, who regularly jogged ten miles into work and followed the marathon circuit. His voice was pitched, like many who work in conditions of intense mechanical activity, at an uncomfortably forceful level for office conversation. The desk was obviously not where he was happiest. I came upon him there examining a biscuit hanging from a human hair. It was threaded through the middle, baked around the human remainder that reminds entrepreneurs that people are involved in production and consumption and that the latter rarely like to see evidence of the former in what they eat. From here, and with the free licence to move around the factory at will, though always dressed in regulation whites and hair cap, a daily diet of images, stories, jokes, ribaldry and sorrow would come my way. It would not be exaggerating to describe as Dickensian the qualities of a factory where generation after generation of a family had entered and only left to get married or retire. Where this was an internal affair the woman had formerly had to leave, there being a prohibition on partnerships in the workplace. On the eve of departure the bride would be given a tier of cake for each year she had been in the factory. In the entrance to the factory stood a replica of the cake presented to a prince and a princess, and in the basement I found dust-covered certificates of triumph in the World's Fairs of the nineteenth century and one of the first industrial films of the twentieth. This spectacle of everyday working life, the residue of production and reproduction, demanded heightened aesthetic forms, verse and music, to transcend the environment without denying its power. Here to ignore the environment would have been to submit to the laziest egotism of the purpose-built theatre, where there is no competition. The point here was to accept what the everyday had to offer as well as the likelihood that it would effortlessly eclipse the attempt to transform its tyrannies. You cannot ask a factory to stop, to be quiet. It goes, and to some degree theatre goes along with it until capital retreats and it closes with no more pomp than the producer of hot air it always was. Here factory and theatre seem to have no greater claim to sympathy: though one paid more wages than the other it also injured more than the other. The factory certainly won more certificates and international accolades for its productions.

The event itself, like many others, was researched over a year, happened on a single occasion after minimal but concentrated preparation, was not recorded and would not excite great interest beyond the audience who witnessed it and those who participated in it, if it were not for the curious relations it throws up between the imagination and production. The dialectic between leisure and work, vision and triviality, is the ground where the alienations of the everyday as well as the pleasures of everyday life are played out. My introduction to the factory had not only been through its connection with the lives of almost everyone in the locality but specifically through working over a year with a group of visually impaired performers. One of my first conversations with a member of that group was about their job at the factory: sorting broken biscuits from good. They knew the place was full of stories but did not grasp the relation between the individual chance event of their task and the complex industrial relations which had segregated their labour from others, their 'disabilities' from others' 'abilities'. Theatre became the means to link the miniature and the massive. It is in this nexus that there is something for theatre to work upon. In the case of this factory there was the added dimension that one of the symptoms of production was an aspect of the sensorium which had long been derided. Hegel would have us believe in his *Aesthetics* that smell is not a category worthy of aesthetic speculation, falling behind sight and hearing as a medium of aesthetic appreciation. But in seeking the boundaries between theatre and everyday life, smell has something to tell. Vision dominates the aesthetic consciousness of those who can see but smell unnervingly reminds those living in places where such an amorphous phenomenon is left, of a world that has been lost to today's hygienic regimes. It is necessary in a book about theatre and everyday life to consider how the sensorium of theatre has been removed from that of the everyday, with the complete eclipse of the chemical senses at the behest of the higher-order faculties of sight and hearing. This oculocentrism is the object of the next chapter. These were not predominant thoughts when the theatre described above was being made. It was after all a verse performance with a musical score, with a seated audience and other trappings of theatrical convention. But it was infused by its environment in ways which a backdrop or photographs can hardly begin to suggest. The event was as much made by its setting as it made that setting anew and in so doing reproduced the relations between people and nature that is the fruit of labour and politics.

In these two approaches to work, both involving local histories and

geographies, integrating work between different generations, entering institutions and leaving them, moving between the street and the interior – in
these negotiations between places and people the poetics and politics of a
lay theatre become discernible. The examples are always parochial given
the limited resources and contingency of people's sporadic availability;
there were after all other commitments and most who became involved
had other more pressing family or work demands on their time. One
theatre can always be replaced with another more fruitful model and in
this way the examples simply invite other experiences from the reader. It
is not perhaps the events in themselves that beyond their moment were
of interest to anyone, perhaps not even those who participated in them,
but rather the occupation of the terrain of theatre as a place to conduct
operations, try out tactics and resolve difficulties that had previously been
thought the prerogative of other dimensions of life.

To conclude this chapter I want to talk about these dimensions, for
they provide certain boundaries which define what I can discuss as theatre.
The first dimension of life which was poached upon, and it remains that
most elusive dimension, was that of everyday life itself. It was this discreet
area of habit and custom that provided the most stimulating boundary
with which, and against which to work. It would make itself known when
people would disappear because dinner was ready, or dinner needed to be
prepared, when older people would leave to attend a funeral or recover
from an illness, and therefore was first apparent through the absence of
an individual or group. If theatre was not being made it was likely that
everyday life had reasserted itself elsewhere and for a while would have
to take precedence. It was not appropriate to appeal to the structures of
the professional theatre as a separated institution from everyday life, the
expectation that rehearsal times would take precedence over meal times,
unless of course the object was to rid the work of those whose involvement
demanded a continual negotiation with the expectations of the everyday
world. Unlike 'professionals' whose lives revolve around a more or less
limited purpose, institutionally centred and separated from everyday life,
the lack of distinction within the community between theatre and other
activities of equal merit, the lack of a hierarchy, would mean that theatre
was to be negotiated at every turn by those involved, with those who
were more involved elsewhere.

This of course meant that the quality of what was being made, if it
aspired to do more than separate itself fatally from the neighbourhood,
was of a different nature to that of a theatre which was the single-minded
raison d'être of the participants. There was rarely a flattening of experience
that is often the experience of an established theatre, the tendency here
being rather to wild oscillation between the wondrous and the wicked.
There is perhaps some expectation that those involved in an activity,
particularly an art, would wish to dedicate themselves to it, to separate

themselves from other diverting activities in order to specialise and to refine their technique. But this is not true in professions which call themselves expert, falsely hoping their specialisation differentiates them from the everyday, and not true in the terrain where everyday life meets theatre. For in all these places there is more or less involvement at different times with negotiating the terms of this balance between specialism and generality. It was this continual sense of definition between something worth doing and something worth exchanging that made the work consciously one of commitment and choice. Such judgements are not necessarily as apparent when these terms and conditions within a profession begin to be institutionalised and expected as the precondition for involvement – this does not mean they don't exist, they are just more covert. This was often why events would happen once, if at all. To repeat the event would have aspired to perpetuation of a set of relations which were so contingent as to be impossible to hold together. The extrapolation from processes of this kind to look for solutions to society's problems is therefore a fraught one. For all this model would offer would be a shifting and anarchistic enterprise where the rules of engagement are no more lasting than the particular work being undertaken in a certain time and place. But this does accord in some ways with the description postmodernism has provided of the contradictory nature of experience beyond reason: a 'parology' of voices, 'rhizomatic' responses, and the possibility of '*différance*', and while not needing academically to endorse those terms to give credibility to practices already justified, it is interesting to note how the most everyday life bears out and questions the most recent abstruse theoretical endeavours. For this reason the critical endeavour associated with the term 'postmodernism' is not to be rejected because of its apparently ineffectual relativism, but rather put in perspective. Given that all knowledge is relative it is dialectically obvious that this partiality is given any meaning it has by 'absolutes'. Therefore judgement is critical to the process of conducting relations between the approximate and the normative. In the pages that follow the links, connections and transitions between such theories and practices are examined with the aim of ascertaining what relevance judgement derived from criticism and the everyday has for the theatre, and whether the judgement being shown now is good judgement. I reiterate, it is not theatre's purpose to offer models for societal arrangement, it is theatre's purpose to antagonise official views of reality which answer for such arrangements, and in this it shares a welcome affiliation with recent theoretical endeavour. Judgement however remains a central critical capacity for those wishing to consider how good the theatre is, and historically how good it has been.

The relation between such theories and theatre practices, like those of the lay theatre, is one which has not been thought in the past to be worthy of serious or extended consideration. It would appear that while literature and other documented forms of cultural activity are, by their very immobility, given the attentions of these conceptual revolutions, more abstruse forms such as theatre are in their own ways ruled outside this domain by their very shifting nature. It is important to reassert the possibility that the most avant-garde texts are of more use in these local and apparently modest contexts than the dogmatisms of definition which answer to purely political and sectarian objectives and are the critical remains, leftovers, cast aside for the community and all its works. These dogmatic perspectives have little of the fluidity that everyday life and theatre demonstrate, for what these two quite incommensurable objects demand is a constant realignment between necessity and imagination, between tactics and strategies and between producers and consumers.

Theatre and everyday life are incommensurable because the conditions for meaningfulness for the descriptive terms of one language, the point of view which arises from theatre, do not permit the use of the descriptive terms of another language such as that of the everyday. It would appear on first sight that the two terms and their frames of reference are mutually exclusive, the one only being possible at the eclipse of the other. This would seem to present an impossible conundrum for a study of this kind. Like the actor who doubles up parts but then finds both characters meet in a final denouement, talking about theatre and everyday life together apparently demands rapid entrances and exits. But this does not mean that the terms of both mean merely different things, or that they are completely disconnected – there is on the contrary a subtle and interesting relation between their conditions of meaningfulness.[8] It is these relations which mark out the changing divide between the written and unwritten theatre that is the object of study in this book.

As well as taking people from and to the theatre, everyday life has other more obvious conditions of association with that theatre. Theatre poaches on everyday life for its content, relationships, humour, surprise, shock, intimacy and voyeurism. It takes for its forms unities of time and place, domestic settings, landscapes and speech patterns that are often identifiable because they are drawn from everyday life, and are celebrated precisely because they are somehow true to that world. But 'that world' is interesting because its codes and conventions are under a continual process of transformation often leaving the naturalism of theatre beached and irrelevant in the wake of its modernity. Everyday life can be stubbornly non-Aristotelian when it tries. It is all very well to quote the Marxist refrain 'Philosophers have so far interpreted the world, the point is to change it', but what 'world' is to be changed – the rarefied and specialised or the despised everyday? The identification of relevant theatrical forms for certain times and places was not therefore the point, but rather the constant attention to the shifting relations between two incommensurable entities, the theatre and the everyday lives of those it sought. An explanation of theatre and everyday life is not enough, given the ethical questions which the relations between the two pose. Rather an understanding of everyday life can provide a basis for a critical response to theatre. The purpose of identifying these incommensurable objects is to transform their possible relations through criticism. Not recognising the existence, never mind complex nature, of the one, will always inhibit the understanding of the other.

Incommensurability does not make things difficult for practitioners of theatre or livers of everyday life. It simply makes it difficult for those writing about the two activities in order to ascertain their relations with the purpose at one moment to bring them closer together, at another to keep them apart. For in writing there is thought to be the need for stability of meaning throughout an argument, whereas practices depend upon both the interpretation of situations and the constant need to change them. Writing has never been a simple supplement to practice, yet it endangers the specificity of practices in its categories and classifications. For instance, for the sake of consistency and for reasons of confidentiality, reference is not made in the foregoing to people by name, but by type. But all practices immediately confront the individuality of groups. The lay theatre has a curious relationship when put into writing with an idea of 'people', a relationship which demands attention before it is possible to proceed with discussion of other theatres. The space in which this theatre occurs is after all populated. The people there should not be confused with an idea of 'The People'. The everyday is placed alongside theatre for consideration in order to avoid constructing yet another reference to the people through whom so much has been justified and with whom so much less achieved.

The question is not so much 'who are the people?' For the lay theatre it was all those who in any way whatsoever participated in its practices – and surreal lists were compiled to say to supporters and detractors, this is what the theatre is and this is who does it. But why 'the people' are referred to in that way is important if the lay theatre is to have any significance. As the French theoretician Pierre Bourdieu makes clear, in his reflexive mix of sociology and anthropology, the nature of the people and the right to speak in their name is what is often at stake in the struggle between intellectuals. This struggle can be extended to a theatre where issues of cultural democracy, accessibility and popular forms over elitist attitudes mark out a complex terrain stretching from survival to subsidy. The lay theatre by its nature would appear to dispose itself to one kind of person and not another - to those outside the domain of legitimate professional status, outside institutional orthodoxy. But by its proximity to these fields of specialist discourse it understands well their languages and without mimicking them uses them as it sees best. The lay theatre, after all, took its place between the remains of the Globe and the National Theatre and understood the power of their cultural traditions. It would be a foolish theatre that did not acknowledge the relative cultural power of speaking in the name of Shakespeare or the Nation. It is aware that 'accessibility' or 'popular' definitions are ones which disqualify its products and devalue its intentions in a cultural landscape where what counts as theatre is understood to be less a matter of negotiation and more a matter of definition from its most conspicuous producers. Cultural status here derives often from flagrant inaccessibility and difficulty.

But what if in these late days of a second Elizabethan age, there were a deeper understanding and a recognition of the continuance of the kinds of negotiation which occurred around Shakespeare's theatre. Would this not throw much of what the most conspicuous producers consider theatre to be into jeopardy? Appeals to 'Shakespeare' as inviolate, or the right to speak in the name of the Nation, would become contingent upon the questions that a lay theatre asks, rather than the other way around, defining the remainder that is left for the lay theatre to be. After all, according to Stephen Greenblatt, the boundaries between the Shakespearian theatre and its world were not unlike those of the lay theatre – a sustained collective improvisation. The home of Shakespeare's theatre was barely a mile from the terrain the lay theatre worked and there is every reason here to consider its willingness to transgress limits as well as its self-regulating submission to boundaries of what theatre was meant to be:

> Life outside the theatre is full of confusion, schemes imperfectly realised, arbitrary interference, unexpected and unpredictable resistance from the body. On the stage this confusion is at once mimed and revealed to be only scripted. Of course, we may say that even onstage there is no certainty: the actors may forget their lines or blurt them out before their cue or altogether refuse to perform, the clown may decide to improvise, individuals in the audience may abandon the voluntary submission expected of them and intervene in the performance, the scaffolding may collapse and force the cancellation of the show. But this absurd, almost entirely theoretical contingency only gives the touch of freedom that seasons that disclosure of necessity.[9]

But in the lay theatre, in the second Elizabethan era, these were, for good or ill, precisely the negotiations which were underway, not the exceptions to a theatrical rule. They were neither, I believe, absurd, nor were they theoretical. They were contingent on understandings of the relations between the everyday and the people taking part. Would the fulfilment of all these conditions of transgression simply deny the status of the event as theatre? No, for the same contingency gives its own touch of freedom and discloses the necessity of the theatre that emerges in reverse from these transgressions. In other words, the lay theatre is the shadow of a theatre that is very well known to us – it is not inept, but neither can it deny the reality that stares all theatre in the face. That when something goes wrong in the theatrical fiction, a corpse here, a collapse there, it rarely forces cancellation but an *increased* level of attention and participation from the audience. This curious anomaly is no justification for the inept, but it hints at the misplaced investment in another ineptitude that so much theatre represents.

It remains that speaking for the people would provide the lay theatre with a powerful referent. No such ambition can be fulfilled without subjecting the lay theatre to the same contradictions that have impoverished other theatre definitions. It is most obvious in politics and concomitantly most obvious in 'political theatre', if such a generic thing exists, that what is most at issue is precisely this question of the people. These positions adopted to the people are in cultural fields always adopted from a position within that field. At stake, when the positions are taken up, is not just who 'the people' are exactly but the definition of the professional's own competence to speak about, and act towards such a group. This in turn depends for its efficaciousness on strict adherence to the boundary between the professional and the profane. The layman of course challenges this professional status as does a lay theatre which is always and everywhere assertively denying that most dangerous of descriptions: amateur. Admittance of the 'amateur' is the acceptance of a segregated culture where play and work have been finally divorced, where what is 'left over' for those outside the specialised and professional is so trivial as to have become the site for distracting alienations – jealousy, gossip and power. This is not to deny that some of the best theatre occurs under this inauspicious sign.

What is 'popular', that other referent so closely aligned to people somewhere or other, becomes a block to the professional's legitimation of their own position. Often the popular is adopted by just those professionals whose own position is most insecure within the cultural field of which they are a marginal part. This is not always the case, as those who work out of television or opera and into theatre demonstrate, bringing with them a different cultural capital to that of the community artist or educational theatre maker. But for some 'the people' and the 'popular' have become a safe haven against failure. The people have quite enough to be getting on with despite this unwarranted burden. In turn a double bind occurs for the practitioner whose appeals to the people jeopardise both their position in the cultural field in which they thought they had a role and conspicuously exiles them from the realm of the people they refer to. It is not perhaps surprising that it has been in the definition of a political theatre since the 1950s that the most acute battle for the people rages, and it is not a battle which can either be forgotten by the lay theatre or accepted uncritically as though that were its own terrain. For built on an idea of the people it cannot be. The terms of the argument are precisely outside its existence, circulating as they do around a set of polarities to do with anti-intellectualism and artistry which deny the terms on which any good theatre can thoughtfully and artistically revision everyday life.

What would be the purpose after all of justifying, supporting and encouraging people to exclude themselves from the most potent and enduring forms of art, whatever they might be? Where alternatives to the 'canon' involve the same kinds of social and creative energy as Shakespearian texts then there is good reason to. But where such distinction simply reinforces the menial nature of so many cultural forms available to groups and individuals, to the people, the rejection of what is perceived as culturally dominant is to deny major genres to those who already are most dispossessed. Like forms of popular language, slang for instance, the dominated is defined by relation to the dominant. Slang would be meaningless without the language it departs from. Pierre Bourdieu believes there to be a confusion here as to the nature and effects of resistance: 'if in order to resist I have no other resource than to lay claim to that in the name of which I am dominated, is this resistance?'[10] Does in turn the adoption of mandarin tongues and Queen's English, the language of the dominant, amount to submission to inauthenticity or power? Examining the idea of the people demonstrates that it is rarely the destitute who are in any position to resist in the first place, for resistance in itself is predicated on a store of cultural capital that some people simply do not have. On the other hand those who were most active in the lay theatre, young and old, commanded considerable cultural capital – nothing I have said should suggest there was any need for ministry here. It was simply a currency that far too few would recognise as having value.

The people, like theatre, brings in its wake its own shadow which is worth looking at. The role models the lay theatre most regularly confronted were those which depended for their influence on deep levels of identification and in some cases hero worship. Where there is the strongest sense of a 'people' there is often discernible the clearest examples of those who 'made it', for instance a Bermondsey Boy called Tommy Steele, or a saintly singer called Max Bygraves. In this case 'A people is a detour of nature to get to one or two great men.'[11] Any idea of the masses is confirmed by these extraordinary individuals who are literally larger than life at the same time as being 'no different from you or me'. It is not the names that matter, as in all hagiography, but episodes which are passed on like lore from one character to the next. This makes people's lives particularly prone to imitation, and where these lives are exemplary can lead to social responsibility and profound social development. Not far from where Tommy and Max were born had lived a Doctor Salter whose reputation was, like other doctors in the docks, legendary, an exemplary life lived among those he cared for. But where these lives arise from other values of commerce and avarice the saintly demeanour becomes an ironic and playful, though deleterious, theatre of imitation. Whether Max or Tommy had any choice in their lives is open to question; it is not so much that they created their chances, but that their success, once it was achieved, was a foregone conclusion – 'he always had it in him'. If they are saintly they are careful not to lose anything which was there in the first place, not even an accent which reminds one of origins in the absence of effigies. The Bermondsey Boy also happens to be a popular local statue making haste to, or speedy retreat from, the local library outside which he stands.

The passage from the private community, isolated and inward looking, to the public sphere of entertainment, is undertaken by the star who becomes a saint through the means of personal lonely trials and public shows of strength or miracles. Deeds of goodness, giving to charity, local returns from the distant land of success in show business or television are all treated as exemplary and to be revered. They also provide the clearest role models, far more assertive than any ethical writings or religious direction of the present day, to those left behind. The founding place of the star is left: not to leave is inconceivable and success is predicated on such a departure to allow for the celebrated return. That place of departure, the exact location of the flat in the estate, becomes something of a shrine. The conversions that occur here are ones of imagination for those who remain. The fact that Tommy and Max 'have not changed' is testament to a space of potential success, with which, even if they are not exactly around that much any more, there is still a connection felt, and a pleasure taken in their deeds. These deeds are after all for the edification of a community which never forgets its own. The terms of this remembrance are ones which inflect on the lay theatre, and are used to judge that theatre's minority appeal, hesitant progress and apparent disregard for success. Caught between this hagiography and 'the people' who write it with their respect, the lay theatre has to 'make do', poaching on the circulating energies of everyday lives which always deny the comfortable and comforting extremes of stardom or banality.

Lay theatre is not therefore another term for a popular theatre or a vernacular theatre, a poor theatre or an amateur theatre. It is at ease in the use of major languages and techniques of performance if those are ones which bring desired ends. It is from these sources that cultural capital circulates most energetically and it denies these in favour of a spurious object at its peril. Lay theatre is a minority within a majority, always political by the very nature of its relation to the major contents and expressions of theatre and constantly redefining the places in which theatre occurs. It is in this tract, by no means a no man's land for it is the layman's world, that theatre and everyday life are worth negotiating and contesting. This tract is one which is spatial, physical and ethical. Like the word tract itself, the lay theatre has three characteristics which are important in contesting official views of reality and negotiating other ways of seeing realities. One is that it occurs in a region or area of indefinite extent, unpicks geographical niceties and reconstitutes places and populations in critical ways. Second it is constituted by the area of bodily organs, the tracts of olfaction and respiration, which are the capacity for human expression and reception, and are the reminder that theatre after all is about human being. Lastly, it is a theatre only articulated by the writing and discourse of belief, it remains unwritten until this belief is shown in it, not because it is make-believe, but unlike so many discredited religions and politics, has the power to make you believe. So how, in this tract where theatre and everyday life occur, can the value of performance be located, written and regarded? That this tract is from here and now also an imaginary landscape should not divert our search for its incidental glories.

2

REGARDING THEATRE

Seeing, watching and looking at theatre do not begin to explain what happens between an audience and a performer. Regarding theatre is both the vision of theatre and the care the body takes in the presence of theatre to understand and value what is happening, to have belief in it. But the cultural predominance of sight as a medium of aesthetic reception hinders this ethical and political dimension of the perception of theatre. Vision has a history that profoundly affects the way theatre is witnessed. This history perpetuates the fallacy that an audience can remain aloof from performance. The political model that such distance endorses, an intellectual disengagement for the purpose of thought, seems to me a less than adequate response to the complex relations between theatre and its audiences. This discussion of vision and visionality is the terrain where the relations between the mental and the material in theatre are played out. This terrain raises questions of the image and imagination which this chapter takes as its object.

The theatre image is composed of material elements – bodies in action and speech articulated in places, and a receptive audience for that action and speech. The images of other arts are constituted in quite different ways. This engagement has a metaphysical aspect in that the image between the performer and the audience adds up to more than the sum of its various parts. A materialist criticism that does not recognise these 'metaphysical' qualities of theatre is lacking critical force. For the 'beyond physical', the numinous, the spirit, the aura of art, however it is described is a material response to art not just ideological or 'imagined'. This 'something more' than the thing itself is attested to by too many people without deference to gender, race or class. And to ignore it, as though it will go away, and leave us with the quantified, the material and the manipulable, in the name of dogmatic sectarian objectives, is to impoverish the terms on which theatre might be most valuably and pleasurably thought and practised. This metaphysics of theatre is what is not seen, beyond the mind's eye it remains unwritten. It is the domain which both makes theatre worthwhile and simultaneously jeopardises its effects. For it is in

58

this hinterland of the undocumented and discreet that the fallacies of theatre are nourished. This 'something more' of the image does not disconnect the experience of theatre from its place of performance, nor from the everyday. Theatre remains bound by its context precisely through the unique relationship images create between audience, performer and everyday life.

Regarding theatre then entails more than just looking at this theatre, it requires a poetics which will allow political and ethical judgements to be made. If judgement is to be possible it is no longer sufficient to say how one knows what is real, but how one knows what one is seeing and experiencing and its relation to reality. At a time when seeing has become believing it is worth reminding theatre that its responsibility is still to disrupt, not to acquiesce with this spectacle. Theatre images carry this potential, but unmoored from ethical and political consideration, they can be disregarded as aesthetic niceties. The common argument about the efficacy or entertainment of theatre is one which revolves around these unresolved issues. The point of this chapter is to relocate theatre images in the context they have been artificially removed from, that is the continual negotiation between what we 'know' and our means of expressing that knowledge. For this purpose it is impossible to go on ignoring that other mystical reservoir, second only to the everyday for its uncharted depths: the imagination. The imagination is not in my view an untethered human phenomenon, but directed by, and towards, the service of the ethical and political operations that make up everyday life. For that reason images and imagination have to be placed within the poetics, ethics and politics that inflect on them and in turn are shaped by them.

But before I can continue with this admittedly expansive task I have to clarify a popular misconception which threatens everything that follows. Arguments have been made that the 'something more' of the theatre image occurs across the spectrum of communications, that there is little to differentiate the experience of high or low art, operas or soap operas. Taking issue with such a conflation of forms would seem to me important on grounds of ethics and politics, regardless of the aesthetic reservations one could have. There is obviously good and bad television, as there is theatre, but the constraints and institutionalised production processes of television make it an unlikely medium through which truth telling can flourish. It is one of the most likely sites for official views of reality to be perpetuated and it is now the first target for control by any coup likely to succeed. At present there are many theatres which lie wholly outside institutional orthodoxy and make alternative broadcasting look both mainstream and conservative. Unless the communications media are to take a radical departure from their current authorised practices and state-licensed operations this situation appears to determine the near future of anything approaching a nonconformist medium. I would then draw a line between believing in soap operas, their stars and their stars' futures, and believing through participation in the fate of a character in whose presence is experienced the process of live theatre, the tragedy and humour of its action. The distance of television allows for a gratuitous sympathy while the theatre through the power of images will never produce more than an empathy born of intelligence and feeling. And it is this limitation of theatre, the defining limitation of its form, never much more or less than a school play, that distinguishes it from the excesses of television. The metaphysics of performance cannot be explained away as easily as the mysteries of the cathode ray tube, and that in itself makes them worthy of more attention.

This does not deny that theatre can be many things, but if normative questions about theatre such as ethics and value are to be given equal thought alongside empirical evidence, it is my responsibility to clarify what I consider game for consideration. I am here interested in all forms of theatre which:

> stimulate debate and pleasure;
> provoke reaction;
> provide resources for living;
> engage emotions and intellect;
> confound expectations.

I am not here talking about cultural forms which:

> deny discussion and feeling;
> reinforce passivity;
> belittle belief;
> disengage emotions and intellect;
> confirm expectations.

I will not divide these expectations of performance between categories such as high and low, popular and traditional, mainstream and alternative, environmental and auditorium, elite and community. There can be no *a priori* categorisation of which features are apparent in musicals, dance, performance, nor theatrical manifestations within everyday life. Any genre of cultural activity may, because of particular properties peculiar to it, have specific social usage made of it, but this does not stop a diversity of use being made of the most apparently constraining forms. This is what is so enduring and essentially democratic about theatre. Disciplinary boundaries undermine this democracy. They are already well enough entrenched and such division does not necessarily help in ascertaining whether an activity is meaningful, relevant or not. Given that theatre is always and everywhere historically and geographically changing, that it is contingent on the most local concerns, and is not immutable or achievable where dogma has prevailed, it would be reckless to judge which generic kinds of activity are more or less likely to meet the above criteria.

It is however possible to make some comparisons that point to the problem in thinking that theatre shares anything with cultural forms which have made use of its operations. While television is often 'banal' in its sophistication, its pleasure is a knowing banality and deprives us of naive and simple responses which are important to any range of expressive behaviour. A relevant theatre is truly banal without any sophistication. 'Banal' is used here in the sense of a commonality – a potential meeting site for people in a common culture.[1] It is not sophisticated because of the connotations of 'artifice' that word brings with it. For theatre is an act of presence and presentation, and if relevant it confronts and confounds pretence and representation. Theatre images are of a qualitatively different kind to those phenomena produced by television. Theatre is irreducible to mechanical reproduction and invites us back to consider its unique place every time we wish to speak of it. And in an age when there is little that is new but much that is reproduced on a scale inconceivable a decade ago, this call to the distinctiveness of theatre, in each of its unrepeatable elements, is of course an aesthetic, an ethical and political statement.

What do I mean by these terms in this context? The aesthetic is considered here to be a contributory element of a poetics, which as a 'defence' of poetry or the 'dramatic', in Aristotelian terms, is the position beyond an understanding of the workings of value and pleasure which aesthetics describes. Thus the aesthetic category is incorporated within a poetics which is its activity 'in' and 'on' theatre and the world. This is not only an internal question of theatre's mechanics because a cultural poetics has to account for the exclusions, conventions and practices which determine the identity theatre can negotiate for itself in any one time or place. My conception of poetics is inseparable from ethics and politics. But to make discussion possible I have broken it down into three aspects which maintain a relation with the other two realms. Poetics is made up of witness and documentary, testimony and knowledge and belief and imagination. I will not be concentrating on this or that manifestation of ethics in theatre, but on ways of introducing ethics as a valid concept for theatre in the first place. Without such a rationale it would be impossible to insist on its relevance in a climate where it is little discussed, or indeed thought to be downright irrelevant to a 'political' theatre. An ethics of theatre after all, at this time of negation and denial of norms, might appear to be a contradiction in terms, but the transactions of theatre are deeply bound to negotiations between the self and the other which are themselves the definition of an ethics. Equally my discussion of politics will not enter into detail concerning the very real manifestation of political conservatism that has become increasingly widespread; rather I will concentrate on broader conceptual understandings and imaginings of this place and this time. This will require considerable abstraction from the pressing historical circumstances considered in the discussion of what a lay theatre might be. This does not deny these realities, it is simply another way of talking about the same thing. This chapter ironically represents another pair of eyes, hoping to see another perspective on the same problem.

These questions are asked with a degree of scepticism about the critical context of postmodernism and its offspring. Theatre might occur in an intellectual landscape of proliferating heterogeneity, but simultaneously transnational finance increases the likelihood of its traditional venues being 'taken over', 'bought out' and subsumed within multi-corporations. As knowledge and information systems escalate this heterogeneity gives way to the suspicion that no more of all available knowledge is understood than it was at the advent of the printing press. Storage and retrieval of information is a highly prized operation but has little to do with understanding. Theatre does not work in the time–space of this deep binarism, this acceleration of the encyclopaedic tradition. It is rather 'rhizomatic', it makes disconcerting and unpredictable associations, has nothing to do with representation and oscillates between the material and metaphysical.[2] In this it shares something with everyday activities threatened by the homogeneity of modern life. Theatre is nothing if it is not understood. To understand is not a dry theoretical capacity but a practice which combines the physical and the mental in equal measure, and denies that a solely intellectual response to experience is ever possible. For understanding is the premiss for the accretion of experience and knowledge but more obliquely, for those brought up in the everyday environment of a circus family, the supporting act of the person who provides the base for the human pyramid. And this 'understanding' is not limited to those who make a profession of being well balanced. Like those in the Catalan festival who rush to shore up the toppling Castillos in Sitges, knowing why you are understanding and the dangers of understanding are never divorced.

To 'think theatre' is to transgress disciplinary boundaries in the name of a more relevant theatre.[3] To do otherwise is to speak in the name of disciplines which are not in themselves of the theatre and will not advance the theatre in desired ways. If this suggests that I believe there is an 'essence' of theatre then that may not be wholly reactionary. For to be without your own understanding of what that 'essence', or 'Idea' of a theatre might be, as Francis Fergusson referred to it,[4] is to consign theatre to an adjunct of its border disciplines: literature and physical education. Debating this essence is not to confine theatre as an inert fact of nature, nor to subscribe to an overarching essentialism, but to set about liberating the discussion of what it could be from the restraints of literary boundaries. As Martin Heidegger says of technology:

the essence of technology is by no means anything technological.

Thus we shall never experience our relationship to the essence of technology so long as we merely conceive and push forward the technological, put up with it, or evade it . . . we are delivered over to it in the worst possible way when we regard it as something neutral; for this conception of it, to which today we particularly like to do homage, makes us utterly blind to the essence of technology.[5]

Resisting the 'neutrality' that Heidegger speaks of both demands a sceptical attitude to what is described and accepted as theatre and requires perspectives from outside theatre's domain to sustain doubt. But where are these to come from if not the social sciences? In this chapter these perspectives come from texts but do not return the theatre to literary antecedents – the texts considered are ones which speak more of the multifarious realm of the everyday than the seclusion of the study, are more concerned with discursive practices than the apartheid of theory and the world. But perspective also comes from the nature of the struggle to write the previously unwritten – the apparently mysterious thought 'beyond' human reason and therefore the domain of religious explanation. The relevance of a scientist describing the ascension of a balloon or attempting to talk about what happens 'below space' may not appear to be of first importance to theatre. But all disciplines strike breaking points and the essence of theatre will only be understood in the company of other attempts to chart the imaginary.

The friction between a static entity, the conventions and accepted traditions of theatre, and a constantly evolving form which requires evaluation, that is theatre as I have described it, can be clarified by looking closer at the discourse that surrounds this realm. If the essence of theatre is in its images, theatre no longer resides as an object of study, separated from its audience for it is in their imagination that images occur. Theatre images are by definition a 'transaction' which are part of an economy of symbolic exchange. The forms and contents of this transaction change continually in apparently unpredictable ways, but certain logics do become apparent on closer scrutiny. The image is central to the act of theatre, the analysis of its logic is the thought of theatre, and is to be given priority here over dramatic textual exegesis or historical research.

POETICS

Why should grappling with the nature and composition of images precede engagement with two such established strategies for describing theatre as literary criticism and historiography? The first foregrounds an element of the theatre process above others, namely the dramatic text, and contributes more to the field of literary studies than it does to the practice of theatre itself. The second relies upon the archival record to reconstruct a theatre that once existed but is now, by definition, dead. A poetics of theatre cannot be devised initially from either because the essence of the theatre, its distinguishing feature, is concealed in both. As Terry Eagleton is only too aware in his brief encounter with dramatic literature in *Criticism and Ideology*, there is a clear distinction to be made between the evaluation of the dramatic text and the discussion of theatre. It is a distinction which runs in the twentieth century from the writings of Edward Gordon Craig to the contemporary theatre and bears reiteration once again:

> A dramatic production does not 'express', 'reflect' or 'reproduce' the dramatic text on which it is based; it 'produces' the text, transforming it into a unique and irreducible entity . . . Text and production are incommensurate because they inhabit distinct real and theoretical spaces.[6]

As with the relations between theatre and everyday life, text and production are incommensurable but not unrelated; simply the language and terms of one resist the expressions of the other. It is the real and theoretical space of production that is of interest here, not that of the dramatic text in the study, and that space is far from irreducible to analysis. I have already begun to explain why it should not be considered an empty space in the first place. Images may, and often do derive lasting reverberations from textual elements but an image is not wholly dependent on any text and often arises without and despite textual preparation.[7] This thesis questions the characterisation of theatre of the contemporary period as a 'literary' form, a proposition which is already and continually confirmed by the relations between verbal language and physical imagery in all theatre. If it were literary it might be thought the most appropriate means with which to address it would be drawn from literary criticism. And this remains one of the widespread ways in which people first come upon the conventions of theatre, the shape of the language on the page being the only hint that something about this text is different from prose or poetry. However, though certain playwrights have been associated with the theatre, in what have become isolated as periods of theatre's ascendancy from the point of view of a history partial to 'writing', this does not make it a literary genre. Indeed John Arden in his essay: 'Playwrights and playwriters', made some time ago the fundamental distinction between the setting down of dramatic dialogue and the working of the production itself: 'The playwright works drama just as the Millwright works mill gear. And working on making a play includes what are now thought to be the activities of the Director as well as those of the Script-writer.'[8] The analysis of images does not shift attention irrevocably from the text but considers the text as one element in a signifying field.[9] It dispels the hierarchy of the word with equal recourse to the action that brings the image into being. This task is one of a composite nature, like the image itself, a complex phenomenon with its own conventions and systems but quite distinct operations from those of literature.

The inevitable danger in analysing images at all is the division of the audience's perception into fragmented and artificial containers that suit the boundaries of different disciplines but bear little relation to the dialectical nature of theatre. The pleasure of thinking about theatre beyond this simplistic model is that it poses so many problems. Unlike the immediate and pressing realities of unemployment, censorship and compromise, it is not always clear where these come from or how to solve them. Like the continual return to the question of language, the problem of theatre imagery is compounded by the uneasy relations between the perceptual and the sensual, objectivity and subjectivity. A theorist of iconology, the study of the discourse of images, W. Mitchell, has summarised the breadth of the problematic by breaking the image down into the following categories: mental and optical, perceptual and verbal, the relations of visual images to linguistic terms, and the relations between objects and visual images that stand for them. Robert Morris concludes that what is implied by this problematic is the enquiry at the heart of Western metaphysics: 'Representational theories of the mind revolve around such issues and imply the persistent division of mind from body, subject from object.'[10] Even in writing about images, and the work of both these figures attests to the problem, there is the contradiction that a medium of representation, words and ideas, is being employed to adjudicate over another representational form. These problems are incitements to understanding and should not be confused with any pessimism or solipsism. For if images are central to theatre, if they are the medium through which the transaction of theatre occurs, then understanding their nature can only, as with the imagination, challenge the persistent and detrimental division of intelligence and feeling. Once challenged from within, the pressing realities of what is worth defending about theatre can also be contested with less prejudice. For what is worth defending and surely warrants particular care are those unanalysed and unwritten forms of theatre which border and define the documented and widely known. This distinction pertains to the discussion of imagery itself for it is often precisely because a theatre event has foregrounded imagery that it is ignored or belittled in a writing faint from its own limitations. The length of the library shelf bearing volumes of Shakespearian textual analysis as distinct from the coffee table bearing the few volumes on theatre 'in production' attests to this dereliction.

There has been a vast literature concentrating on the literary connotations of the image, on the nature of poetry as contrasted for instance to the pictorial tradition. But the theatre image's presence in time and space has, until recent work, been neglected. To move away from the bias of considering the problematic of the image to be one solely between the textual and the visual is the first necessity. Later I will take up the relations between text and image from the point of view of artistic practice where there is by definition, in composite forms of expression such as theatre and film, a continual violation of the boundaries and relations between the two. This 'violation' is precisely what makes theatre possible in the first place. The supersession of the dramatic text over physicality has marginalised research into these boundary areas for too long. The body in theatre has been elided, as though it were somehow unproblematic, and in its place the written word has been set upon for all it has to say. For the moment it is this 'composite' nature of theatre that interests me, that is 'essential', and this must be considered before trying to return it to any one of its elemental parts.

Just to add to these already complex problems of definition, the ascendancy of the visual in the aesthetic sensorium with which I began this chapter is a fundamental limitation which compounds the basis for discussion. If the desire is to think of theatre as an act which is as discursive as it is visual, and then again as olfactive as it is auditory, the accepted hierarchy of representational modes, where the visual is privileged over other elements, has to be reconsidered. The privileging of the visual, through Western culture's preoccupation with objects and texts, demands rethinking from the perspective of theatre's corporeality, its sensuality and multivocality, and it is in this realm that the work of theatre anthropology has been compiling an innovative inventory.[11] This serves as a reminder that theatre images are not just visual, but a composite of the visual, aural and nasal. Olfaction will be considered in the next chapter, the visual and aural here. Applause is the audience's consolation to themselves that touch is more often than not precluded from their experience of performance.

It is clear that the image and imagination are not the prerogative of the theatre but a complex of relations between the theatre event and the context in which it occurs, and an oscillating arrangement of other representational forms not in themselves named and separated as theatrical operations. Images are therefore as much a part of everyday life as a product of specialised activities, though it is in the duration and longevity of performance that they become most accessible to observation and reflection. These, using Antonio Gramsci's popular phrase, are the 'formations' of theatre and ones which have a particular bearing on the status of theatre within culture at any one time or place. The relations between artistic forms and social formations are central to all cultural activities but particularly significant to an understanding of performance. Gramsci's thought has been widely adopted in cultural analysis as an antidote to the simplifications of the base/superstructure model as derived from Marx. For this reason any discussion of a 'composite' form such as theatre, which moves beyond the determinist analysis of society and its cultural artefacts, is in special need of the kind of subtleties which inform Gramsci's thinking. As he says: 'It is not enough to know the ensemble of relations as they exist at any given time as a given system. They must be known genetically, in the movement of their formation.'[12] The popularity of the phrase should not obscure the real advances such an understanding of the practices of theatre would bring. It provokes us to think the 'before' and 'after' of the image, the coming to be of the image and the relations between the image as an 'ensemble' and the wider context of its emergence into expressive cultural forms in society. This is by no means a semiotics of theatre, and can make no claims to scientific validity, but is perhaps a simpler more contextually responsive starting point for analysis which rethinks rather than ignores the metaphysics of performance. Let me briefly place this in the context of the lay theatre.

Before and after events which occurred as part of the lay theatre I had the opportunity to speak to many audiences about what they expected, what they saw, and what they felt. The last was often the first to be expressed, the most human and biological response to theatre. The question of whether the theatre was good superseded the question of what it might have meant. The place of images in these discussions was always central. In normal conversation one often isolates and identifies, brackets and separates with the words: 'I liked the bit where . . . I didn't like the part that . . .' These divisions will often fall around a perception of rhythm in the performance as sophisticated as any language analysis. The problem was not defining for oneself the strength of these parts but making a complementary judgement as to their relation to a whole, and the relation of that whole to others. This experience of theatre is a common one in the everyday and, despite the sophistication of critical languages that have been made available to those who wish to regard theatre as more than a nicety, remains an elusive skill. There is a complex relationship between what constitutes imagery in other cultural expressions, what is thought to be worth knowing, and how best to retrieve experience of the senses in language. I have considered the first with regard to television and in the lay theatre this remained a continual point of reference. But the second and third issues are worth considering in more depth. To speak about images is to document the discreet in a discursive practice. It requires speculation and the willingness to stake something on what you believe, not just from what you have seen, but more importantly what you have not seen. This in turn derives its force from saying what is worth knowing. How an image conveys knowledge is important not because theatre is educational but because the cultural forms with power in society both economically and mentally are ones which claim a relationship to this knowledge. The knowledge of theatre is perhaps more a know-how for it combines the simplest physical demonstration with the most complex mental adjustments. At the simplest level in the theatre the hand of the woman moves towards a man under a table, as she speaks to her husband. The image is neither hand, speech nor table, but the realisation of the expression of infidelity and the feelings consequent on this revelation. It is a cheat, not a knowledge of marital relations, but an awareness that something's up. This sense is the sixth sense of theatre and while it is metaphysical it is commonly shared and understood.

The problem is of course, as this simple example demonstrates, that the image relies ultimately on the verbal and the textual, if it is to be transmitted by way of description beyond the witness of the individual who sees, hears, experiences, its occurrence. That this is not just any language but 'a way of speaking that we inherit from a long tradition of talking about minds and pictures' compounds the problem.[13] My own example, to back this up, is a retelling of David Hare's image of how theatre works. The permanence of theatre relies on this intermediary language to perpetuate its momentary existence, for it is often only by verbal record that what has been seen and experienced enters the public domain. It is this transition from the image to its record in the everyday that is particularly problematic and significant for a study of the relations between theatre and everyday life. Reviewing, the predominant discourse surrounding theatre, is one means by which theatre is transformed by being critically transcribed, but it is a genre which for economic and structural reasons is not suited to the discussion of imagery in the kind of depth that such an elemental part of an arts process might otherwise demand. It remains however the relationship to theatre that most people maintain, given its place in the daily paper. This chapter and the next outline a poetics of theatre imagery that moves beyond the journalistic as well as the anthropological and semiotic, towards the discursive structures and paradigms of everyday life, beyond the internal, structuralist discourse to the contextual, and then towards an understanding and participation in the transformation of that context. This cannot remain a purely 'objective' strategy, nor a subjective 'impression' but draws on the spectrum between these two artificial extremes, in the same places of thought and feeling that the image itself operates from. The images I am about to consider do not, unlike those I have just spoken of arise from a culturally separated domain called theatre. At the risk of being diversionary I take examples from the everyday which have fascinated the interpretive sciences.

Who, or what, might one say, brings us closer to the everyday than disciplines designed to interpret the everyday world for us? Stepping outside the specifics of theatre temporarily will allow for a sense of where its boundaries might adjoin other practices where the nature of the image has distinct but associated problems of definition. A problem shared is not a solution to what constitutes a theatre image but the relations between images of different kinds constitutes what a theatre image can be within a set of relations called culture. One strategy is to ascertain the connections there are between knowledge-forming operations such as those of the 'sciences' and their reliance on imagery, another to look at other 'arts' where the relations between images and context have been given special consideration. In order to ground this discussion I will examine the work of two individuals with a concern for the meaning of images, Humphrey Jennings and Gaston Bachelard, within the context of two cultural movements with particular relevance to the image-forming nature of theatre: Surrealism and phenomenology. Both figures are often cited by theatre practitioners as in some way influential on their work, though their precise influence is rarely clear. For me it is the profound relationship between their understanding of images and everyday life which is of interest. But in very different ways both contributed to a body of work which was unusually provocative to imaginative practices. Their work, and this is perhaps a key to its provocation, is multifarious, interdisciplinary, in the sense that it creates an object that belonged to no one and therefore is peculiarly adaptable to use in the most prosaic circumstances of making theatre – where poetry is most needed. Given this plurality it is necessary to concentrate on two key questions that return in their writing. Both are central to an understanding of how images work and how an unwritten theatre can be taken note of.

The first question concerns the relations between 'witness' and 'documentary'. In this emphasis the earlier discussion of what constitutes the object of theatre studies, the documents of its enquiry, will be developed, first by rethinking what the witness of images entails. I will examine this aspect of Jennings' work and the part his particular conception of the 'image' plays in that process. The second question is concerned with 'testimony' and 'knowledge', and what kind of knowledge the image conveys. I will examine Bachelard's discussion of the 'image' in science in relation to epistemology, the theory of the grounds of knowledge, and its distinction from the image of poetics. Between the two is the trajectory modernism followed from documentary to the interpretation of the discreet. Witness suggests what is seen is taken note of, testimony that what is heard is spoken up for.

The 'something more' of images, the metaphysical, cannot be allowed to consign theatre to the margin of all that is scientific. An epistemology of theatre is defined by the framework of knowledge that defines other image-making processes. The questions of 'documentary' and 'knowledge' are important in order to make claims for the potential ethical and political role of theatre. Documentary, because unless we are in a position to reread the past with reference to the future, a radical project will be destined to repeat itself, as the old saw goes, 'the second time as farce'. Thus I am seeking forms of 'documentation' which do not betray the complexity of the theatre process, particularly the witness of images, and in this Jennings' work is provocative and exhaustive. Knowledge, because unless we understand better the ways in which the image operates, including its metaphysical qualities, and the kinds of knowledge it creates, as distinct from say the use of poetic metaphors and images in science, the particular value of theatre will remain arbitrary, to be defended endlessly with recourse to irrelevant rationalities by unreasonable practitioners with other work to do. What is discreet is only accessible through such interpretation and that which is most elusive to heavy-handed disciplines is lost to a theatre. In short, how can we get our hands on the theatre we value, how can images be documented without losing a sense of their incidental glories and how can such glories be understood as integral to everyday life?

Witness and documentary

Humphrey Jennings' use and theorisation of images was inextricably linked to his practice as film-maker, artist and critic in Britain in the 1930s–50s. His media were canvas, celluloid and paper and while such materials mark a wholly different realm to theatre, the words used to describe this work and the role of the image in it are nevertheless worth detailed consideration. Further, the formation of an idea of nationality, the everyday practices which make up 'Britain' itself, owes something very distinctive to the work of the 'Mass Observation' movement of which Jennings was a co-founder, a movement which I will look at in the next chapter.[14] Jennings was a practitioner and theoretician, his wartime interests as a film-maker giving way to a variety of artistic, poetic and critical operations in the years before his untimely death. He is central and contradictory to any debate about the absence of 'modernism' from Britain during the inter-war years, his work representing a rupture from a conservative romanticism to a critical modernism. The contention that modernism never reached England with its characteristic traits intact is a commonly made. There is much in the perception that the evolutionary and linear nature of English culture took the 'catastrophic' reading of history and tradition at the core of modernism and 'domesticated it within its own sympathetic eclecticism', that unpredictable poetic forces were 'naturalized, within a patient and accommodating gradualism'.[15] Perhaps for these reasons the work of Humphrey Jennings appears now doubly out of context. It first requires a social and historical setting to emphasise the importance of this eclectic work to a nonconformist tradition of English intellectual and artistic life, built as it was on an unusually subtle cognisance of the ethical, aesthetic and political. It was this work, reaching back to William Blake, and now forward to contemporary performance, that tells another history for the British arts and provides possibilities for rethinking its theatre. Here history was the realisation of human imagination, a history that supersedes the provincial theatrical watershed of 1956 and sets its dam on the gradient between a Surrealism of France and the political modernism of German criticism – the work of André Breton and Antonin Artaud and Walter

Benjamin and Bertolt Brecht. If intellectual currents can generate a sufficient head of water for critics to install their power stations on them, as Benjamin said, it is this more eclectic European tradition of critical work, rather than that of the angry young men, that would seem worthy of a sub-station now. For here a theatre which derives from imagery, presentation and juxtaposition can be discussed rather than a fascination with literary texts and their representation of social concerns.

Beyond a number of influential films made during and after the Second World War including *Fires were Started*, Humphrey Jennings is now perhaps best known for his collection of 'Images' which were published posthumously under the title: *Pandaemonium, The Coming of the Machine as seen by Contemporary Observers*.[16] The title should signal an immediate interest in the work from the point of view of a study of everyday life, namely his placing of value on witness and contemporary testimony. This was an archaeology of reception of the apparently ephemeral and unwritable phenomenon of an industrial revolution and its relations to the human being. Central to the work was the place of the imagination in industrial society and the role of science within the social space of knowledge. Jennings had been taught by I.A. Richards, whose own concern had been to seek connections between science and poetry. Foremost in this work was the creative capacity that derives from making 'connections' and this lay behind the modernist juxtapositions of the material in *Pandaemonium*. His structuring of the myriad texts that make up the book was guided by the idea that each excerpt, or Image, as he called these parts, should be included unedited to limit the possibility of losing some unnoticed coherence or interest that might come from their juxtaposition. He countenanced complete excision of an Image rather than internal editing to protect the integrity of each element of the picture of the relations between vision and production during the Industrial Revolution. *Pandaemonium* represents the most 'open' of texts, a long-term, never completed project by Jennings, which even in its truncated form as a book, assembled by Mary-Lou Jennings and Charles Madge, remains a resonant source-work. The published work only hints at the vast remainder that Jennings collected and confronts the question of what is always left out, or partial about knowledge. This notion of 'Images' was a personal one particular to Jennings and was governed by his research into poetry and painting through the medium of psychology, literary criticism and Surrealist theory. His 'imagery' could not be categorised as simply poetic or sociological: he drew across disciplines mixing the arts of theory, images of the historical and the artistic. His pursuit was a public, or collective imagery which beyond the patriotic necessities of the Second World War was most needed and yet most difficult to achieve.

To give an impression of the kind of material collected in *Pandaemonium* I will quote what might be considered an 'image of the image'. It is drawn from Michael Faraday the physicist, is dated 1850, and is titled 'A stream of golden cloud':

> A Balloon went up on Saturday Evng. (22 instant) from Vauxhall. The evening was very clear and the Sun bright: the balloon was very high, so that I could not see the car from Queens Square, Bloomsbury, and looked like a golden ball. Ballast was thrown out two or three times and was probably sand; but the dust of it had this effect, that a stream of golden cloud seemed to descend from the balloon, shooting downwards, for a moment, and then remained apparently stationary, the balloon and it separating very slowly. It shews the wonderful manner in which [each] particle of this dusty cloud must have made its impression on the eye by the light reflected from it, and is a fine illustration of the combination of many effects, each utterly insensible alone, into one sum of fine effect. If a cloud of dusty matter, as powdered chalk or road dust, were purposely poured forth under these circumstances, it would give a fine effect both to those on earth and those in the balloon.[17]

The first and most obvious thing to say about this image, like all others in *Pandaemonium*, is that it does not occur within parameters that mark it out as theatre. Yet it has certain qualities that are associated with theatre and it maintains the possibility that theatre can occur in the unlikeliest settings. How does the page relate to this stage? The image as described by Faraday is not *one* of the many elements that contribute to the diary entry but their totality and relation. As Charles Madge, a prominent poet and colleague of Jennings points out: 'it is not in the elements but in their coming together at a particular moment, that the magical potency lies'. Whether one is able to analyse the various elements in turn to establish their overall effect as a structuralist method might propose, the question remains as to the creation of this magical potency. What is it about that combination in a particular time and place that endures? The question equally pertains to theatre. Each of the elements is insensible and non-sensical alone. The sensual arises from their relation to the whole. For Charles Madge the combination of the image and the imaginative eye that seizes that image is a point of 'ordonnance', and this gives us a starting point from which to ask questions about the theatre image and its construction without irrevocably splitting the individual's perception. The fine effect is apparent to those on earth and brought about by those in the balloon. Though discreet, the presence of the balloonist and the onlookers marks out a human bracket which does not so much contain the image as bring about the image, in the way that the presence or absence of the brackets of an equation alters fundamentally the meaning of its contents. The question is not only how is one to 'read' this bracket, but how is one to experience it? Ordonnance helps with the sense of a reading which moves beyond simple hermeneutic speculation. According to general definition it is a systematic arrangement, especially of a literary or architectural work. It is this aspect of the image, the balloon and the sand, which can be addressed by methodologies such as structuralist theory and semiotics and is available to sight. It shares a useful linguistic association with ordinance: an authoritative decree of enactment. Further, another associated word, ordnance, is the preparing of detailed maps, an authoritative guide, and it is this combination of directive and mapping which comes closest to the observation of images by the imaginative eye, deconstructing and reconstructing the part–whole relations of the image simultaneously and dialectically. It is here between definition, power and arrangement, that the relationship between the apparently stationary phenomenon of balloon and sand can be thought.

But it is clear that the image as described by Faraday is one consequent upon chance elements, coincidental juxtaposition, in so far as it accumulates as a 'fine effect'. There is a value judgement in this description which moves beyond the structuralist impasse to a differential world of value and pleasure, moves from the objective maps of the contemporary age to those of the medieval where the emotions and tribulations of travel were discernible. And most importantly it is an observation that moves beyond the limits of vision. For beyond vision there is a comprehension born of the mental and the material, the gap between the virtual image and its significance and the 'experience' of Faraday in its bodily presence. Given Faraday's spiritual convictions, the permeation and influence over his science of the Sandemanian religion, there is an element of the transcendent about this vocabulary. The Sandemanians believed that the Bible and the natural world were both God-given and could be read and understood by those who studied them. As an Elder of that church, Faraday approached his science expecting to find order and simplicity in the laws of nature, that could be read like a text and interpreted accordingly. This combination of the material and the spiritual, a combination which profoundly affects the ways of seeing that are open to the human being, is what produces the metaphysical dimension of the experience of images. In my understanding the spiritual is not to be associated with the conventions of a specific church or religion, as in the case of the Sandemanians, but as Joseph Beuys has said, 'one of one's own power'. The advances of the sciences of structuralism, a materialism of the image, has at some point to be superseded by a further dimension which takes on the image's fine effect:

Materialism has two functions. One is to bring old emotional energies to a complete standstill, and the other is to establish intellectually precise criteria of knowledge for all scientific undertakings. After that intensification of the human intellect a link must be reestablished with the spiritual – but one of one's own power . . . and no longer

out of the gift of traditional power . . . You must attempt to achieve
a precision of 'belief'.[18]

Achieving this 'precision of belief' is next to impossible in cultures where
the belief available has retreated into the crevices of journalism and broad-
cast news. Here theatre is left behind, no longer transportable to the
domain where belief resides and therefore consigned to the margin of
superstition and personal conviction once the prerogative of the possessed.
The funds of belief previously assigned to religion and politics have fragmented, leaving their historically tense relations with theatre confused. In
this abeyance of values the ironic significance of theatre and the credence
afforded it by other belief systems (churches and governments) is lost in
a presumption that it has nothing whatsoever to do with real issues and
the beliefs they imply. Images that challenge these official views of reality
provoke questions about what we believe in, how we know something
and the contents of such beliefs and knowledge and it is through them
that what is good about theatre comes about.

But let us return to the stream of golden cloud. The imaginative eye
on the balloon has a double. The first witness to the event is a physicist,
Faraday, and his curiosity is indicative of the observational qualities of
the developing science at the time. Nineteenth-century science was forging
a language of scrutiny assisted by the rapid development in instrumentation
and galvanised by the Industrial Revolution. It is here that the possibilities
of regarding theatre were superseded by the power of sight in the 'need
to know' – from Galileo's mischievous use of the telescope to 'prove' a
Copernican revolution to the role of the microscope to see below space,
the relations between knowledge and sight have been intimate. This oculocentrism dominates perception of theatre and is popularly expressed in
applause for the 'first sight' of set or star on stage, the anachronistic relic
of its power the opera glasses clamped to the back of the seat. This
observational language consistently emerges through *Pandaemonium* as
though the second eye on the records, Jennings himself, was exploring the
frontiers between the sciences and the arts, and placing one discourse at
the service of the other. It is his eye which cuts out Faraday's report,
from the everyday crowd of which he was a part, turns it over and places
it in another context. From 'onlooker' he is turned into 'seer'. That act
links the representational languages of physics to a poetics with profound
implications for the relations between two partitioned domains. Faraday
was a witness to change in the sensorium. From within everyday life, the
crowd, he retrieved images that distilled both the significance of vision
and the contingency of that vision on questions of belief and knowledge.
The sciences of optics and light might explain the phenomenon of apparently stationary sand suspended in mid-air, but cannot begin to explain
the effects this has on the witness. The relationship between Faraday's act

74

of witness and Jennings' act of documentation is the significant one for an unwritten theatre. Faraday was witness to the palpably material yet its effects were intangible – his revolution, and Jennings' interest in him, was not to turn away from the mental aspect of phenomena but to write the unwritten.

In this project Jennings has responded to the central Surrealist urge to explore the incongruity in the juxtaposition of objects, the notion of chance within the rational. Indeed Jennings writing about his own painting described what was needed as: 'A new solidity as firm as Cubism, but fluid, not static . . .'.[19] Jennings' project was to liberate human perceptions from surrounding literature and to investigate the nature of the image and its relationship to the subject that constitutes its heart. The parallels with a theatre bound by sight, literature and the convention of reading are apparent. An example of such a subject was the dome of St Paul's, a recurring point from which many images evolved, and one which through his wartime filming became a potent symbol of national endurance. These subjects were worked by the artist and metamorphosed through the artist's imaginative practice, a concept which reflected Jennings' relation to the Marxist concern for the transformation of the other means of production.[20] Here the relations between the poetic imagination and a liberal politics become clearer, a conjunction that is not unproblematic. If it is the 'imagination' which is the organising principle behind Jennings' selection of texts for inclusion, he perceives the building of Pandaemonium itself as expressed in the conflict of 'animism and materialism'. The soul of nature has been concealed by industrialisation and this is reflected in the 'expropriation of poetry' and 'the repression of the clear imaginative vision in ordinary folk'. The tenor of Jennings' language, as well as his film language, has suggested to some a patronising quality which may have contributed to his neglect. It is my assertion that it is precisely the structures of feeling in Jennings' work, his un-patronising association with the subjects of his work that signifies its radical departure. Further it is Jennings' nonconformist, yet socially oriented politics which are of interest, his distinctive way of subverting Marxist categories to achieve desired aims. As he says in the introduction to Pandaemonium: 'Man as we see him today lives by production and by vision. It is doubtful he can live by one alone.' Here eating, sleeping and loving as everyday activities are joined by the necessity for imagination as an indispensable function of life. Vision moves away from the solely optical and opens into questions of belief and aspiration more associated with the 'visionary'. This 'poetic' owed something to Surrealism which provides both a context for Jennings' work and a reference point which a study of the relations between theatre and everyday life cannot ignore. It is important briefly to return to the well worn path of this movement if only to distinguish that aspect of its work which remained within the everyday and that better known part of its operations which became mere 'literary techniques'.

Surrealism

The coalescence of the political and the psychological in Jennings' work, the constant tension between the two, is reminiscent of the debate between the legacies of Freud and Marx that characterised the history of Surrealism in the inter-war years of the 1920s and 1930s. It is this movement which provides the context both for Jennings' work and for his specific under-standing of the workings of images and the imagination. His association with Surrealism was formalised by his involvement in the International Surrealist Exhibition in London in 1936.[21] While this event marked Jennings' direct involvement with André Breton it also occurred when Surrealism had moved beyond its most profound moment of development, if not influence. Jennings, writing about an article by Breton, com-mented:

> He [Breton] continues to say that Surrealism has replaced the 'coinci-dence' for the apparition and that we must 'allow ourselves to be guided towards the unknown by this newest promise'. Now that is talking and to settle Surrealism down as Romanticism only is to deny this promise. It is to cling to the apparition with its special 'haunt' . . . Coincidences have the infinite freedom of appearing any-where, anytime, to anyone . . .[22]

Here Jennings advances the idea of the 'coincidence', as contrary to the 'ghostly', the need for ethics and politics to endure because of mystery and against mystification. It is in this matter-of-factness that the image has evolved from a number of intangible elements throughout *Pandaemonium*. Jennings' modernist resistance to the Romantic undercurrents of English Surrealism denied the eccentric dimension of coincidence and reinforced its profound potential and purpose in intellectual and poetic practices. The claim that all this work represents is a strain of English eccentricity, the peculiarities of the English, has to be repudiated. Here was the chance to outwit the habitual through the juxtaposition of objects: the everyday could be disrupted via the mundane. Further still, the coincidence is seen as grounded in the everyday. The central position that coincidence and chance held within Surrealism is paralleled by their persistent influence on the arts since, and while having been remorselessly analysed in the fine arts they still remain to be fully examined from the perspective of the incidental nature of theatre imagery. Maurice Nadeau, the contemporary chronicler of Surrealism, describes the influence of chance in the following way:

One of the few values that remained at the centre of Surrealist thinking was 'objective chance' or loosely coincidence... poets have long lingered over such chance occurrences... randomness coupled with the hidden order that surrounds us was the only true reality and described as Surreality... for Breton, objective chance, the geometric locus of these coincidences embodies the relationship of necessity and freedom and therefore is the problem of problems.[23]

That formation, the relationship of necessity and freedom, describes the relationship of composed and coincidental elements that go to make up all images. The changing nature of audiences, the changing circumstances in which images occur and the coincidental relationship between this geometry all question the notion of a theatre that can wholly control its meaning. This is the theatre of mistakes, the accident that makes theatre images possible and resonant for changing audiences and so difficult to capture by the metanarratives of analytic theories built to understand more orderly fare. The problem of Surrealism for an ethics of performance, and one which Jennings' critique of its development points toward, is that in the celebration of 'coincidence' and the 'marvellous' was lost the real which was to be superseded by the surreal. Surrealism marked an escape from the everyday not a return to it, a belittling of the landscape of most people's existence in a process familiar to other avant-gardes predicated on minority status. Though influential within cultural parameters the claims of Surrealism were much more ambitious. As Henri Lefebvre has pointed out these claims were not only unfounded but dangerous: 'the real world is accepted since it is *transposed* instead of being *transformed* by knowledge'.[24] The Surrealists' revolt against 'the prose of the world' became simply that, a battery of literary techniques. But Jennings' fascination with the sensibility of the scientist, his keeping open the relation of imagining between the 'arts' and 'sciences' found echoes in Surrealism and points to the true significance of his work for understanding the imaginary realm of theatre metaphysics.

The Surrealist enterprise was not of course solely one governed by literary forces though de Sade, Baudelaire, Rimbaud, Jarry and Ducasse were central to its history. Coterminous with these literary influences Nadeau points out was the significance of the intellectual climate of the time for the central theses of the Surrealist moment:

New ways of thinking were being simultaneously created by the scientific, philosophical and psychological discoveries of Einstein, Heisenberg... and Freud... notions of universal relativism, of the collapse of causality, of the omnipotence of the unconscious, breaking with the notions based on logic and determinism.[25]

While the interface with scientific discovery of the period is clear the

Surrealists nonetheless mistrusted the habitual procedures of scientific method such as the 'logical apparatus', and resorted to the means traditionally utilised by the poets: intuition and inspiration, chiefly concretised in images. As Walter Benjamin quotes from Breton and Apollinaire in his essay on Surrealism: 'The conquests of science rest far more on Surrealistic than on logical thinking.'[26] In this the Surrealists have been vindicated by the contemporary philosophy of science. It has become increasingly evident through the work of philosophers such as Paul Feyerabend that the logical nature of scientific discovery has been widely overestimated, many real advances being made coincidentally to main lines of enquiry.[27] Further, 'Copernican' revolutions often come about through a combination of ingenuity and chance discovery, the context of discovery often being quite at odds with the logical procedures and languages used to describe that discovery after the event. Seemingly insignificant branch lines of thought and experiment grow to become main trunks while other arterial routes become forgotten side roads.[28] This realisation, which has found prominence over the century in the philosophical writings of Thomas Kuhn, was intuitively and explicitly stated by Jennings in his working methods and in his drawing from Surrealism.[29] The contribution here to a poetics is significant as this challenge to logic and scientific dogmatism demands constant vigilance. A 'consistency principle' has always to be resisted if new working methods are not to be jeopardised by appeals to tradition, or longevity used as a rationale for the compromise of experiment. When I say theatre is unreasonable I mean that the standards of reason as derived from science are themselves prone to contradiction and doubt, and to foster those standards within theatre is to jeopardise the most innovative phenomenon it shares with science: the radical possibility that the irrational will more often lead to the increase of rationality than not. These are all criteria well known to the research-based sciences and are equally relevant to a theatre attempting to renew itself. The procedures that legitimised science's status as 'nature's own language' have been exposed during the twentieth century to increasingly critical attention. The relationship between research, science and storytelling, the propaganda ploys of scientists from Galileo's defence of his discoveries in the vernacular, to current justifications of nuclear power safety with recourse to populist demonstrations, has been underestimated. It was these paradigmatic shifts that provided the social space for the opportunistic postmodern phase of multi-vocal, conflictual, polemical stances, where rationality and progress were presumed to have given way to diversification and pastiche. These contemporary philosophies of contingency were however deeply rooted in longer-term movements which stretch back to the beginning of the century and beyond and inflect on everything of interest that the theatre achieves today in the name of the 'postmodern'.

The inevitability of human emancipation was profoundly challenged by the First World War and the Surrealist enterprise rejected any notion of 'authority' or 'continuity' by choosing to act on flux, juxtaposition and rupture. Charles Madge's description of Humphrey Jennings' art corresponds with this loss of faith in the continuum and a new adherence to chance and change:

> The art that Jennings was seeking must reflect cosmos in flux. In this flux are assemblages, or shapes, or patterns of relative intensity and fixity, and certainty. Paradoxically solid and fluid, the images are moments in the flow of human experience.[30]

It is clear that Surrealism had from its beginnings drawn not only on the intellectual climate of its time but incessantly on its language. This was particularly evident in the metaphors it took from physics to describe the disequilibrium it sought to harness: 'interference', 'short circuit' and 'communicating vessels', terms which were widely used, all derived from the sciences and in turn connected with the developing language of the newest science; that is psychology and particularly Freud's *The Psychopathology of Everyday Life*. It is in this interest in the language of science and its use of metaphor that there is a clear connection between the theories of the 'Images' elucidated through Jennings' artistic practice and the theory of the image developed through the philosophy of science of Gaston Bachelard. Jennings' work traces a historical relationship between reason and imagination, science and poetry as modes of knowledge, indeed what has been described as a microphysics of the imagination. The Surrealist moment marks a certain ironic logic, from the threat to theology by science, the 'death of God' and the need for a belief in progress as an emancipatory dynamic in the absence of higher-order principles. And yet, with the contemporary developments of science, and the effects of the First World War throwing scepticism on such an optimistic project, the role of a philosopher of science such as Bachelard, in a tradition which reaches to the present day, began to be one of ascertaining increasingly the 'relative' epistemological claims of the sciences and their creations, the kinds of knowledge and feeling, that the arts produce. It is in this shifting context that the continual transformations of theatre, the progenitors of what is good about theatre today, need to be placed and valued as vectors of change. Theatre cannot be extricated from this tapestry of forces and securely placed within this or that philosophy without mortally compromising what is most distinctive to it, turning it into a truly absurd theatre. Unless one wishes to follow the logical positivists and exclude aesthetic criteria along with ethical concerns from philosophy, to question the possibility of an art form conveying knowledge of a perceivable kind, it remains to ask what sort of knowledge images are able to convey. How can you value something you cannot see in the theatre, instead of blindly believing in everything you can on television?

Testimony and knowledge

The history of thinking and writing about images speaks of a continual transference across disciplinary boundaries. Gaston Bachelard would have resisted the notion of a theory of the image, explicitly stating: 'The image in its simplicity has no need of scholarship.'[31] The latter half of his life was committed nonetheless to producing a series of works that inaugurated just that project. Jennings and Bachelard were in good measure contemporaries in their working lives, although Bachelard was twenty years older. They are linked for my purposes by an unusual awareness of the relations between the poetic imagination, the discourse of knowledge and the elision of everyday life from both. They tell us why the know-how of theatre is 'scene' *and* 'heard'.

Bachelard demands attention in the arts for his work on the poetics of the most commonplace features of life, namely his major works, *The Poetics of Space* and *The Poetics of Reverie*. In these works the poetic qualities of everyday space, from cupboards to corners, are identified and examined. Like the problematic 'empty space', Bachelard reminds us it is impossible to 'imagine' an empty drawer or cupboard, only to 'think' it. Imagination will always come up with the 'lavendered' sheets that are at home there. It is less widely appreciated from a cultural perspective that his career, in the first third of this century, had to the point of *The Psychoanalysis of Fire* been concerned with the philosophy of science. The duality of his work therefore shares a common concern with the nature of images both in the arts and the sciences and simultaneously challenges, and then from innovative perspectives redraws, the boundaries between such categories.[32]

The work of philosophers of science, from Bachelard to Feyerabend, has been central to the understandings of contingency which ironically underpin the anti-foundationalism of postmodern theory. Further, his writing connected him implicitly with the Surrealists although from a very different direction than that of Jennings. For his concern was with concepts of 'break', 'rupture' and 'metaphor' and specifically the imagery of Lautréamont whose *Maldoror* was a profound influence on the Surrealists and which Bachelard analysed in depth through its bestiary.

Bachelard was central to, and formative of, a growing awareness as the twentieth century proceeded that the certainties and continuities of science were being eroded by discoveries in physics. Bachelard's own specialism was micro-physics and as we shall see the sub-space nature of this enquiry made his interest in images all the more intense. His was a science of the most discreet realm. The regard for thinking and understanding this volatile and, in its day, metaphysical region, shares some resemblance with a current state of theatre thinking which attempts to locate the distinctive forces of the imagery of performance as distinct from its literary effects.

This reformulation requires an *epistemological break*. That is, the framework of knowledge systems that surround theatre are unnecessarily wedded to the objects of literature and need to be dislodged from their moorings in that foreign harbour. The concept was introduced by Bachelard in *The New Scientific Mind* to challenge those inclined to thinking of science as a continuum with the argument that science was only installed and established by 'breaking with itself'. The object of science, for Bachelard, was not an immediate given and did not pre-exist the process of production.[33] Bachelard identified the scientist as one who through rationalist effort brings about the formation of the scientific mind – an existential rupture that breaks with the spontaneous interests of life. This individual would constantly approach obstacles which produce breaking effects in the scientific practice itself. For Bachelard certain concepts such as 'obstacle' and 'rupture' indicated how philosophy entered science. They would appear when an existing organising principle of science was in danger and thus consequently structured the relation of the scientist to their scientific practice. This analysis extends for my purposes to theatre where it illuminates the institutional orthodoxies that prevail in order to guarantee its survival as an adjunct to the literary and therefore worthy. This rethinking of how knowledge develops from within disciplines is useful for reorientating a discussion of theatre which has become prey to a seeming continuity, a natural state and order, that is resistant to experiment, change and influence from alternative sources. This does not just mean the predominance of the classics in the repertoire, nor the lack of 'new writing', it refers to all conservative structures including those that afflict the most apparently radical groups. The theatre mind can only be established by a discipline 'breaking with itself'. The current inflation of terms to describe a forthcoming performance, a hyperbole of promotion backed up by nonsensical photographic images before anything is made, is as dangerous to any radical theatre seeking an audience as the most turgid rehearsal or the deleterious effects of long-runs. To initiate a re-evaluation of current theatre is not only to have to accept the 'epistemological break' that Bachelard identified as central to, what he considered to be, the most rational processes, but to demonstrate the existence of such a break between one theatre and another and the social reorientation that this demands. It is in the analysis of the formation of imagery and its relation to the contexts of everyday life that I believe the 'epistemological break' of theatre becomes apparent. It is here that knowledge is seen to be dependent on criticism not just from within theatre. Judgement derives its meaning from a set of associations that are as linked to well-being in the everyday as they are to the specialised advancement of a separate cultural domain.

If this language sounds metaphoric Bachelard saw this as one of the central concerns and limitations or potential liberations of science. On

asking scientists what they took to be the philosophy of their practices
Bachelard discovered that scientists maintained an imaginary relationship
to their own practice and that metaphor, language and philosophy played
a central part in that relationship. This is evidently a key departure from
the understanding of the scientist translating for the world 'Nature's Own
Language', and one which opens up the sciences to potential affiliations
with the arts. This was, it should be acknowledged, the reacquaintance of
old colleagues who since the division between arts and sciences in the
classifying project of the *Encyclopaedia* had been considered divergent
entities with only romantic hopes of reacquaintance. But what in this
metaphoric spiral can be said to be the reality that is sought? For Bachelard: 'To separate oneself from images one must act on the real.'[34] The
double range of Bachelard's work, in philosophy of science and poetics,
shared a concern for the use of images, metaphors and their shrouding of
the 'real' – the value of their effects in the fields of science and poetry.
In *The Rationalist Activity* Bachelard proposed a qualitative perception of
images that would threaten a theatre of repetition and long runs: 'Images
like tongues cooked by Aesop, are good and bad, indispensable and harm-
ful by turns. One has to know how to use them moderately when they
are good and to get rid of them as soon as they are useless.'[35] This
qualification is understandable given that the starting point of Bachelard's
epistemology, micro-physics, relied heavily on metaphors to describe work
being done 'below space'. Here Bachelard believed the imagination to be
'under torture', an inverted view of the 'happiness of the imagination' that
he expounded in his *Poetics*. Here the image intervened in the abstract
process as a concretising phenomenon – almost the opposite of how one
might normally consider the image mediating between the physicality of
the world and its expression. But it is a view which corresponds with
Humphrey Jennings' perception of the image. Bachelard speaking of the
separation from images in order to be able to act on the real was concerned
with shifting attention from the algebraic space of his enquiry to ordinary
space which would be 'no longer . . . taken for anything more than a
means of illustration, a propitious site for our images, but never possibly
the adequate canvas for the complete relations'.[36] This 'adequate canvas'
demands not just an understanding of images in their isolation, and their
mental milieu, but a grasp of the material relations between images through
composition and the relationship of that composition to its context.

By concentrating on the poetic image Bachelard was concerned with
language and its relation to the image. He was not however tempted to
consider composition, the 'grouping together of numerous images', in
preference seeking a pure phenomenology of the image as 'detached entity'.
But for theatre the phenomenological image in its isolation is insufficient.
Indeed theatre rests precisely on the relations between the materiality of
images and the mental capacities of audience and performer. Theatre is

after all a process of dialectical relations between images and other images, in other words concerns that Bachelard felt in his study to move beyond the purely phenomenological and therefore to risk obscuring the project in hand. The relations between Bachelard's phenomenology and Jennings' Surrealism are interesting here as both found themselves moving into each other's field to further their understanding of the image. It was Jennings the painter and poet who was quoting the physicist Faraday while Bachelard the physicist was quoting the poet and painter. Here interdisciplinarity is seen for what it always is, the identification of already catholic borrowing and influence that occurs between practices and their theories. The perception of images which Bachelard identifies in the arts and sciences is one which informs everyday perceptions of the images of theatre and determines the credibility which theatre is able to accrue to itself from one time and place to the next. This credibility does not come from an infinite store but from a cultural economy where belief ebbs and flows between different objects.

While dismantling certain boundaries, others require reinforcing on behalf of theatre. There is for instance a clear distinction to be made between the processes of literary criticism and those of 'reading' images. Jennings wished his images: 'to succeed one another as contrasts playing upon the responsive mind of the reader, and to promote in that mind some (undefined) synthesis.'[37] The difference between images of this kind, which can be connected with the process of theatre, and the literary criticism of I.A. Richards and William Empson, who influenced Jennings, is apparent: 'The close textual criticism of that school demands the exercise of faculties more explicitly diagnostic than does the responsive attention to the images of film.'[38] Jennings and Bachelard question the relations between these 'diagnostic' faculties and the 'responsive attention' of the perceiver in the theatre act. It is the former which have held privileged status over the latter in theatre theory, which now requires refocusing towards the 'responsive attention' to the image-making process. This is what regarding theatre is.

There are further direct connections to be made between Bachelard and Jennings' understanding of images, particularly in the introduction of *The Poetics of Space* where Bachelard discusses the nature of the image, its opposition to causality and connection with 'reverberation'. This audio concept was an idea drawn from Eugène Minkowski, the phenomenologist, who had written:

> the sound of a hunting horn reverberating everywhere through its echo, made the tiniest leaf, the tiniest wisp of moss shudder in a common movement and transformed the whole forest, filling it to its limits, into a vibrating, sonorous world . . . What is secondary in these images, or, in other terms, what makes these images only

images for us, are the sonorous well-spring, the hunting horn, the sealed vase, the echo, the reflection of sonorous waves against the sides – in a word all that belongs to the material and palpable world.[39]

Here the vertical metamorphosis of Faraday's balloon and sand, recorded by Jennings in *Pandaemonium*, is achieved by the lateral effects of the sound in the forest. The 'material' and 'palpable' gives way to a 'sonorous' world through the reverberation of the sound. This concept of sound carries the image into time and space simultaneously and importantly moves beyond the visual into discursive realms of the sensorium, opening up the relations between the visual and auditory aspects of the image. The concept of reverberation might appear to open into questions of context and politics but these implications of imagery are resisted by Bachelard for fear of contaminating the purity of phenomenological pursuit.

Bachelard saw in the image a novelty and action that denied its interpretation as caused by something else. It simply could not be explained with recourse to a history. Rather he sought within the image an ontology, in the manner in which it creates in the perceiver a sense that one could, or should, have created the image for oneself. In that process he believed there to be a 'becoming of expression' and a 'becoming of being'. The statement that theatre is always as good as it can be derives from this perception, the sense in which the audience as critic always must concede the act of theatre as one they might have made. In engagement with the image, through the imagination, this expression creates being. In this understanding of the image as becoming, Bachelard turned to phenomenology away from psychology and psychoanalysis, declaring: 'Doctrines that are timidly causal ... can hardly determine the ontology of what is poetic.' He sought recourse to a phenomenology of the imagination to found a metaphysics of the imagination.[40] Where the concepts of physics and science were 'constitutive', 'essential', the poetic image was seen by Bachelard as 'variational'. An image was not an object but a specific reality that came before thought, from reverie. If this was preceded by language, by logos, it was not language of the objective interpretive kind, but a poetic logos. The imagining consciousness was seen as an origin, and it was in bringing out the quality of this origin that the phenomenology operated, through the consideration of various poetic images. Here we can see the breadth of a field which iconology, interpretation of the writing about images, seeks to address, where the theatre image and its materiality is increasingly caught up with questions of ontology and the metaphysics of the pre-expressivity of the actor and audience. It is here that ethics contrary to the isolation of phenomenology is of primary importance and has to be addressed.

Bachelard believed we should be receptive to the image at the moment it appears, describing this state as 'a sudden salience on the surface of the psyche'. He believed as we have seen that the poetic act had no past in which its preparation and appearance could be followed. The problem is Bachelard was not willing to concede the 'future' possibilities of the image – its political potential in the contexts in which it occurred. For that reason the following considers not the recent past of the image but the context of the image, the reverberations it might establish with that 'imagined community' in which it occurs through the medium of the imagination. We are thus not yet primarily concerned with a 'history of images', but with a geometry of their occurrence, of how they make us believe in them.

Belief and imagination

If the preceding discussion of imagery points to anything it reiterates that theatre is not a transparent medium for conveying dogmatic opinion or didactic messages. It is peculiarly prone to being interpreted by its audience in quite distinct, individual and anarchic ways. A poetics of theatre accepts with relish this diversity of communication and seeks to place the images in a thorough cultural context rather than to predict or diagnose how those images might transform the context itself. This acceptance does not imply a relativism for critical judgement is not denied by pluralism. Post-industrial society has been described as a place and time where the real and the imaginary have become almost impossible to distinguish. This makes Bachelard's turn from the image, to work on the 'real', highly problematic. In this society reality has apparently become a pale reflection of the image, a contention which has raised critical questions for the place of the imagination and the ethical operations it guides in such a society. The widespread use of advertising and the predominant use of imagery, including the extensive influence of Surrealist techniques within that medium, raise broad questions of appropriation and the role of the image maker. As Sue-Ellen Case says in conclusion to *Feminism and Theatre*:

> In the age of television, computer languages and communications satellites, the production of signs creates the sense of what a person is, rather than reflects it (in the traditional mimetic order). The mode of cultural production is reversed: signs create reality rather than reflect it. This condition means that artists and cultural theorists may be the activists and revolutionaries. Modes of discourse and representation may replace the Molotov cocktail.[41]

The 'laboratory' that Case hopes the 'feminist in theatre' might create could well signal 'a new age for both women and men'. But the aestheticis-ation of this discourse is precisely what will keep, if not its practitioners from becoming revolutionaries, then the everyday world on which such a revolution would be predicated, firmly in its place. The word 'may' between Modes and Molotov, opens the question 'how?', and what connections and distances there are between the politically active project and the theatrically active subject. Whatever the poetics of theatre being discussed, and whatever pressing concerns it might be utilised for, the surest way to separate that theatre from everyday life, to a laboratory, is to ascribe overarching privilege to a metanarrative drawn from the academy. The preference here is for the dialectical construction of a theatre theory derived from the relations theatre holds to the everyday lives that are to be revisioned. That begins by taking issue with the image of the laboratory, from de Broglie to Grotowski. The interest of a more detailed examination of imagery is the complex way theatre itself, as a material process with its own operational logics and discursive practices, conceals and distorts the most optimistic hopes placed at its practitioner's threshold. It is therefore in the space opened up by the word 'may' that the following seeks to move on from the creation of the image to its contexts. The imagination is the medium in this process, it is literally the human faculty for image making, and given the insecurities surrounding the term it is this human capacity for being that will require attention first.

In turning from a philosophy of science to a philosophy of art, and in particular a poetics, Gaston Bachelard had above all wanted to draw scientists' attention to the significance of the material imagination. He distinguished between two forms of imagination: the formal and material, both of which were at work in nature and in the mind. In his concern for the material, Bachelard echoed the connection made by Jennings, who had written in relation to the phenomena of *déjà vu*: 'The use therefore of images and serial objects is important as a debunking of idealism and furthers the cause of materialism.'[42] Jennings' work was political in purpose, exposing the ignorance that lay at the source of superstitions and mass 'wish situations'. His means were those of the Surrealist ministering blows to the habitual world of the everyday and its objects. For Jennings the basic problem for the film director was the question of imagination in an industrialised society. It was through imagination that the 'Pandaemonium' that Jennings had retrieved from history might be transformed into William Blake's 'Jerusalem'. The historian E.P. Thompson responds to this dilemma and its relations to a political perspective:

> we are left to mediate upon the imagination. What the hell is it? Where is it? The modern socialist movement scarcely seems to be Jennings' imagined vector, since it knows so much more passionately what and whom it is against than what it is for. Few people in these latter days, like to talk about such a shabby, old fashioned, suspect, uncerebral thing as the imagination. It is time that we imagined it once again.[43]

Historically there have been two aspects to the concept of imagination, as Richard Kearney in *The Wake of Imagination* points out: 'as a representational faculty which reproduces images of some pre-existing reality and as a creative faculty which produces images which lay claim to an original status in their own right'.[44] Both have referred to everyday activities as well as artistic practice since the Greeks. In the context of the above it is the second notion of the imagination as originally creative that is of particular interest for it is from here that belief in something can occur. While one can recognise the corrective nature of much Marxist criticism of the post-war period, it is harder to accept the complete loss of the concepts of image and imagination from the discussion of arts and particularly theatre. It is as though left to think for ourselves alternatives to official views of reality conveyed by theatre might be more attractive to us than the political discourse of opposition which was once meant to speak in our name.

The loss of the concept of image and imagination from criticism is reflected in the questioning of the nature of humanism at the heart of the postmodern debate. Through recent Continental philosophy, the work of Louis Althusser, and Michel Foucault in *The Archaeology of Knowledge*, there has been a challenge to the anthropocentric philosophy of the nineteenth and twentieth centuries and the creative imagination, which was seen as a passing illusion of Western humanist culture. The concomitant rejection of Romantic notions of individual genius has profoundly affected the way in which arts practice and production can be thought. The word 'production' itself began to hold sway over the analysis of creativity and gave rise to a mechanistic lexicon to describe the processes formerly passed off as mysterious and impenetrable. It is this vocabulary I attempt to take issue with here, believing that it overemphasises the productivist aspect of cultural activity and falsely denies the central part the material nature of species' being and biology play in the formations of theatre.

The impulse to remove humanity from the centre of history and question its privileged source of meaning had been enhanced by Jacques Lacan and Jacques Derrida, and what followed was the questioning of the idea of humanity making its own history. Richard Kearney asks in summing up this philosophical tradition whether one can any longer speak of an imagination, whether the notion of a postmodern imagination isn't a contradiction in terms. What he believes is necessary is a 'poetics of the possible': 'a move beyond humanism while remaining faithful to its intentions'. Further he rightly insists 'we should be wary of slipping from a healthy scepticism about humanism and progress to denying the creative subject any role whatsoever in the shaping of history.'[45] Theatre cannot deny humanism, it is a species-specific art, but the humanism it espouses can only be derived from an intimate knowledge of humanity which requires familiarity with the tedious as well as the tragic.

The predominant imagery of postmodernism, the stylistic connotations of its form, pastiche and parody, repetition and involution, are reminiscent of an internally reflective mode rather than one of expression, less theatre more cynicism. This is not to say that postmodern literature or works associated with that genre lack spectacular imagery and metaphor derived from the performative. But this is doubly perplexing given the creaking contradictions of the theatrical model. The work of Jean Baudrillard on 'simulation' and Jean-François Lyotard on 'narrative' have much to offer an analysis of this nature. But the overarching term 'postmodern' conceals rather than illuminates the very real and persistent homogenising tendency of the multi-corporations that have now superseded the industrial age and its relative heterogeneity. It is this homogenising tendency that the 'poetics of the possible' will have to work upon. The imagination is a tool in the creation and reception of images. Unless its relevance is better understood it is hard to see quite what purpose there could be in reaching for a deeper meaning from a work or understanding its mode of production more accurately. For in the last analysis it will be the individual imagination that creates the image in question, in collectivity with the theatre performer and the audience, neither one nor the other. The ethical possibilities from such a meeting therefore become of central importance. Theatre values the creative individual and that individual's relation to the 'other', while recognising the overall need for ethical responses to possible actions. These are the implications of the space between 'modes' of discourse, and the 'weapons' of revolution they might be asked to replace, and while asking questions of them is tentative and prone to the threat of the 'religious', not to ask them is to deny the metaphysics and therefore the imagination of theatre.

ETHICS

Equity, the name of the British theatre union, is a word which derives from the ethical domain and establishes the already intimate link there is between the belief of religions and oppositional politics. Equity is a form of right which does not carry with it the authority to enforce it. Ethics is not divorced from political purposes, but is rather a theory of the social duties of the individual. Though attempts to marry ethical operations and political purposes have been fraught and are rightly suspected, it is useful to quote Karl Kautsky's formulation of a political ethic to emphasise the undogmatic possibilities of the term:

> no ethic is absolute . . . moral rules can change . . . ethical rules are necessary for particular times, societies and classes . . . ethics are not a matter of convention, nor something that the individual chooses at will, but are determined by powers which are stronger than the individual . . .[46]

It is in this sense which I understand an ethics of performance to link with a politics of performance. Individual belief and social good are associated by the question of how best to debate and organise what is right for people. Fear of ethics has left this debate to others with no interest in the results except those of profit. The two words, theatre and ethics, are anyway inextricable. To indicate why they are demands a brief historical perspective.

In the modern period, that is, since the early seventeenth century, there has been a continual debate between theatre and issues of morality, and one from which theatre does not emerge unscathed. It is a debate which has recently intensified from within theatre with 'religion' and 'moral rebirth' being hawked as the ascendant themes of a *fin de siècle* theatre. But while these issues infiltrate the contents of theatre the critical context of performance has lost the bite of belief it once presumed its prerogative. In the seventeenth century William Prynne's notorious *Histriomastix* described stage plays as 'heathenish, lewde, ungodly spectacles, and most pernicious corruptions'. Prynne was the unfortunate target of a true subversive who circulated in his name a defence of stage plays and a retraction of his previous assault. Prynne was drawn to refute these 'scandalous papers and imputations' as forgeries, though between the two sets of papers, in 1633 and 1649, there is the anarchic possibility that Prynne could have surreptitiously commanded both sides of an argument. For discussing a morality of theatre, or as I wish to do an ethics, is to value the power of theatre to affect life, emotionally and biologically, and with this belief in theatre there is responsibility to ask how it does this and to what purpose. It is not sufficient to mobilise the church against the stage by adopting the latest blasphemous title, for all creative work derives from a path between blasphemy and curiosity. Goading institutions in this way is the confirmation of their power over a stage awestruck by an apology for religious ritual. These are cyclical affairs which require thought from within theatre in defence of the truly radical, experimental and nonconformist. William Prynne, by the turn of the next century was superseded by Jeremy Collier, whose *Short View* constituted the most serious attack on the 'immorality and profaneness' of the stage at that time. And so on until the present, when television fixates the censorious eye by being so much more a public phenomenon. The absurdities of *The Romans in Britain* trial at the Old Bailey in London in 1982 did much to resuscitate theatre's memories of days of prominence and the dangers of notoriety. These are transient and recurrent phenomena for one culture, yet the life-threatening, everyday conditions for another. Returning to first principle questions of ethics and theatre does not deny these real histories of censorship and compromise, but seeks out ways to deny them sustenance.

Ethics not only raises questions of normative conduct and lawful behaviour, it also traces out the possibility of its own shadow, the negation and defiance of norms.[47] Here the importance of an ethics of performance becomes clearer, given that the characteristics of a postmodern context would appear to derive from the destabilisation of norms, the dissolution of certainties. Theatre is a process that constantly revisions this normative frame in ways that release us from the polarity between what is considered ethical, and what is not ethical behaviour. It provides narrations which are exemplary and radical. These stories of other people, and their lives, open up a venue for ethics which is not a conceptual anchor, simply 'good' or 'bad' with all the power relations such statements imply, but a living arrangement of material needs. Ethical discourse itself has had very little effect or bearing on ethical acts. By contrast 'exemplary lives' guide by way of practice, and theatre inside its fictions and out, and in its personnel, are perceived to be made up of such lives. As Michel de Certeau says: 'Ethics is articulated through effective operations and it defines a distance between what is and what ought to be. This distance designates a space where we have something to do.'[48] This is the place where theatre occurs. Both ethics and theatre are concerned with possibility. On the contrary representation is the reflection of an 'existing' proposition as though it were fact, and this is never what the theatre achieves. The theatre image unlike any other is always a possibility without closure, like the ethical relation which awaits creation.

What then are the relations between an ethics and a poetics of theatre imagery? The convoluted spiral of postmodern theory with its floating postponement of judgements has led critics back to re-explore the work of writers such as Emmanuel Levinas in whose philosophy ethics plays a central part. It is the contemporary nature of this retention, in resistance to its marginalisation in other philosophies of the time, which is of interest. This move may seem unwarranted by theorists who claim that it is not postmodernism itself that is the problem but how it is used. There is of course good and bad theory, politically or otherwise to be drawn from such a widening movement of diverse thinkers. It remains, though, that the bewildering assertions that have come to be associated with contemporary theory leave the actuality of theatre, the face to face encounter that distinguishes theatre, largely unthought. The biological underpinnings of this absence are looked at in the final part of the book, the ethical aspects here.

Kearney, whom I have referred to in reflection on the imagination, links that faculty very specifically with ethical considerations. He uses 'ethics' in the broad sense of a 'personal and social responsibility to others' and argues that this should not be confused with the more limited sense of morality as 'a dogmatic system of abstract "oughts" '.[49] Further there is no sense here of an individualist notion, but rather a framework that surpasses the epistemological statement 'I think' with the statement 'I stand', thus grounded on and inclusive of the 'other' as its indispensable precondition. This conception of ethics being centred in the 'face to face' relation is particularly appropriate to theatre, and Kearney develops this theme in a useful direction by recalling the original sense of ethos as disposition:

> The face to face is a relation of disposition rather than position . . . The face to face can never be a complete or closed relation. The face of the other is always irreducible to my relation to it, or my representation of it . . . It is clear that this notion of the ethical subject as a dis-position before the face of the other is radically social and political in its implications.[50]

The secular nature of the term is therefore asserted, it is a dimension through which a theory of behaviours can be elaborated. What it asks is, 'where are you?' and thus privileges practice over theory in such a way as to redress the predominance of theory, some would say 'the poverty of theory' that has characterised the postmodern period.[51] This philosophical stasis, a form of social paralysis, can be countered by what Kearney describes and deconstructs as 'the poetic imagination': 'The first and most effective step . . . is to begin to imagine that the world as it is could be otherwise . . . It is not enough to state what might be done. We must also reckon with the practical factors which militate against us doing it.'[52] Poetics in Kearney's use thus combines the political, ethical and the playful in a broad sense of invention drawn from the root of the word *poiesis*: the 'willingness to imagine oneself in the other person's skin', the classic 'as if' of the theatre.

Kearney's concern for ethics, in his discussion of the genealogy of the imagination, is influenced by the later work of Michel Foucault, as well as Emmanuel Levinas. Both in quite distinct ways see ethics as an interaction of theory and practice. Thinking and acting are connected in an ethical sense and give rise to results which are political.[53] As Michel Foucault says:

> it's not at all necessary to relate ethical problems to scientific knowledge. Among the cultural inventions of mankind there is a treasury of devices, techniques, ideas, procedures and so on, that cannot exactly be reactivated, but at least constitute, or help to constitute, a certain point of view which can be very useful as a tool for analyzing what's going on now – and to change it.[54]

This is an important qualification of the unwarranted mediating role of 'scientific knowledge' in what is thought to be worthwhile. The 'treasury of devices' is for me apparent in the everyday, and while Bachelard wished to retain the significance of scientific rationality his arrival in the quotidian world of houses, cupboards and drawers was an acknowledgement of how influential this apparently irrational domain remained over what was worth knowing in the first place. Ethics for Foucault is a practice, ethos a manner of being, and both constitute: 'a very strong structure of existence, without any relation with the juridical per se, with an authoritarian system, with a disciplinary structure.'[55] A discussion of the relations between theatre and ethics need not automatically raise materialist eyebrows without attention to the specific terms I have laid out for their discussion.

Kearney is able to address the conceptual nature of imagination through its genealogical mutations while retaining much that is useful from postmodern theory. His approach is one of involution and reflection in the way that he characterises postmodernism's project as being not an evolution of modernism but 'involving' of it. By raising the question of the relationship between the imagination and theatre I am reasserting the need for a mechanics of images as well as the theory of images developed earlier. Not just what images are, but how they work and how they are received and appropriated by the precondition of their creation, the audience. Such a mechanics draws from phenomenology the framework in which this ethics of performance needs to be situated.

Phenomenological and existential philosophies have had a decisive impact on the thought of theatre during the last century. The latter was unified and explicated through a variety of playwrights under the title *The Theatre of the Absurd* in Martin Esslin's book.[56] This piece of audacious critical comparison nonetheless remains an example of literary critical, dramatic exegesis, rather than theatre theory. Phenomenological theory, however, has informed the practice of theatre in more diverse ways with particular reference to the body in space, and deserves further explication for what it offers an ethics and poetics of theatre now. It was a generation of phenomenologists that dominated European philosophy between 1930 and 1960, and it is therefore consistent that their work contributes to the understanding of theatre in subsequent years. With each of these philosophers there remains the question – as has been so critically and cruelly exposed in the case of Heidegger – of the testing of their theory and the modification of that theory in the light of practice and experience: 'The key to the personal poetic attitude of a philosopher is not to be sought in his ideas, as if it could be deduced from them, but rather in his philosophy-as-life, in his philosophical life, his ethos.'[57] Referring to the French philosophers who participated in the resistance during the Second World War, Foucault remarks: 'None of the philosophers of *engagement* – Sartre, Simone de Beauvoir, Merleau-Ponty – none of them did a thing.'[58] This does not deny the relevance of their thinking to a politics of commitment, but it does problematise the relation between 'situation' and 'position' which I understand as central to the theatre act. For if theatre's internal coherence is that of the body in 'situation' as image, its outer coherence is one of 'dis-position' in context. It is this 'placing' of theatre, in an ethical dimension, that marks its social and political project.

Phenomenology shares with 'Imagist' poets of the same generation, Ezra Pound, William Carlos Williams and later Charles Olson, a wish for philosophy to return to 'things in themselves', thus phenomenology: the phenomena of meaning as constituted by the human consciousness. This consciousness is an activity of intentionality, a consciousness by definition of something other than itself, and a reflective logical operation presupposing a pre-reflective lived experience of the world.[59] The relevance of phenomenology for theatre arises with its attempt to describe our 'situated experience' as 'body subjects' who creatively experience the world before ever analysing it in abstract terms. But the temporal question of the relationship between theory and practice, the consequence of the one upon the other is not here sufficiently contextualised for a politics or ethics to provide a framework for the theatre activity.

An ethical understanding of the 'other' opens up such a theoretical space for reconsidering the relations between the theatre performer and audience as well as the relations between both and criticism. The presence of an audience is a defining characteristic of the person, becoming performer. Without their presence in time that transformation would not take place as expression but would remain in the therapeutic, private domain. It would here remain meditative rather than expressive. Further the presence of an audience is also by definition a non-presence, a non-simultaneity, for while the real time of performance is shared, the theatre time of the event, which marks theatre off from Happenings and Performance Art, reimposes itself and in turn establishes the space and time of theatre as separate from, and to be re-entered by, the audience.[60]

The question of how one conducts oneself in relation to the other, how one behaves, is a first philosophy, the precondition for life and the exchange between lives that I assert is theatre's domain. Here it is not simply language as the capacity for dwelling, as Heidegger said, but criticism, for it is this activity which signifies a primordial relation with the other. Where theatre is an expression constituted by the moment and space of the image, criticism communicates through concepts. For Emmanuel Levinas: 'criticism exists as a public's mode of comportment'. But if criticism creates the 'knowledge' of art, art itself disengages from the world and knowledge, evades that world through substituting the object for the image. In this process Levinas believes Art 'lets go of the prey for the shadow.'[61] Theatre through the corporeality of the body and its objects, the fact that it is a living instant open to the possibility of becoming something else, makes different demands on this shadow world, however. The transparency that Levinas sees as the characteristic property of the image is substituted in theatre by a renewed and deepened presence, which separated from the arts in general locates theatre in a unique cultural realm. Instead of completing the world, art completes its shadow – there is no necessary relation between art and commitment but rather a potential for the critic to link the disengagement of art to history, the artist to their world. This process of criticism and comportment is revisioned by the act of theatre and its ethical disposition. Theatre is both the shadow and the echo of the everyday. It is not a reflection and does not complete this realm but distorts it while remaining intimately linked to, and inseparable from it.

Further still, ethics deepen the problematic of what is the essence of theatre. Do there need to be many present or just one witness and one performer, in other words two, for theatre to occur? For ethical understanding:

> There are always at least three persons. This means that we are obliged to ask who is the other . . . the first type of simultaneity is the simultaneity of equality, the attempt to reconcile and balance the conflicting claims of each person . . . As soon as there are three, the ethical relationship with the other becomes political and enters into the totalizing discourse of ontology.[62]

This entry into the political and ethical through the power of three is the privilege of theatre. There is, in the act of theatre, the performer, the audience and you, and it is this tripartite, dialectical nature that demands distinct responses from the ensuing event. That event is quite different when undertaken between a performer and 'you' alone, entering the religious, the ritual and the therapeutic. This relationship, three as a crowd, maintains the essence of 'difference' and counters the European Romantic tradition of two becoming one 'in love'. This binary pairing is where the theatre as propaganda begins to work and is the antithesis of what I believe a relevant theatre to be. The myth of togetherness of an earlier generation is deposed by the dynamics of difference.

The poetics of 'difference' have been inaugurated by the pluralism of the milieu, the circumspection towards the possibility of making truth statements and the emergence of powerful influences of feminism and ethnic examination of the ideas of gender and nationhood. Any theatre entering this terrain cannot presume the unitary, fusion or sameness beloved of another more innocent era. Indeed the thinking being is no longer pre-emptive of existence, I think therefore I am, but rather I think of you therefore I might be: 'the ethical rapport with the face is asymmetrical in that it subordinates my existence to the other . . . Ethics is against nature because it forbids the murderousness of my natural will to put my existence first.'[63] Here is distilled the dialectic of the performer's ethic: the constant interplay between the 'egological' of the individual and the 'cosmological' of the world as audience. The urge to be seen as separate but dependent upon the will of the other, the recognition of the observing eye and its relation to the 'I' of being human, the listening ear and the 'here' of the place of performance. This ethical stance is not depersonalising, but defining of existence precisely because of the relationship with the other, in Levinas' terms: 'The ethical I is a being who asks if he has a right to be!, who excuses himself to the other for his own existence.'[64] The 'bow' of theatre surely resides in this 'excuse to be', the right being garnered from the other. The dispensing with the bow, the inversion of the bow as clapping of the audience by the performer strikes an unfamiliar and uneasy note for it often has nothing to do with the ethics of the theatre contract as established by the performance itself. For the bow as acknowledgement of applause also carries with it the bow of submission and the 'bowing acquaintance', that is the slight degree of acquaintance that theatre initiates, but which stops at that, and distinguishes theatre from the domain of imitation and hagiography.

Ethics here leads us away from the post-structuralists and the 'demise of the subject', to a terrain which is the opposite of a political acquiescence. The audience are rediscovered always coming before the performer however early the performer might be. For the spectator's eye is watching for an entrance, to their place, and when that entrance is denied by the performance it is waiting for an initiating movement and when that movement is denied by stillness it suspects the dance within that stillness, and can sense the discreetest breath in passage. And where there is no breath, there is no life, the funeral rites begin and the audience witness the entry of the priest to the body and so everyday life and theatre continue albeit with understudies and the heightened theatrical expectations sudden substitutions of the unknown for the known often bring.

Theatre that is unwritten, that is beyond the scriptural economy in the black market that is the everyday, relies on a 'saying' rather than the 'said'. The said is the discourse that is translatable, transferable and performable. The saying is the speech act itself that resists removal from its context however banal that arena might be. Saying replaces the inert object of literature and language with the process of enunciation, as words which remain the property of users though infinitely hearable in the everyday babble of conversation. Saying is more than speaking, it is a way of giving everything, of not keeping anything for oneself, and here embraces and challenges the politics of quietude. The 'said' of theatre exists in its repetition and reproduction; the 'saying' in its improvisation and innovation. It is in the everyday that the saying often discreetly occurs in and around the ethical relation. It resides in the micro-gestures of society, not in its flamboyant theatrical expressions concretised as the discourse of theatre. This is the challenge for the theatre: to enter the quotidian and leave without coercing or constraining it nor equally for the theatre to be coerced, dis-posed, before its departure. Where the theatre relies on audition, repetition and representation it can barely begin to face up to these ethical propositions. Antonin Artaud in *The Theatre and its Double* testified to this when he fundamentally challenged the role of theatre as representation, indeed the perversion of theatre that imitation entailed, and the obfuscation of the world which it sought to 'reflect': 'rarely does the debate rise to a social level or do we question our social or ethical system. Our Theatre never goes so far as to ask itself whether by chance this social or ethical system is iniquitous or not.'[65] From within theatre the first ethical system to be addressed is the one it inaugurates itself – the actor's ethical relation to the space in which theatre takes its place. It is this that relates an ethics back to a poetics and out to a politics of performance.

POLITICS

Considering the ethical imagination in this abstract way reaffirms the complex relation between performer and audience, both active in the process of image creation at a point somewhere between the two, but never wholly within the territory of one or the other. The question of bounds leads me to ask the more concrete question of what the contextual nature of this exchange might be, what kinds of terrain the imagination works? A relevant and provocative theatre is one which has recognised the local and particular nature of this terrain, valuing time and place as preconditions for the criticism of universal values. This is not a rejection of the modernist preference for space over place, but a rethinking of what has been lost in increasing homogeneity under the duress of international capital. The imagination at work here participates in the formation of images that are a dialectic between the particular part, the material of the locality and the mental whole in which this place has meaning. This is a move from the centre to the periphery, towards regional pluralism with particular commitment to local initiatives.[66] The relationship between imagination, the image and these manifestations which are internationally widespread, is the sense in which communities are themselves constructed imaginatively and symbolically. The context of theatre making itself thus operates within codes that in turn fold back on the operational paradigms of the act of theatre.

To recognise this structural acquaintance between the theatre process as image creation and the dynamic of communities to 'imagine' themselves as much as being constructed from outside, reinforces theatre as an inevitable manifestation of all societies rather than a specialised and coded activity separate from the society in question. The naming process of theatre is rather like the naming process of towns and villages in that it places identity on the entity and allows others to see it and speak to it in those chosen parameters. The naming process entails an ethical dimension in its willingness to be identified and criticised, to be 'stood up to'. The opposite is of course true where the naming process removes the entity from criticism by recourse to higher-order principles such as national authority or royal patronage. This entails not a 'saying' or 'naming' but a 'said', a 'named'.

The question as to whether there can be such a thing as a 'national' theatre is a salient one. That a theatre exists that operates under the aegis of a national title cannot be questioned. Nor can the very real material and spiritual effort and investment that has been directed to that entity. But there is a contradiction in the idea, and it remains an idea, of a theatre reflecting something which is in itself in good measure 'imagined'. Here really is the 'Theatre and its Double', an imagined response, theatre, to an imagined formation, nation. The conundrum is deepened by the addition of royal approbation, in the entitled and top heavy 'Royal National Theatre'; the House of Windsor here allowing their official recognition, patronage, to be bestowed on that other house of enchantment, the theatre. While the latter has a long historical precedent, the former is a relatively recent phenomenon, and understandably so. For the concept of the Nation has for too long been problematic to allow a theatre to speak in its name and on its behalf.[67] A study of theatre in places with nationally representative bodies takes on this enquiry if it is not to ignore the problematic site of its existence. If the Royal National Theatre has entered into the life of the nation, been accepted as part of that nation, readily identifiable by visitors to the country, it remains in its hegemonic state problematic for a study of theatre and should be treated as such if only to make more likely its conscious, continued and better existence.

The problem is both a spatial and temporal one. The words nation and national are of course connected with the word native, which implies being born into a settled place. To jump from this to a conception of nation state, as Raymond Williams points out, is artificial and denies the very real 'placeable bonding' that occurs on a local and immediate level.[68] The language of the Arts Council of Great Britain in the 1980s speaking of a regional priority further enhanced this notion of an entity which is national, from which are abstracted regional identities. Here the movement is one backwards from the larger generalisation to the distinct regional unit, which is subordinate to and dependent on the nation rather than constitutive in its own right.[69] It is clear in this analysis that the larger identities are meant to prevail. The terms and images of identity flow down and govern what it is to be British. As other peoples have shown in recent years this is for many an unacceptable imposition of identity. So to speak of a theatre in post-industrial Britain is to speak of an entity that conserves this relationship between people and their imagined national identity or challenges it. Imagined, because as is so evident in periods of war such as the Falklands/Malvinas dispute, a unification, generalisation and devotion to the entity of nation through patriotism is not a natural nor everyday occurrence. It remains to be constructed in successive and changing periods. Consistent with such periods of reaffirmation of nationhood is the belief that radicalism is associated with opposition to such conceptions of nation, and hence is unpatriotic.

This leaves a theatre that is radical in spirit and practice in a complex relationship with the milieu in which it occurs. While such a theatre might rely on the immediate 'theatrical' environment it cannot presume the nature of the relations of its audience to the shifting perceptions of wider loyalties. Further, such perceptions, once directly drawn from the relations between individual, collective, home, county and country, have now been superseded by the imagery and dynamics of commerce, what Raymond Williams describes as: 'an artificial construction which increasingly had to be defined in generalising and centralised images because the only effective political identity still apparently compatible with the dislocating and relocating processes of industry was now at the deliberately distanced level'.[70] This is not just a simple external oppression of multi-corporation finance but also, like hegemony, an internal one of imagination, for those to whom it is being 'done'. The system that is advanced by the images of advertising is one which relies on continued consumption, where systems quite other than those of community and settlement now operate. But beyond this consumption, supported by the free-trade capitalist economy, other relations and conceptions of people are necessary and it is to these identities that theatre most actively contributes. These are cultural needs which in turn rely upon other peoples not as producers but people from places identifiable in relation to one's own settlement. Here the idea of nation returns, and supersedes that of the world economy, that borderless place which otherwise is supported and striven for in the interest of consumer choice. And it is here that a modernist but belligerently local theatre can be imagined, as it has been for many years in places like Tbilisi, Manila, Belfast and Ljubljana.

This concept of nation is difficult at the point where it becomes established in a particular figuration, as the entity called the National Theatre implies. Its very existence is what stimulates attention because it is in its form that its limitations are so noticeable. To confront a theatrical institution with these questions of identity seems a peculiar target in one sense. But it is precisely the existence of national theatres that governs the relations between other emerging local theatres that in their plurality might be considered constituting what is truly 'national' about any theatre. Here we would need to address the marginal and fringe theatres, what I have referred to previously as 'micro-theatres' in constant states of emergence and disappearance that reflect the diversity of ethnic background, gender and physical constitution, that determines another understanding of Britain and its theatre today. We need to understand more clearly the persuasive character and attractions of a National Theatre – from which much theatre of note has arisen. A study of theatre cannot ignore nor deny this work, for it is central to any estimation of the contemporary theatre in Britain.

It places it alongside, rather than over, the manifestations of theatre whose presence it shadows. It is not the 'evil' antipode of the 'other' theatre, it is its neighbour, no less and certainly no more.

Such an analysis bears directly on the relationship between a predominantly textually based theatre and one which derives its coherence from the construction and interplay of images. Predominant, because as we have seen there is nothing intrinsically untheatrical about a text, and texts themselves have interactive qualities. Indeed when texts are produced their medium will inevitably be one of 'images'. Rather, the canon of literature from which theatre texts emerge is still not 'variable' in the sense in which Williams uses that word. While the accessibility of theatres to writers 'becoming writers' has enormously widened since the advent of the English Stage Company at the Royal Court, there remains an inevitable predisposition to those writers who have established themselves, from Shakespeare onwards. I resist here using meaningless terms like 'new writing' to avoid the fallacious division between the most significant writing of the past and the most significant writing now.

We 'all', of course, have an imagined relation with Shakespeare which mirrors that of our interest and commitment to what is national. Shakespeare is immutably connected to what it is to be 'English' or 'British', and any theatre that derives its impetus from that set of relations knowingly, and often radically, plays upon that commitment and legacy. Indeed while our relations to nation, nationality and nationalism might prove notoriously difficult to define, the relations we hold with the nation's poet remain an 'uncomfortable anomaly' within that confusion. It is again in large measure an imagined relation for one could count on the fact that the majority of British people have never read, let alone seen, a Shakespeare play in its entirety. This does not of course stop anyone from having an opinion about his writing, of which opinions there are as many as people in the country. As Oscar Wilde says:

> in the case of Shakespeare it is quite obvious that the public really see neither the beauties nor the defects of his plays. If they saw the beauties, they would not object to the development of the drama; and if they saw the defects, they would not object to the development of the drama either. The fact is, the public make use of the classics of a country as a means of checking the progress of Art. They degrade the classics into authorities. They use them as bludgeons for preventing the free expression of Beauty in new forms.[71]

The politics I speak about, whether theatrically directed to the Royal Shakespeare Company or the Royal National Theatre, or to the wider sphere of the contexts of those theatres, therefore operate within imaginative paradigms as well as everyday realities. In this they share with cultural relations an ideological aspect. To return politics, questions of nation, only to their material parts, is to miss the complex of their operations in the mental sphere, the subconscious as well as the cognitive realm. As this is equally the domain of our relation to the arts it is divisive to 'think' a solely material politics. Tactical investigations drawn from the border disciplines of theatre can expose these simplifications and disrupt their generic separation from everyday life.

Benedict Anderson, in his book *Imagined Communities*, allows us to press these connections further, and to look more closely at this quality of imagining that informs the context of the theatre.[72] It is an imagining of a distinct kind from that under consideration by Richard Kearney, Gaston Bachelard or Humphrey Jennings and has been described by other theorists as 'ideology' or 'doxa'. But the strength of using the term 'imagined' is the sense in which the positive, the possibility of agency, is not lost. For it is not the community or Shakespeare that is the problem but how we construct and then use these various, and obviously quite distinct entities for ethically guided purposes. The construction of these entities is what is in question, and the theatre contributes a dynamic of imaging which is central to the construction of any reality, and the transformation of that reality in turn into desired ends. Groups as diverse as Collettivo di Parma, Rustaveli, and the Comedy Theatre of Bucharest have demonstrated how Shakespeare is not only our contemporary but anyone's own.

For Anderson, nationality and nation-ness are cultural artefacts of a particular kind that command profound emotional legitimacy and yet once created take on a 'modular' capability of being transplanted to a variety of social terrains. This sense of transition, between the particular and the universal, is clearly associated with the description of images considered earlier in the work of Humphrey Jennings, and resides at the heart of any poetics. Again like the image, Anderson describes the nation as constructed from innumerable elements which do not meet except in the mind of the beholder: '[the nation] is *imagined* because the members of even the smallest nation will never know most of their fellow members, meet them, or even hear of them, yet in the minds of each lives the image of their communion'.[73] The optimism of Anderson's stance can be seen in comparison to Ernst Gellner's critical use of the word 'invents' in the following: 'Nationalism is not the awakening of nations to self consciousness: it invents nations where they do not exist.'[74] Here there is an element of falsity rather than imagination and a direct contrast is made with 'true' communities which can be advantageously juxtaposed to nations. This position could be said to have permeated Raymond Williams' earlier work, and Benedict Anderson takes issue with its terms of reference: 'all communities, larger than primordial villages of face-to-face contact (and perhaps even these) are imagined'. Anderson goes on to say that the distinction to be made is not as Gellner implies between the falsity and genuineness of such constructions but by the *style* in which they are imagined.[75]

Where the nation is always imagined as limited, bounded somewhere however far away by other peoples with their own boundaries, communities can be conceived as a deep horizontal comradeship. Here community, nation and audience coalesce in their imagined state of collectivity. Unless more is understood of this imagined constituency little can be achieved in its best interests. It is theatre which provides one of the most valuable means through which communities understand themselves and become understood by others. One aspect of this, the specific relations between theatre and mining communities, is considered later. Images and the imagination are, if Jennings and Bachelard are taken seriously, the means through which the material needs of communities and their mental aspirations form and disperse, at each point allowing a break with past dogmas and the expression of intangible possibilities. These do not, until they have been expressed through images, have credence in the domain of rationalities that science marks out, but it is precisely through images that the first tentative transformation of everyday existing realities is first conducted. Beyond Bachelard it is here that the ethics and politics of constituencies become paramount. So, equally such constituencies need to be thought for the actual, material differences that reside in each, as well as the styles in which they are imagined, otherwise there is little hope for their imaginative survival. And it is this thought that the 'Esperanto' of the image, its internationalism, often fails to address. Where images have been treated as cosmopolitan constructions, an international style for a theatre to speak across boundaries, the need for the precision and distinctiveness of locality is reasserted. For the image derives first from those specific particulars before proliferating in meaning and significance. Where theatre speaks in dialects, outmoded languages of theatre analysis seek an Esperanto of universal understanding and lose sight of their prey.

The images in question throughout this chapter – a woman reaching for a man, a balloon ascending, sand descending, the reverberation of a forest – like others add up to more than the sum of their parts, they have physical depth and imaginative height. They are not solely literary, visual, or poetic images but potentially theatre images, and as such are produced by the relationship between bodies in place, made space, and the presence of more than a seeing eye; they are regarded by a perceiving audience. The presence of the body in this theatre is one of becoming, through action to image, but a becoming in the world which presumes the participation of the other. The theatre here is a 'face to face' relationship, an ethical relationship, which moves beyond the visual to the sensual, which provokes the question, not is the image true, but is it good? This question of worth carries more than just an evaluative sense, but evaluation is central to it. To defend cultural plurality there is the expectation that value judgements will be made, and that relativism is coincidental with nihilism. Without the concepts of criticism derived from beyond the arts the theatre image might be mistaken for a shadow, and one which determines the theatre's inability to catch its prey. Theatre is the shadow of the everyday from which performance attempts to take its leave. It is important to return to this realm to ask why it is everyday life which determines what theatre can be. Without this return there could be no response to Luce Irigaray when she asks: 'And what if what he were asked to judge were only a "shadow"? How could he do it?'[76] Regarding theatre entails judgement and judgement derives its force and meaning from everyday life.

3

EVERYDAY LIFE

To value theatre is to value life, not to escape from it. The everyday is at once the most habitual and demanding dimension of life which theatre has most responsibility to. Theatre does not tease people out of their everyday lives like other expressions of wish fulfilment but reminds them who they are and what is worth living and changing in their lives every day. The lay theatre derives from these convictions and can be examined through the nature of images and their relation to an ethics and a politics of theatre practice. While I have considered the potential of these categories for a language of theatre, there is the concern that such a vocabulary remains twice removed from the theatre I set out to examine. This is a problem given my emphasis on practices of theatre, where the traditional axes of production and consumption demand rethinking. It is not surprising when one considers the divisions driven between understandings drawn from everyday life and those considered endemic to cultural practices and intellectual pursuits. The languages available to us derived from these pursuits are ones which in discreet and subtle ways make sure that divisions between the professional and the profane endure. In other words, theoretically it is only 'in other words' that theatre and everyday life can be acquainted. In practice, if the lay theatre is a viable example, they are infinitely linked and negotiable. It is however necessary to enter the tract between these practices and theories if only to demonstrate that the central problem is not the split between them, but that which is documented and that which remains unwritten. The purpose here is to explore the provocation to theatre of the everyday realm, that is when the everyday itself is taken to be a set of identifiable practices which have more or less logic. If the importance of the imagination has been concealed by criticism reaching for objectivity, equally the everyday, left unthought and unwritten, threatens to exile theatre to an inconsequential margin. Conceptual advances achieved on behalf of theatre only by the exclusion of the everyday are retreats for theatre from life.

This concern arose from theatre practices conducted in a particular place over a number of years, and was a response to the subtle and unpredictable means by which audiences became performers, and communities wove a theatre practice without regard for disciplines' boundaries, or theoretical loyalties. Here theatre and everyday life were in continual negotiation and there was no foregone conclusion as to their possible equilibrium or as to which would prevail. Theatre would serve causes such as political and social needs, it would be used to provide comradeship and community for those who were isolated, it was an excuse to eat together and to conduct relations outside and away from the family circle and home, it was an opportunity to confront neighbours with long held complaints and express prejudices against those who were not welcome, and it was an opportunity for those who felt prejudice and disrespect to redress wrongs visited on them. This was a utilitarian theatre because everyday life was not expected to cease on entry to, and participation in it. But it would be wrong to surmise that theatre was simply here being used as a way to continue politics by other means. It was known to be an expressive medium which articulated desires, and generated pleasures through aesthetic operations.

How were these operations conducted? Performances were devised, or texts chosen, which appeared to accommodate these needs, were adapted unceremoniously when they failed to go on meeting these needs and were sacrificed as soon as they stopped being appropriate to those needs. Constant use was made of those storytelling forms which appeared to convey truths and expose concealment. For some this inevitably meant drawing on the fictions of television where the currency of storytelling was most apparent in everyday life and in turn through soap operas and 'sitcoms' drew upon apparently everyday stories. Theatre exposed these tales to another, more critical mode of expression where apparently 'true' life stories would solicit laughter and criticism for being absurd and irrelevant to the everyday lives of the participants. On occasions when nothing so critical was achieved, theatre derived from the most trite caricatures of the everyday and was accepted as fantasy and escape for those who saw it. Theatrical forms themselves were appropriated including pantomimes, postmodern dance forms, music hall, quiz shows, improvisation, and the canon of dramatic literature adjusted to new ends. It is these narratives and local participation in a lay theatre that are the reality, and practice, returned to throughout the following; not the demands of an academy for another 'newer' apparatus with which to deconstruct the separated and privatised text. There is a pressing political need to discover ways of valuing and creating with the stories of neighbourhoods and stories from visitors to those neighbourhoods. This will remain in theatre a voluntaristic activity as long as qualitative theory is kept at arm's length. The lessons of the following have already been derived from practice, and therefore the danger of an austere convention might give way temporarily to a more playful invention around those experiences.

Where this activity named itself as 'theatre', and located itself in a building, the weaving of everyday life and cultural expression became a knotting, increasingly concerned with divisive, separatist politics and institutional concerns. The gap opened up by this movement from a minority expression of everyday creativity to a majority imposition, an official vision of what that expression could be, provides the impetus for me to explore the theoretical dogmatism of theatre. Here is a chance to conjecture about the limitations of theatre's critical vocabulary for an emergent and minority theatre practice. What has been described previously as the micro-theatre, the rhizomatic response of audiences in their relation to that theatre, can be located, with some patience, in the everyday where it is most discreet. But in any discussion of texts, contexts and imagery, it becomes obvious that the theatre which is 'available' for discussion is primarily that which is 'documented', that which is accessible at a certain place and time, in a 'theatre' that is named and separated from daily life, precisely beyond the everyday with which it cannot be allowed congress. Where there has been an attempt to define imagery 'outside' this context, for example the community play, carnival, site-specific events or pedestrian dance, there has simply been a reformulation of institutional parameters around the chosen object, separating it from the context which the analysis seeks to understand. The purpose of speaking of a lay theatre is to define theatre in relation to forces it should resist, the pressures of conservatism and cynical commercialism, rather than to something it is, or should be. Without this critique being reinforced at all times, it is quite impossible to conceive of theatre as a transformative project in and on the world. And given the socialist principles stated as the premiss of this study, such a condition for theatre is unacceptable.

Everyday life is both the social space from which this argument arises and for my purposes the conceptual entity which is most provocative to its cultural questioning. The proposal that everyday life be considered conceptual at all demands a clarification. It is conceptual in the sense that concepts were considered earlier: the everyday provides a tool box with which to open up the nature of theatre. The tools or concepts it offers are unusual ones in that they have provided the vast remainder 'against' which academic disciplines define themselves: common sense, local knowledge, tactics and ruses all derive from the everyday and its discursive operations. They are not random but have a logic which can include coincidence and chance encounter. The problem is that being of the everyday, commonplace and familiar, these logics remain unwritten, denying their relations with other operations they might say something about. The theatre is one such operation, cooking, eating, walking and talking are others.

But whose everyday life am I talking about: mine or yours? They are after all different. Everyday life is without a subject in that it is not only 'my' everyday life, nor only the everyday of an 'other' that is immediately in question. But in recognising this, as in the ethical relationship, there is an acceptance of the reciprocity of identity. My everyday life inevitably impinges on someone else's and it is there that the pleasures of human interaction occur and the possibilities of theatre begin. It is also here that issues of racial oppression, sexist discrimination and censorship manifest themselves, and the concept of everyday life is expected to reveal these fundamental politics, not conceal them with vagaries. It is though, a common denominator that resists being broken down into the components of its operations – vehicles, cooking utensils, tables, beds, are the technology of the everyday, but not the everyday itself. The everyday is stubbornly human and though it is bound by natural phenomena, light and dark, heat and cold, it is most apparent in the domain where such constraints are least consciously felt, if not for some physically endured, in the urban milieu.

We can look back towards the antecedents of the thought of everyday life, the emergence of a position regarding its spatial and temporal characteristics. This 'removal', to see, presents us with the first contradiction of what might appear a contradictory exercise. If everyday life is that which is most difficult to discern, and if our looking for it removes us from it, does this not jeopardise the project in the same way that traditional separation of critical disciplines from their objects of study has compromised their claims to be speaking of anything except themselves? Certainly the quantitative, statistical approaches of theoretical sociology for instance, would appear to define life only in terms that statistics allow, and while this is an obvious example, reservations might be held about a range of academic disciplines designed to speak in 'Nature's Own Language'. I have made play of this separation and have to demonstrate why 'everyday life' constitutes a critical advance by providing an alternative more conducive to contexts. Considering everyday life as a critical concept is dissimilar in one important respect to the disciplines I criticise. There is no 'language' or single critical stance associated with everyday life, it is precisely a term which is thought to be outside the domain of specialist vocabulary and is therefore the milieu which is least likely to conceal the object under scrutiny with its own historically mediated languages. This is not to say it does not have a history, but as the following diversity of approaches to it will demonstrate, there is no simple Esperanto of the everyday to which theory can appeal in moments of interpretive crisis. Given it is at these breaking points that most is at stake, the lack of theoretical release from the stubborn complexity of practices is, in my view, an advance for theatre and life. The everyday is a world of dialects not mother tongues, utterances so apparently inconsequential that they have avoided the attentions of the academy. It has its own logics and tactics but these are changeable entities, are qualitative in nature and demand to be reformulated in each case where theatre occurs. It is therefore insufficient to speak of this or that theory of everyday life having critical potential beyond the immediate relations established between each occurrence of theatre and the everyday from which it distinguishes itself. For that reason I cannot propose a theory of everyday life which will be amenable to general use, I can simply define its genealogy as a concept having in the description of the lay theatre indicated some of the ways it has inflected on my own practice. This is not the same thing as saying 'anything goes'; there is a specific ethical, political and aesthetic purpose to the choice of the everyday as the realm within which the theatre is to be most usefully thought – a hypothesis which is central to this book and my work.

I will not perpetuate a mystery about what Maurice Blanchot called: 'what is most difficult to discover'.[1] The problematic of everyday life needs to be considered temporally and spatially. Reconsidering the conceptual coordinates of everyday life provides not just a sense of the context that gives rise to theatre but poses questions about the transformation of that context. What could be said to be its history? Can something as apparently habitual and uncontroversial as everyday life have a history? If its practices are evasive its theorisation can be traced out. It is these writings which are worthy of consideration as an indication of its usefulness as a concept for theatre to be related to. It also of course remains a historical reality for theatre to work within. But the purpose here is to move thought as far as possible from a predominant image of the everyday perpetuated by memories of history classes where the cross-section of the medieval keep would give way to the romantic panorama of everyday life in the castle. Shaker colony, Indian reservation and igloo are flattened for our curiosity and pleasure. Here talk of everyday life does not increase knowledge but conceals it. From another more conducive extreme Patrick Wright in his work, *On Living in an Old Country,* which inaugurated a field of enquiry in Britain centred on the meaning of 'heritage', traced the antecedents of a conceptualisation of everyday life by recovering an 'academic' lineage of the theme through Agnes Heller to Georg Lukács and his concept of trivial life: 'Alltäglichkeit'.[2] The problem with this lineage is that its philosophical rigour swamps the very practices and everyday voices which gave rise to it in a distant past. Here the abstraction of life in the medieval keep is substituted by the abstraction of philosophy spiralling away from its context. Wright's own work while owing a conceptual debt to these sources is, in later studies such as *A Journey through Ruins,* closer to the tenor of nonconformist thinkers such as Henri Lefebvre and Michel de Certeau, which to my mind are more conducive to a critical theatre, being more finely tuned to the practices which gave rise to thoughts.[3] Between 1940 and 1960 Lefebvre was writing his major works, the Mass Observation movement was attempting to establish what everyday life was, while the Situationists in France having discovered what it was were attempting to intervene in it. Michel de Certeau's work, more recent than Lefebvre's but still only now becoming widely disseminated through translation, covers an eclectic field drawn from the discursive sciences and their relations to the everyday. It is a combination of themes from this work which supplies a provocative vocabulary for a lay theatre.

Historically then, a cultural lineage for the understanding of everyday life can be drawn from the problematic discrediting of the everyday by the Surrealist movement through the restorative work of Humphrey Jennings and the inauguration of 'Mass Observation', to the quite distinct, but not dissociated Situationist activity of the 1960s. Geographically a complex interrelationship was inaugurated by the Paris/London Surrealist exhibition of 1936, the 'construction' of everyday Britain in wartime by Mass Observation and Humphrey Jennings' documentary films for the GPO film unit, the links between the 'London Psycho Geographical Committee' and their Europe-wide situationist interventions of the 1960s. From these various writings of the everyday I will focus on the English phenomenon of Mass Observation, two French theorists of the everyday, Henri Lefebvre and Michel de Certeau whose work opens up potential areas of everyday creativity and imagining, and more broadly to complete the chapter, the cultural practices of cinema and theatre in which the everyday is marked.

While movements, people and practices might appear an incongruous mix, ascertaining the breadth of the everyday demands tactical investigations drawn from a variety of sources in order not to conceal the real that interpretation seeks to capture. Where these were drawn in the previous chapter from industrial documentary and the philosophy of science, here it is an idiosyncratic version of consumer research and an alternative strain of French cultural theory. This theory, in the hands of Lefebvre and de Certeau, is alternative in the sense that their work resists the 'panopticon' procedures and conclusions of Michel Foucault whose discourse analysis emphasised the all-pervasive influence of power over agents. Here agency is considered, akin to experience within the lay theatre, to be infinitely improvised and tactical, and though oppressions cannot be discounted, neither can they be considered wholly constitutive of the operations of society. To deliver society over to that fate theoretically is as inadequate as discounting the place of the imagination in the politics of being human.

Throughout the following the purpose of identifying a conceptual legacy to everyday life is underwritten by the expectation of transforming and improving that everyday life by, and for, as many as possible. There is no such thing as a critical approach to everyday life which can be separated from the expectation that criticism is undertaken from within that domain. In this sense the identification of everyday life as a position from which to speak is implicitly to question the other places from which people speak including the academy, it remains a common-sense referent with which to judge the validity of other social constructs, and finally, despite the conceptual use made of the everyday here, it remains the domain of cooking, eating, sleeping, sitting at home, walking the street, that is the remainder when the specialised activities associated with work and play have relinquished their hold on the imagination and the body. But where is one to find these casual, apparently inconsequential moments, and how is one to take note of them once they are discovered between the rationalities of the everyday? Looking and listening is only a beginning but a place to start nevertheless.

Observation

Mass Observation was initiated through a letter to the *New Statesman and Nation* published in early 1937. Charles Madge, the poet whose connections with Humphrey Jennings were considered in the last chapter, wrote of 'An anthropology at home', and speaking of what he described as the 'mass wish-situations' of the British people at the time of the abdication crisis of 1936 defined the possibilities of such a movement:

> The real observers in this case were the millions of people who were for once, irretrievably involved in the public events. Only mass observations can create mass science. The group for whom I write is engaged in establishing observation points on as widely extended a front as can at present be organised.[4]

From these beginnings Mass Observation became an independent scientific organisation. Its origins were in two focused areas of activity, in northern English 'working class' environments and the broader record of national phenomena such as dreams, clothing and daily life. Mass Observation became for some participants an habitual activity with a totalising aim – the complete record and understanding of modern society. Its roots lay in Surrealism and the documentary fiction of George Orwell, coupled with a faith in the contribution that science could make to the liberation of humanity as expounded by H.G. Wells. Mass Observation was not issue based but holistic in that it sought observation of the unobserved, resisting the pastoral attitude to the 'people' by being not only about them, but by them and for them. The inauguration of Mass Observation seems to have been predicated on three concerns: a distrust of the press and how events of the crisis years before the war were being reported to people, a perceived gulf between politics and those people, and a fascination with the part that myth and superstition were playing in the everyday accommodation of crises. This peculiarly English yet evocative phenomenon, was to attract the participation of never more than 3,000 'observers' with a hard core of between 300 and 700, among them being Humphrey Jennings. Their methods were unconventional, combining over-heard conversations, diary accounts, field work, questionnaires and reports supplied by professional observers. When referring to Mass Observation it is these texts which are at issue as well as the practices of a movement, for it was a practice conducted through listening, looking and writing, and one which now comprises a Mass Observation archive.[5]

It can hardly then have been called a comprehensive movement, and the word 'mass' brings with it as many problems as 'the people', though its strategies for information accumulation are more interesting than its minority status. The focus of observation included the events of a single pre-ordained day, the behaviour of people in pubs, intimate relations in seaside towns, customs in the workplace, popular dances and leisure activi-ties. The movement gave rise to a wealth of 'everyday' research whose limitless scope made it until recently literally unquantifiable, research that was to be commissioned by the Ministry of Information in the Second World War, and 'consumer research' organisations after. It was in many ways an unorthodox ur-sociology with a remarkable appetite for the trivial and mundane. But its nonconformist, non-commercial beginnings are worth re-emphasising in a book which seeks to reacquaint theatre analysis with the recognition of its processes of consumption. The archive it gave rise to is a complex, contradictory and juxtaposed project reaffirming the modernist potential of the exercise. The question here is how one can ascertain what 'people' do, how they make do, and what they make of operations like theatre without consigning these researches to rigid strategies that miss all that is coincidental and therefore most telling about them, that turn people into 'the People'.

The 'wish-situations' that observation would reveal were connected with just such coincidental features: 'Clues to these situations may turn up, in the popular phenomenon of the "coincidence". In fact it is probable that in the ultra-repressed condition of our society they can only materialise in this form . . . '.[6] The connections with Humphrey Jennings' perception and involvement in Surrealism are apparent, for at the same time as the inauguration of Mass Observation, Jennings was defending Surrealism against its appropriation, its 'use', by those such as Herbert Read who were rereading it in the service of an overarching Romanticism. As Jennings said:

'Coincidences' have the infinite freedom of appearing anywhere, any time, to anyone: in broad daylight to those whom we most despise in places we have most loathed: not even to us at all: probably least to petty seekers after mystery and poetry on deserted sea-shores and in misty junk-shops.[7]

One such coincidence that influenced the constitution of Mass Observation itself was the meeting point between the work of the ornithologist and anthropologist Tom Harrisson and the founders of the movement. The publication of his poem on cannibalism which appeared in the 2 January 1937 edition of the *New Statesman* coincided with the call to an 'Anthropology at Home' in the letters column of that week. But having met somewhat coincidentally, the movement's founders were by no means united in their attitudes to the relations between 'research' methodologies and findings. For Humphrey Jennings, if not the other founders of Mass Observation, documentary observation and social investigation were perceived as continuous with the realm of poetry and imagination. The artist and the scientist were no longer to be split by their domains of expertise, nor were they to be divided from the masses. Of the founders it was Jennings who resisted the Romantic and eccentric potential of the movement, seeking the aestheticisation of documentary and the politicisation of Surrealism. Mass Observation has been described as Surrealism in reverse: 'Surrealism wants to project the imagination onto the objective world in order to transform it; Mass Observation tries to recover the imagination that produced the vulgar objects and images of the everyday world.'[8] This is a telling inversion for the reacquaintance of theatre and everyday life for it reverses the defeatism of Surrealism, the emphasis of the worst of the everyday and credited the reality of everyday life with its multifarious and often celebratory pleasures.

Central to the work of Mass Observation was the detailed documentation of wartime leisure pursuits, pantomime, jazz and dancing, which provided the focus for many reports. Mass Observation's organisers directed its personnel to chosen topics, from rumours to wrestling. The latter was published in one of the few completed Mass Observation publications *Britain*, pre-empting by many years its later television exposure, and analysis by cultural interpreters such as Roland Barthes. Pantomimes were indicative of this holistic approach, the reports concerned to record the minutiae of the audience's responses, their coughs, laughs, talk and even the timing of laughter and clapping. Where the qualitative is about to give way to the quantitative in the reports the coincidental detail reimposes itself, as with this description of the hilarity caused by the appearance of household objects on stage: 'The mere appearance of a large iron . . . or a large bar of soap created six seconds' laughter.' Also documented at length and in extraordinary detail is the emergence, growth and international proliferation of a popular dance 'craze', the Lambeth Walk. This provides a comprehensive set of analyses of the relations between a theatre form and the social space in everyday life from which it derives. The texts that make up this record provide a vector of the move from the pedestrian practices of everyday life to a formal dance. Thus these writings provide a key both to the workings of Mass Observation and its archive and to the potential both present for tracing the emergence and disappearance of theatrical forms over a specific period of English history. It seems to have been understood at the time of their writing that this element of their work might have wider implications, the *Yorkshire Post* announcing: 'The Lambeth Walk may yet prove the master key to – to whatever the Mass Observationists hope to find out.'[9]

One way of looking at the phenomenon of the Lambeth Walk is this: first there was a song that began: 'Anytime you're Lambeth way/Any evening any day/ You'll find us all doin' the Lambeth Walk', and then a walk and then a dance. But the genealogy the observers trace is far more confused and contradictory, it is complex and refutes single stories of how theatre forms arise from neighbourhoods. The dance spread in popularity throughout Europe and reached New York to great acclaim in 1938. For the early interpreters of the information coming in about the dance it was used to explain the responses to oncoming war: 'We may learn something about the future of democracy if we take a closer look at the Lambeth Walk.'[10] From its 'origins' in the West End musical *Me and My Girl* which had been produced in 1937 with Lupino Lane, through the elaboration of the characteristic walk into a dance by Adele England, to the dance halls nationwide where the swagger, roll and 'Oi' of the walk were adopted, observers submitted detailed records of its mutations and idiosyncrasies. Charles Madge and Tom Harrisson in *Britain*, identify the transition of a dance from the local and particular origins of its south London culture in Lambeth, to the masses who have rarely ever 'been there' but know all about it. It is an inverted invitation to people to come and see for themselves – the perfect icon of an anthropology at home. The observers' reports emphasise the longer history of a dance which simply had a different name – the jig or even the twist. The interpreters of the reports, though, overlay this detail with their own anthropological interests, likening the Lambeth traditions of dancing with 'primitive dancing' and noting its proclivity for cross dressing and mimicry of animals; a dance where beer was important and where the gender of partners was immaterial. The everyday was still not immune from the interpretive zeal of disciplines which, judged alongside the observations themselves, appear the least effective aspect of the project.

Me and My Girl had placed a cockney 'out of his class' in the context of dukes and duchesses, and from this conceit derives the distinction drawn by Mass Observation between natural behaviour and affected mannerisms. The connection is made between William Empson's view of pastoral where the fool in contact with nature transcends misfortune. This understanding of the pastoral was an important one, as it described for Empson a genre of stories which are always 'about' the people but rarely 'by' or 'for' them. The relationship between 'natural' and 'common' for the observers is the locus for a gamut of value judgements about the dance. For some 'vulgar' meant good, for others bad. Mass Observation tracks the growth of the dance and its value systems via its progenitors, but also through the communications media promoting and playing it. For wireless listeners of the day there was the sense that it was something different. When they heard the dancers shouting 'Oi' at the end of the chorus it had become participatory radio of sorts. For one of the observed, and interviewed, what they particularly enjoyed was 'doing what you are singing'. Many of the reports point to the pleasure in the lack of conformity in the dance – that nobody does it quite the same and no place organises it in quite the same way. It was though, a dance specific to a place, combining the distilled and stereotyped gesture, speech and action of a cultural group and thereby providing a link between dancing and acting. Here one 'class' would appropriate the dance as their own, mimicking another class, an unusual inverted snobbery and downward mobility, a cultural code put into reverse. This was not court dances finding their way down but street dances finding their way up. It was not an apolitical movement either being used to break up a Fascist march in the East End and providing the base for a series of large-scale open air dances in the parks of London in the summer of 1938. From 3,000 to 20,000 people would group in the parks in inner and outer circles in an activity that was described by one observer as 'more like a cattle stampede than a dance'.

The interpretation placed on this genealogy points to the strengths and weaknesses of the Mass Observation approach. Here is one of their conclusions: 'It proves that if you give the masses something which connects with their own lives and streets, at the same time breaking down the conventions of shyness and stranger-feeling, they will take to it with far more spontaneous feeling than they have ever shown for the paradise-drug of the American dance tune.'[11] For all the simple sophistication of the analyses of the dance, the timing and location of the interpretation prior to war overrides other concerns. In the face of Fascist propaganda the purposes of Mass Observation are clear – the separation of facts from fantasy at all levels of society, the deconstruction of wish situations that imperil a nation in a time of crisis. As a mass observer said, the conditions needed for rumour to flourish were 'dread without knowledge'. The interpreters of the Mass Observation texts betray a pastorally democratic attitude which retains a historically specific idea of the people as prone to wish situations and superstition. Interpretation does not however elide the observers' texts themselves, which in sheer volume alone are always discernible beyond the analyses put upon them.

The strategies of Mass Observation and the archive which has arisen from its work speak of a palimpsest, like that of the cartographers of Jorge Luis Borges' story drawing up a map so detailed that it ends up exactly covering the territory surveyed.[12] Or as the organisers put it in their earliest publication, observers would be: 'meteorological stations from whose reports a weather map of popular feeling can be completed'. But this project was no simulation, nor abstraction of the social real. The

territory here precedes the map and survives it – the Lambeth Walk has since reappeared in the West End and on Broadway and never went away from the shows put on by older people in their own lay theatre. The real is surveyable to Mass Observation and, as it pulsates outwards from street counts to queue analyses, the everyday in all its complexity survives. It does so despite the abstraction that all writing entails and this, after all is said, is a movement of a myriad texts. But here 'being' and 'appearance' have broken down as a complex and contradictory exercise sets out to see everything. It is an attempt at a complete account but celebrates its modernity by flagrantly being a version of the reality, an archive of unstable materials – notes, interviews, observations, diaries, and photographs – which refuses to fictionalise the reality it sought. Although there were directives to observe very specific phenomena, chosen by the organisers, each report in the archive, in a different hand or typescript, is the work of a self-reflexive observer whose eye and ear brings back to this motley collection an individual's experience of being part of a mass, that silent majority that poststructuralism gave up on as a spongy referent and unsurveyable.

The archive is a reminder that the mass is made up of individuals but with directions and velocities that meet and agitate around causes and celebrations that derive their energies precisely from the masses: the reports on the opposition to Fascist marches speak of causes, and reports on the Lambeth Walk speak of celebration. They conjoin where reports detail the use of popular dance to drive out Oswald Mosley's supporters form the Bermondsey back streets. 'The Public' is taken apart and reconstituted in these papers at a moment where there were real reasons for a 'need to know' beyond the caricature of the Mass Observer with his or her 'furtive note book', 'licked pencil' and 'earnest preoccupied expression'.

Inadvertently the archive presents theatre with a resource and a challenge, a genealogy of performance forms between the years 1937 and 1950 that demands attention for what it says about that other 'revolution' in the theatre of 1956. For that revolution in Britain was one of contents, the domestic and the everyday struggling to be seen in theatre's places. But the places of performance that deny this watershed and stand as a veritable dam of the everyday in performance are the evidence of the Mass Observation Archive. Then there is the specific formation of audience responses and habits. Here really is a record of what 'audiences' do with theatre and it would make unerring reading for those who believe theatre begins and ends with the performer's art. But more importantly for my purposes is what the archive presents to a nonconformist, modernist project in Britain, like Humphrey Jennings' work with texts and images in *Pandaemonium,* a modernist antiquarianism providing the fragments of reality and putting them into collision within the archive. They remain beyond classification and in so doing reveal much more of the real they seek to capture in their diverse script. Theatre being a transient phenomenon is in special need of archives of this kind, built out of the museum's ruins, not rigidly classified and programmed but responsive to its diversity. The only way to ensure this is to accept everyday life as the site of the study, for it is from here and back to here that forms emerge, distinguish themselves from daily activity, are transformed through media into distinct shapes with a fragile longevity, before they subside into the pastiche of the street, the growl of the traffic.

Interpretation

If as Fernand Braudel says, everyday life consists of 'the little things one hardly notices in time and space',[13] it is to these coincidences, anecdotes and occasions that analysis might turn, to determine at least their relation to a history of 'events' that has told a different story for theatre. The provocation of Mass Observation is a concern for observing something which is not only recognised as 'everyday life' but is described with fidelity to that life and its hesitant and discordant voices. Interpreting and intervening in that life was not the premiss of an organisation whose purpose was a science of people. This marks Mass Observation from the Surrealists and Situationists who in different ways both sought everyday life and intervened to transform it.

It is not perhaps chance that the academy, while accommodating the myriad diversions of French structuralist discourse over the last three decades, almost completely ignored its concomitant developments, always more politically and contextually bound, namely the concern for everyday life which the contemporaries of Roland Barthes and Jacques Derrida were developing.[14] This influence is clearly evident in both, and yet was superseded when their work was adopted by education for other textually responsive strategies. Many of Barthes' essays and Derrida's continual return to everyday objects in his analysis were indicative of more than a flirtation with the everyday. Despite their cultural capital the academy remained profoundly suspicious of this aspect of their work. For this was not the emphasis which could be given priority for 'literary studies'. From the French perspective writers such as Henri Lefebvre have until recently been given truncated critical treatment by prominent critics.[15] It is also significant that it was two women from the American academy, Alice Kaplan and Kristin Ross, who have recuperated the question of everyday life, and its merits for reassessment against the trend towards structuralism which they characterise as the normative academic project. It is a symptomatic intervention, because if anything, as Lefebvre pointed out many years ago, everyday life sits most heavily on the shoulders of women.

To move beyond the role of observation to that of interpretation and intervention is to reflect the Marxist challenge to philosophers not only

115

to interpret but to change the world. The purpose of examining a position from which to consider everyday life, to advance theory in its name, is: 'to elevate lived experience to the status of a critical concept – not merely in order to describe lived experience, but in order to change it'.[16] The reference points of a conceptualisation of everyday life indicate a specific engagement with Marxism which draws upon the philosophical movements discussed in the last chapter. It is a Marxism challenged by the Surrealists to embrace the psychological realm of the everyday, a Marxism reinterpreted by the subjectivities of phenomenology and existentialism and it is a Marxism reformulated by the playful sloganeering and anarchy of the Situationist International. From this genealogy can be traced an equal and opposite development in the academy. While the critique of everyday life was being initiated by Lefebvre and others in post-war France, so structuralism and its successor semiotics were being accommodated and tuned for ultimate performance in the University system. It is this tradition which has inflected on European theatre studies attempting to theorise performance practices beyond literary analysis. The critique of consumer society that everyday life theory held at its centre was symptomatically marginalised for the 'textual' felicities of a socially disconnected critical strategy. As Kaplan and Ross point out, it was existentialism that remained the pervasive paradigm when 'conditions of life' needed to be thought, otherwise the word was thought as material as the world and criticism began to be confused with action on that world. Here talking became a substitute for acting, performative utterances replaced performance and negated the need for action on what had already been said. This inclination has escalated with the increasing isolation of the academy from the everyday. Languages are heightened to include all manner of sensitivities to distinction, at the same time as the subjects of that language become less and less able to enter the debate themselves, or to gain entry to the academy where the debate is taking place. Where this was not the case, and there are rare but prominent examples, there were telling reconsiderations of that politicised everyday world and its relations to criticism; I could recall here Edward Said's criticism and the exchanges between Marshall Berman and Perry Anderson as to what constitutes a revolutionary project, the cultural criticism of Raymond Williams and Meaghan Morris and the literary theory of Terry Eagleton. Before getting carried away with the optimism of academic resistance however, Pierre Bourdieu has shown the gap there is between the voice of 'Homo Academicus' and the subjects of their institutions.

The cultural conditions of 'literature' were emphasised at a moment when theatre studies were driving themselves more rapidly than ever from the demands of the locality. This contradiction is indicative of the delay there remains between the adoption by literary theory of that which is 'new' in border disciplines, and the theatre whose complexities, as understood by this study, demand different and distinct theoretical structures. Further, contemporary with the adoption of structuralist theory in North America and its filtering into departments of drama through textual criticism, the British academy was engaged in a characteristic phase of insularity, with the 'crisis' in English at Cambridge University being just one, well documented example, of a more generally conservative resistance to 'theory'.[17] In retrospect, such a resistance might have had an ironic and fortuitous effect protecting the theatre from the filtered literary theory which has inscribed the understanding of drama in the North American academy as primarily a literary critical activity and secondarily a fully theorised practice. In both countries there is, however, little room for complacency given the distance that has opened up between theatre pedagogy as derived from the academy, theatre pedagogy as perceived by the 'profession', and the conduct of that profession itself and its relation to the profane commonality of a lay theatre.

These educational concerns are a minor 'internal' reflection of a more important socially rooted phenomenon. That is the division between what is perceived as valid 'knowledge', what carries epistemological weight, and the common-sense tactics and ruses (Michel de Certeau), local knowledge (Clifford Geertz), or doxa (Ivan Illich), which this chapter is about, and which projects like Mass Observation validate. It is no coincidence that the extremities of the theory that I have been considering, the spiral of Jean Baudrillard's perceptions from Walter Benjamin's politics, are themselves rooted in an attempt to come to terms with this split. The best-known progenitors and practitioners of a theory of everyday life were the Situationists, who either included in their number, or were associated with, a generation of theorists whose work in postmodern theory begins precisely from a critique of everyday life. The best-known textual work of the Situationists, not to be considered its rationale or apotheosis, is Guy Debord's *Society of the Spectacle*. This work can clearly be connected with critical texts of Jean Baudrillard, concerned as it is with the reification of the commodity and the incursion of that commodity in the complex social and cultural relations of everyday life.[18] The coincident point for all these writings was the work of Henri Lefebvre, who in a series of books written in the 1940s and 1950s foregrounded the quotidian as a space of analysis. The Situationists were particularly drawn to the spatial praxis that Lefebvre's theory offered, at the time an unusual reformulation of Marx which has since been given prominence in the conception of postmodern geography by David Harvey and Edward Soja. In the Situationist's hands this rethinking of social terrain characteristically led to the perception of the city as a site for *dérive*, a drifting, aimless walking and mapping of the psychogeographical areas and ambience of the streets, the marking of their differential emotional intensities. This strategy was: 'the active study of mental states and spatial ambiances produced by the material organisation of the urban terrain.'[19]

The quotidian is clearly most evident in the city, it is in the urban landscape that what Lefebvre calls its 'organised nature' is most discernible. It is the world of habit, of routine and repetition rather than the recurrence of rural landscapes documented by the Annales School of everyday historiography, that has provided the context and impetus for the theatre from which this study began. I am not attempting to speak of everyday life in the 'world', but limited by the possible, simply speaking of the urban context of less than half of the world's population. For this is the urban shadow of what Fernand Braudel described some years ago when cities accounted for a more modest percentage as follows: 'this layer of stagnant history is enormous: all rural life, that is 80–90% of the world's population belongs to it for the most part'.[20] In the everyday life of a city the polarity of producer and consumer gives way to a web of interconnections that bring the relations of production about in the first place. These are rhizomatic and their relations can be traced, not by isolating their component parts, for instance in the simplest of street settings: the traffic lights, the street corner, the news-stand and the pedestrian glancing at the news, but in their formation, their coming to be, the conditions which brought that possibility and conjunction about. This quality the good street shares with the good image in theatre. All this of course might appear to announce a potentially unlimited area of enquiry, within the urban parameters already defined. But in the spirit of the first botanists and palaeontologists who, without preconceptions traced innumerable species and types, there is a question as to the stamina of a theatre enquiry which has stopped short at three or four generic examples of its contemporary practice. It is against this sense of theatre as an inert fact of nature that an understanding of everyday life most clearly militates.

How is such an understanding of the 'urban', or as Lefebvre would have it, 'city' landscape, conducive to an expanded language for the contemporary theatre? And how does it begin to resolve the split between everyday phenomena and questions of belief and knowledge? To answer this I will interrupt the lineage of the concept of everyday life to take up a position in the quotidian itself. And this position cannot be spoken of in quite the same voice, for it is concerned with a practice, and a way of mapping a city, in a way that does not return the essence of the city to its outer suburbs. As aestheticians have done since Hegel, we could return to the sensorium that we have inherited in the West, and ask whether the way we perceive art as separate and distinct from everyday life isn't wholly disconnected from the hierarchy of senses which separate us from the animals and aspects of our environment. If we are able to ascertain such a fundamental privileging of one realm of the senses over another, for instance the sight and hearing I considered in the previous chapter over the chemical senses of taste and smell, we might establish the grounds to reintroduce theatre to the everyday practices of walking and cooking from which it has been separated. To reacquaint daily life and extra-daily life in this way is not to say they are the same – the rigorous work of theatre anthropologists has shown in detail why this is not so – but rather to allow for the consideration of the liminal states between the two operations of theatre and everyday life as negotiable at every turn.

Olfaction

The closure of a biscuit factory in London in 1989 and, shortly after, a vinegar plant nearby, was a unique loss to the docklands area of the city. The loss was of a different order to that of employment, more difficult to gauge but with a long-term significance for the area. While both factories were synonymous with the manufacturing history of that area of London they were also important for other 'everyday' reasons which require formulation before they are forgotten. Navigation in the city was, and continues to be, jeopardised by these closures. The 'Botanist of the Asphalt', as Walter Benjamin described the *flâneur* on foot, has lost a critical sense of orientation. The nose is being downgraded. It was never esteemed in the hierarchy of senses but now at its lowest ebb for years the nasal apparatus would appear to be almost redundant. What has brought about this demise in the post-industrial period? The loss of an object for the subject. The disappearance of a dimension of the city, through which the reversal of a history is unmistakable. That history is a history of smells. Like everyday life itself it has a temporal dimension and a spatial one which might be described as a geography of odour. Its retreat has been going on for a century but really seriously for the last twenty years. This is not a trivial matter. The collapse of the olfactory is synonymous with the collapse of the old factory.

As manufacturing industry in the city has given way to the hi-tech, computerised pursuit of invisible earnings for the new city, so there has been an equivalent reduction in 'air pollution' – a positive way of looking at a loss. But there is a reciprocity to this equation that suggests a less than wholesome future for the city. An analysis of everyday life takes such seemingly marginal interests as central to an understanding of the space, the city, in which theatre occurs and how it occurs, deepening our sense of that space as specific place.

Deep cleansing assails us from all sides, as Roland Barthes, characteristically, has already felt it relevant to inform us. Here the individual body reflects and predicts the social body. Service industries we are told will provide employment for those to whom factory closure brings redundancy, they make it their aim to dry clean, launder and lavender the apparel and lives of those who come their way. The smell of a computer is unmistakable to those that use them but hardly the complex aromatic that testifies to the differential history of a city and the geographies from which its commerce has been built. The smell of work, often brutal and dehumanised, should not be mistaken for this lost Illyria, this perfumed garden. The point here is not to mourn the loss of particular smells, which in a very real way have polluted the lives of those who live within their circulation, but to register an inevitable loss which will bring with it the loss of an inducement to memory. A loss that will join other forgettings in a city of amnesia, where a theatre will simply become a memory chamber.

Why should this loss be anything but a cause for rejoicing among those within its immediate circumference? As the Situationists in Paris were so aware, the composition of the city and its well-being is a precarious balance that goes far deeper than prognostications about architecture, road-widening schemes and community developments. These are the symptoms of the city, not its causes, and it is beneath these levels, literally to the subterranean that one should go to determine the formations that provide the foundations of the urban conglomeration, the site for the everyday. In the lattice of pipework and ducts that weave beneath the city a Victorian legacy is at work, a circulation of sewage that was the Archimedean triumph of its time. The occasional and embarrassing collapse of this system, an increasing prospect for the future, returns us to the reality of ourselves as producers in more ways than one. It is shockingly abrupt when it happens, as though the medieval has escaped from its mannered immured form, its representation in *The Name of the Rose*, to steam forth a quaint reminder of our biological similarity to those who have walked this path before.

Good cities, ones which people have rated as places worth living in, have often coincidentally been places with characteristic odour. A good city one might go on to say cannot be worth recommendation if there is an absence of smell. Photographs of gondoliers rowing tourists in face masks may be momentarily disturbing, but for those who are able to visit Venice at the height of the summer, all is confirmed is that it is the smell of the Lagoon, a sea air a *buenos aires*, mingling with the feline, that is a reminder of 'place' beyond its cosmopolitan aspirations to international space – and that is surely a point that a theory of everyday life might ask us to reconsider. Do I want to be reminded of where I am, or would I like to think of my city like some sanitised and ultimately interchangeable location? A location, not unlike that of a film, that contrary to the everyday that stubbornly shows up in the background of even the tightest shots, conveniently pans away from the detritus in favour of the statuesque, the fragrant.

The International style did not come merely in the level of architecture, but in a wholesale sensual reorganisation that included the olfactory. How else is one to explain the familiarity of the air in the hotel lobby, the *déjà vu* (or should it be *déjà nu*?) that comes on entering certain shops to be assailed not by muzak but scent, and circulated scent at that? As with other walks, it is the entrepreneur who has occupied the field, to the detriment of those who might promote a responsible, socialised approach to the issue. These are cosmopolitan concerns, as Antonio Gramsci might have said, and not of that other everyday life, where the experience of the International is in a supermarket. They are nevertheless indicative of the way in which the capital is heading at the behest of enterprise. The olfactory is therefore important for a number of reasons. It has not become appropriated yet, nor achieved the hegemonic status of the visual in advertising, newspapers and television, the aural in radio. It is frankly difficult to deal with, notoriously hard to pin down, and of interest only to an analysis which begins from the everyday realm in which it plays such an important yet unthought part. It is a sophisticated reminder of time and place, but impossible to describe in its own terms. It is therefore removed from the economy of senses as we know them and reduced in some people's eyes to the level of the perfumerie, the marginal and therefore politically irrelevant domain.

The efforts of Renault's promotional campaign in the late 1980s to introduce the olfactory to their advertising is marked by its uneasy vocabulary. It is indicative that there is more at stake here than 'meets the eye'. A litany of the sensual delights of the Renault 5 Monaco, the car being promoted, is completed by the suggestion that the vehicle even smells rich. The claim must have struck a deep ambivalence in any potential customer. To be invited to 'sniff one out' at your local dealer only compounded the Surrealistically instinctive approach. Similarly fraught but more imaginative was the introduction of smell to the cinema in the form of 'scratch and sniff' cards, but like the short life of the Sensurround film, these became distractions fraught with miscalculation of the 'users' of the art form. On the contrary those whose work in theatre derives most deeply from the everyday are intuitively able to confront the everyday's most meaningful odours. The miasma that hung over the turf of Pina Bausch's *1980* encompassed dancers and audience in a canopy of nostalgia and unease, and from the epic to the domestic, the smells of Bobby Baker's *Kitchen Show* were a reminder that this was a workplace as well as, for the moment, a play space.

It is perhaps for this reason that the olfactory in this conceptual sense drawn from everyday life, provides us with a guide, a vector of response, a way of examining a change in our sensorium and the environment in which we live. It is notoriously difficult to remember quite what this or that site used to look like on the disappearance of an old and valued building. The success of books on London 'as it used to be', or the more recent transcendent trend for cities 'as seen from above', is testament to this human and in the latter case, divine, aspiration. But ask anyone to describe a place that was characterised by odour, and one is surprised at the depth of that memory, the emotion that it conveys and the very real sense of loss. As though this loss is of a wholly different order. And of course it is. That is the point of an analysis of the everyday. The anaesthetising of our participation in the world, in the life of the city, has followed a trajectory not unequivalent, nor unrelated, to the diminution of the active place of smell in our sensorium. The privatisation of smell through the development of an industry has been thwarted by the olfactory irony that the best place to smell perfume is at a distance from its owner, and by implication the worst is from a position not unadjacent to the owner's nose. The olfactory has again pre-empted its would-be manipulators, in ways not unlike the elusiveness of the everyday continually retreating from inspection.

Writing of the olfactory, as anything from the everyday, invites comparison with those who discreetly inform us in the press of some hitherto undiscovered idyll, only to mourn its loss to mass tourism in the following year. But the scale of the field, the feeling that one is entering a domain in which the precedents for discussion are few and distanced by intellectual bigotry, disabled by dogmatism, is an invigorating one for further analysis. How else is one to explain the critics' surprise at that 'first' olfactory novel, Perfume by Patrick Suskind.[21] The morbid nature of the content did little to prise commentators' superlatives away from the form. There have been, and will be written more subtle evocations of the olfactory than this gothic tourist guide to the genre. The initial book list might begin with Montaigne 'On Smells', Gogol's 'The Nose', and move on to the more specific academic works of the olfactory theorists, Daniel Sperber, Gaston Bachelard and the historian of the field, Alain Corbin. It is indicative that writers like Bachelard, whose understanding of scientific imagery was discussed in the last chapter, provide us with a wholly unprejudiced view of the domain, and in The Poetics of Space he turns the olfactory to decisive theoretical advantage. It is as much this inclination as its execution that is of interest to a study of the progenitors of the everyday, a coalition of theory and practice in the everyday realm.

The olfactory is a reminder of a world that has been lost, that is the everyday world that pertained before today's hygienic regimes. The way these regimes have shaped the theatre historically are considered in the final chapter, but here the conceptual importance of the olfactory has to be established. Alain Corbin is the obvious guide for such thought having written in The Foul and the Fragrant what amounts to a comprehensive survey of the olfactory, tracing the importance of odour for the social imagination. At the centre of this discussion is the contradiction that the human's inability to describe olfactory sensations is a profound limit. For if those very sensations are deemed important the inability to control them through language appears to tie the human to their natural environment. The development of a sense of smell, and its associations with animality would appear to indicate the 'lack' not the 'gain' of intelligence. This interpretation persists despite the evidence that the olfactory is in the forefront of protection against disease and danger; in the presence of decomposition and poison the olfactory is an intelligence of survival. It was in the late eighteenth century at the time of developments in chemistry that there were attempts to establish an inventory of smells, and perhaps in keeping with the need for urban control this was directed at the efficient functioning of the city. As Corbin points out, with entry to the nineteenth century: 'what has been and has in no way changed, has suddenly become unbearable'.[22] Both in France and Britain at this time there was a relation between the purification and standardisation of language and a decline in references to smell and excrement in all but the most twisted syntactical euphemisms. When Père Ubu stepped onto the French stage with the word 'merde!' there was more at stake than a theatrical revolution. Behind this word and its excision from everyday use, was the rise of the concept of the individual against the collective audience, the rise of intolerance and revulsion at the atmosphere of 'the people' that hygienist literature propagated. The conscious awareness of smell 'permits a new interpretation of the rise of narcissism, the retreat into private space, the destruction of primitive comfort, the intolerance of promiscuity'.[23] This, as I will show in the final chapters, is profoundly formative of the twentieth-century theatre.

The personal dimension of perfume and its genealogy is but a fragment of the potential of the public domain. It is significant that Freud chose to talk of the nature of the olfactory in *Civilisation and Its Discontents*. The decline of the olfactory for Freud was equated with the move to erect stature in the human and was an indicator of the growing status of the visual within the libidinal urge. This had been attested to in the aesthetic dimension by Hegel, who discounted taste and smell as dependent on desire and will, and therefore useless to the objective process of aesthetic contemplation. More recently Jacques Derrida has likened the text to 'effluvium', the product of decomposing substances floating as gas in the air, and he along with Gregory Ulmer, Bachelard and Sperber has used the oppression of the olfactory as a starting point for a way of discussing our sensorium, as though it provides a dream world, another site from which to think new thoughts.

But each of these writers has neglected the essentially geographical quality of what Immanuel Kant described as 'taste at a distance'. The olfactory raises questions not just of space and time through memory but as a mnemonic it is rooted in a sense of place. It gives direction to space, and in so doing subliminally provides us with orientation in a changing environment. This is not merely an urban concern, although everyday life analysis takes as its starting point the organised nature of the city, but one which signifies change across all forms of settlement. The baking of bread is international and yet its odour is specific to the local ingredients that are used in its making. Where it is homogenised, as in the production plants that supply the cities of North America, the intervention of capital in the form of additives is as heavy on the air as the smell of the earth from a Moscow rye loaf. But ideological preconceptions are disrupted by the olfactory which sniffs out the survival of a back-room oven in Ohio, a conglomerate in Kiev.

It is these contradictions that make the olfactory a responsive litmus to change, where sight weakened by the visual stimulus through television and advertising gives way on occasion to a less formally educated and therefore perhaps more responsive guide. It is a guide which alerts us to the irrevocable desensitising at the heart of the post-industrial period. These less obvious realms are the object of an analysis of the everyday which seeks to locate, foreground and illuminate the presumptions which constitute the unwritten phenomena of the quotidian and the alienations which arise from their suppression. For what reaches us through the nose is a knowledge, not drawn from the encyclopaedic tradition but a doxa, a wisdom, that belies the splitting of the mental and the material. It conflates such divisions in ways that are only now beginning to be examined and understood. The interest of the olfactory is what it tells us about other times and places, formations previously referred to as production and consumption, and in its subtlety exposes the myth of the passive consumer of the everyday. For what could be a more distinct individual yet profoundly social interface with the world than that conducted through the chemical senses?

It is in articulating this world, the shadow of the predominant sensorium of the arts, that a deep and socially meaningful discourse can be built, one which pre-empts the advertisers in their bid to occupy the olfactive terrain and 'Docklands' developers from sealing its public properties into privatised ones with names like 'Cinammon Wharf'. A walk around Shad Thames, in the same area of London as the lay theatre occurred, still provides subtle yet slowly deteriorating evidence of the persistence of a moment in the history of a city, a moment which refuses to be forgotten, and speaks of a time when the exotic really did co-exist within the domestic. It is time for the olfactory to be brought out of the kitchen and the closet. Aroma and odour are not the sole domain of cooks and hygienists, they are not a privatised pursuit, but as public and political a part of our lives as one could imagine. It is for this reason that they have been worth talking about seriously. The comedy of smell has been running for a long time in schoolboy jokes and West End farce, in reciprocal measure to the tragic history of its unrecorded loss.

An analysis of the olfactory like this suffers from the transition between the identification of the everyday and the 'reality' of its conscious practice. It is always compromised and limited but nevertheless generative of other theatre possibilities, a theatre event described earlier which occurred in the first factory spoken of where a process of 'reminiscence' with older people concerned with the loss of their neighbourhood provided a context for the work, and a language of performance which derived from the everyday experience of this workplace and its smells. Indeed it was through discussion with the older people in the locale of the theatre and the factory that the writing arose, a practice of taking soundings from the everyday and the transformation of those discussions to a position in theatre, beyond reminiscence. There is no empty space for theatre here, but places of performance enveloped in the aromatic of their own history.

Intervention

In this work and writing the aim was, as with the Situationists, to move from a Marxist analysis which focused its attentions on the relations of production *in* the factory, to their social reproduction, that is the conditions which make the olfactory possible in the first place, and the way people navigate around and through these parameters. Here is proposed an alternative to 'agit prop' reaching more for the conditions of analysis appropriate to a theatre of 'dynamic ambiguities' that David Edgar has defined in his theoretical essays. However in contrast to Edgar in his book *The Second Time as Farce*,[24] my hope for critical alternatives would not in any sense be placed in the community play movement, nor in the festivals of the oppressed which he describes. These quite different cultural forms undoubtedly present a certain conundrum for the mainstream British theatre. But both are open to instant accommodation and marginalisation as the fringe remainder to all that is serious, real and important about theatre now. Each is worth defending but without a coherent critical context which can consider both in the same social space as the mainstream, where cultural capital circulates most aggressively, both will remain minor irritations to official views of reality. Rather in the antithesis of the festival, a critical return to the everyday 'real' is overdue. Cinema took its lead from this world, and theatre this century has taken it as its subject matter but neither has critically addressed the everyday as its context. As Henri Lefebvre says: 'transforming the everyday requires certain conditions. A break with the everyday by means of a festival – violent or peaceful – cannot endure. In order to change life, society, space, architecture, even the city must change.'[25] That this arena, the social reproduction of everyday life, also and centrally happens to be a focus for feminist debate retrieving unwritten histories, is a reminder that the analyses of historical materialism can act within the same space as the feminist agenda, and most importantly both are inscribed within the spatial patterns that everyday life analysis exposes. On the local level questions of ethnicity, and at the international level the concerns of what is described ambitiously as the post-colonial debate are also contingent upon understandings drawn from people's everyday lives. There is here no question of recovering an order where separation is desired, indeed theatre and politics often work precisely off such division, but neither can that separation remain unthought, concealing as it does on the most banal level the *actual* differences between academic writing 'on' theatre, and that theatre, and a further gulf between that theatre and everyday life. When these divisions have been addressed then there might be space for the separations of a 'reading room' where one pursues the theory of theatre undisturbed by the clamour outside the door.

If there is some hope that the previously separate issues noted above can be understood to have specific association with a theory of everyday life, there is the possibility of not being bound by the rigid divisions and closed shops of professional practice, but rather to reformulate their collective concerns and interests in relation to the everyday. This would not be possible through the subject/object oppositions prevalent in the academic discourse of structuralism, but rather could be acted on in the tract between 'the subjective, phenomenological, sensory apparatus of the individual and reified institutions'.[26] It was these concerns which were central to distinguishing the poetic and political relations between the olfactory and the old factory. It is here that the action of sculpting forms, telling stories and acting scenes is an everyday miniature event with much larger social implications. Criticism of the trivial is not trivial criticism.

Henri Lefebvre, from whom the critique of the everyday derives, characterised the modern period as one of increasing uniformity at the expense of the diversity of daily life. There is more than a hint of nostalgic romanticism in this perception. But it is worth connecting Lefebvre's view of the crisis of heterogeneity with that of Paul Feyerabend, who shares a resistance to homogeneous relocation. This relocation happens for Lefebvre under the sign of 'rationality': 'Rationality dominates, accompanied but not diversified by irrationality; signs, rational in their way, are attached to things in order to convey the prestige of their possessors and their place in the hierarchy.'[27] For Lefebvre the 'forms, functions and structures' of life were once part of an 'undifferentiated whole', prior to a split between specialised knowledge and the common sense of the everyday. But now the 'functional' element of the trio has been separated off, rationalised, and industrially produced, before being reimposed on subjects through advertising and marketing. Here, as in Feyerabend's analysis of the procedures of science, a 'totalising system' is identified as maintaining an illusion of diversity in opposition to, and extinction of, that which was truly diverse in a previous era. Lefebvre summarises this process, which has a lineage to the Frankfurt School and

126

Hegel's conception of reification: 'The everyday can ... be defined as a set of functions which connect and join together systems that might appear to be distinct.'[28]

Thinking the everyday in this way, considering it as a concept, is to do no more than I have claimed for concepts elsewhere. Everyday life analysis on the one hand designates a 'reality', which becomes available for thought while also, and importantly, it remains 'a sole surviving common sense referent and point of reference'.[29] So it seeks a common denominator, but it resists the trite by considering the very terms which escape the everyday. Lefebvre asks: 'Are not the surreal, the extraordinary, the surprising, even the magical also part of the real? Why wouldn't the concept of everydayness reveal the ordinary in the extraordinary?'[30] The concept of the everyday therefore accommodates a dialectic, between what we have chosen previously to call the 'exotic in the domestic', or in another place 'the country in the city'. It also illuminates temporal patterns and their connection with subjectivity: the long-term repetitive cycles of nature, mortal life, and the shorter-term cycles of work and consumption. Everyday life is bound not only by the cyclical return of natural phenomena, the seasons, elements and climate (it is these to which I return later) but more mundanely by the linear rhythms of life's trajectories through birth, marriage and death, and even more mundanely travel to school, commuting to work and retirement. Any analysis which privileges one cycle over the other is destined to miss the subject of those patterns, and the imaginative passivity that such life journeys conceal.

These thoughts shed light on the characterisation of the period as post-industrial and postmodern. For where the former implies a temporal movement through the industrial age to an 'electronic' future, and the latter seeks to make sense of that proliferation and speeding of knowledge becoming information, so the everyday which after all both strive to describe, provides the social space of this occurrence:

> The everyday is covered by a surface: that of modernity. News stories and the turbulent affectations of art, fashion and event, veil without ever eradicating the everyday blahs. Images, the cinema and television divert the everyday by at times offering up to its own spectacle, or sometimes the spectacle of the distinctly non-everyday; violence, death, catastrophe, the lives of kings and stars – those who we are led to believe defy everydayness. Modernity and everydayness constitute a deep structure that a critical analysis can work to uncover.[31]

These 'blahs' are the narratives which in the absence of metanarratives will have to provide the discourse of a localised and politicised expression. These 'may' be the discursive practices described earlier that give rise to a practice between 'modes of discourse' and political activity, or the

'Molotov'. It is anyway as likely to be this minority language as a 'special-ised' and separated language, a mandarin tongue, that will be relevant to a politics of theatre. The resonance of the everyday is that it reaffirms in many coherent ways that this scenario is clearly further away than the postmodern predictions might suggest. Keeping the everyday in mind reminds us of the reservations held by Meaghan Morris about the seem-ingly politically hopeful prognosis of a crisis in master-narratives, the emancipatory potential of difference, ethnicity, and gender:

> the crisis in credibility of meta-narratives can, in context, simply
> mean the disintegration of motivating arguments for intervening in
> anything at all, and that there are no longer any means of deciding
> in what, when, and how to intervene except by random passion.[32]

The danger of 'voluntarism' inherent in the postmodern condition makes especially welcome the unique quality of Michel de Certeau's theoretical work for an understanding of cultural practice and everyday life. In this work there is an analysis which resists the conflictual form of postmodern argument, a Jürgen Habermas 'lecturing' and a Jean-François Lyotard 'reporting', but involves that conflictual stance within its own theoretical forms. It is a form of writing and action, a tactic, which de Certeau describes somewhat obscurely as 'polomelogical'. Here the surface lucidity of Lyotard's writing in *The Postmodern Condition* gives way to a project of 'Heterologies', a questioning of the problematic relations of theory and practice in the speculative thought that arises from the dialectical tradition of Hegelian philosophy.[33] This is not to say de Certeau's work is 'un', or 'anti' theoretical, trained in theology, history, psychoanalysis, and anthro-pology, that would be unlikely. But rather his writing, particularly strongly in *The Practice of Everyday Life*, returns to the ground which Lefebvre established as worthy of observation and interpretation. Like Lefebvre the theory which de Certeau derives from this realm is shaped by the difficulties of its focus. Or put another way, the context it seeks to be responsive to is by its nature always beyond it. Not here in the sense of Foucault's analyses of power, but more in the playful aspect of 'hide' and 'seek'.

THE PRACTICE OF EVERYDAY LIFE

The imaginative space opened by Henri Lefebvre's critique of everyday life is uniquely developed by the French polymath Michel de Certeau. In a series of works, most obviously *The Practice of Everyday Life*, de Certeau engages with a complex of themes and an eclecticism of sources which seem responsive to the tract between theatre and the everyday referred to at the opening of this chapter. That this work is still, some years after its publication, not widely read, nor at the time of writing was it as influential as other cultural theorists, is perhaps another instance of the academy's proclivity for interpretive strategies which value writers over readers and urban planners over pedestrians. But heterodoxy swiftly turns to orthodoxy and before this work is appropriated against the ordinary man to whom it is dedicated it is worth emphasising the special place given to the 'ordinary' and everyday within it.

Michel de Certeau has been described as working within a philosophical 'countertradition', broadly speaking in questioning the 'identity of thought and being'.[34] As in other discourse theorists the organisation of knowledge is at the centre of his enquiry, but with a divergence in de Certeau's case from the ontological and epistemological emphases of his contemporaries. In *Heterologies* and *The Practice of Everyday Life*, his two generally available translated works, de Certeau is more concerned with elucidating a 'discursive order'. He is able to show in this work, in a survey of apparently 'everyday' features of life, the ways in which the opposition of theory and practice circumscribes disciplines and, further, the manner in which seemingly disparate disciplines function according to paradigms borrowed from their neighbours. Interdisciplinary enquiry in postmodernism has ironically tended to illuminate the distinctions, rather than the connections between strategies for learning and knowledge and it is this that de Certeau rethinks. In the face of the postmodern perspective, in the aftermath of the totalising claims of semiotics, there is no need to promote another embracing apparatus to consolidate the 'inter' in interdisciplinary, but rather to accentuate the already existent and catholic borrowing that occurs between disciplines previously thought in need of marriage, or at least correspondence. Alternatively postmodernism can be perceived as having, in a somewhat illusory fashion, created the impression that a heterogeneous discourse will somehow service those marginal groups, these 'others' for whom 'difference' is not just another critical strategy. This illusion reinforces the distance between critical texts and their intended subjects and de Certeau is at least aware of its implications if not finally able to avoid its consequences.

The recent fact that a domain called 'literary criticism' rather than 'philosophy' or 'theology' has become one of prominence beyond the academy for intellectuals has of course historical roots. Now it would seem the word is as material as the world, a belief that has led to a faith that literature might tell us more of the world than the compromised sciences. Félix Guattari takes this view when he says:

> the best cartographies of the psyche or, if you will, the best psycho-analyses are surely to be found in the work of Goethe, Proust, Joyce, Artaud and Beckett, rather than Freud, Jung and Lacan. And the literary dimensions of these latters' works are surely what remains best in them . . .[35]

But as Terry Eagleton, Edward Said and others have been concerned to point out, the literary is of course bound by institutional 'norms' and 'prohibitions' and it is this alternative emphasis which de Certeau seeks to identify. That is, the way that literature operates as another 'discourse', as actual social interaction, a practice governed by relations. It is in this emphasis on a discourse quite distinct in its logics and emphases from that foregrounded by Foucault, a focus by de Certeau on the 'user', within power relations rather than the mechanisms of power itself, which attracts attention to de Certeau's work from the perspective of theatre beyond literature. The countertradition which de Certeau represents is emphatically summarised by Wlad Godzich:

> De Certeau's conception of discourse, so different from Foucault's hegemonic one, recovers an agential dimension for us in as much as it recognises that discursive activity is a form of social activity, an activity in which we attempt to apply the roles of the discourses that we assume. These may not be heroic roles, but they place us much more squarely in front of our responsibility as historical actors.[36]

The strength of de Certeau's work, for a practice of theatre that does not deny but involves many of the textual resonances from theatre's border disciplines, is that it contributes equally to the theatre from which it borrows its paradigms. Analogies, such as that used by Godzich at the end of the quotation above, 'connect what they compare in both directions', and as Clifford Geertz says: 'Having trifled with theater's idiom, some social scientists find themselves drawn into the rather tangled coils of its aesthetic.'[37] With this in mind Michel de Certeau does at least provide a strategy, or he might prefer 'tactics', which seems uncommonly sensitive to the issues of practice, the 'saying' rather than the 'said' of what a theatre language might be. This language, if the concerns of this book have any justification, would have to reconsider first the importance of speaking about the relation of theory to practice and the role that speculative thought has played in their separation, second the possibility of an 'ethics' of theatre that is secular and avoids the religious implications that would make it unacceptable to a materialist enquiry and third, following from these concerns, a politics of theatre that is able to value the cognitive realm of the other, and the oppositional and conflictual narratives, the criticisms, which arise from such a theatre. These are three questions for theatre and everyday life now which follow from the demands of a poetics, ethics and politics considered earlier, and they are ones which current languages of theatre either have little interest in or have some difficulty in defining.

Starting with the last of the three, the political realm, history has been superseded in the intellectual milieu by questions of subjectivity and the psychoanalytic. But outside that patch, as Paul Feyerabend is wont to remind us, lies a considerable, and, for the academy, surprisingly vast domain, and in that landscape regional identification and liberation politics have been continuing apace on the broadest possible fronts. Often these historical movements have simply been ignored by the procedures of knowledge associated with structuralism and its successors. It is in this political framework that the theatre now reflects the world-wide complex of politics in space, and their relation to the particularisms of place. It is these spatial reorderings that have undermined the universal moorings of a Marxist position, a curious feint being played recently being the equation between the decentring, debureaucratising Conservatism, while the commerce it perpetuates and invigorates relocates its subjects in more subtly multinational, deterritorialised ways. So in politics the relationship between practice and theory is again not a simple split, but the specific elision of everyday lives by disciplines which claim to describe them. In this way politics remain unwritten.

I have already characterised the use of 'ethics' in this study as a disposition to the other. I then sought at least a reconsideration of its claims to be the first philosophy of theatre. In the political scenario outlined above the 'other' has evidently been a 'threat to be reduced, as a potential same-to-be, a yet-not-same.'[38] In the intellectual field where the cultural capital of teaching and publishing is still antagonistic to the threat of the 'everyday', the political acquiescence to the existence of the 'other' as differently qualified and independently thoughtful has been almost wholly denied. The abrogation of responsibility to others was 'always evident in the lay theatre – the admittance of those involved to the 'profession' being fraught at all times. De Certeau, not unlike Paul Feyerabend, emphasises local resistances to the pervasive rationalities of power. Discourses and practices pose in each particular case: 'individual or small group efforts against this machinery, as a mode of interaction that constitutes the lived experience of these people.'[39] De Certeau insists that such emphases do not promote another individualism, the opening of his work *The Practice of Everyday Life* spells this out, but help to foreground social relations as determining of the transactions and operational paradigms of everyday life. The 'theoretical questions and methods, categories and perspectives' that de Certeau seeks from an investigation of 'users' in everyday life is characterised as 'an operational logic whose models may go as far back as the age old ruses of fishes and insects that disguise or transform themselves in order to survive'.[40] It is this curious poetic of making up and making do which is of interest to a study concerned with a lay theatre. For an emphasis on 'users', and their models of action, prepares the conditions which would be necessary to conceive of the audience beyond that of 'consumer', passive and docile and with more subtlety than a politically oriented participatory theatre has previously allowed. For this 'joining in' obviously occurs every time an image is realised and the participation of the audience in the act of theatre is surely a premature festival. Participation in all likelihood conceals as much as reveals the subtle divergence of opinion between audience and performer. The question of the 'other' becoming 'same' in the transaction of theatre suggests an inadequately subtle model of what actually occurs in a differentiated audience. For though as I have said, exemplary lives lead to imitation, each imitation is characteristic of the individual who imitates. Despite the development of 'reader response' theory there is a widespread lack of interest in criticism in the constituencies of 'readers', as opposed to 'writers'.[41] A more varied understanding of these constituencies is required, perhaps along the lines of Mass Observation's ingenuity, to enable 'ruses' of the audience to be identified and valued.[42] This is an ethical and poetic question for the theatre. This is not an argument that prostrates at the altar of the audience the sacrifice of the performer. Edward Said's warning in 'Religious criticism' is well taken, the dangers of the 'theologizing of the Other', and the resultant impoverishment of a critical discourse pertaining to 'the secular, historical world' is always present.[43] But while this is concerned with the 'other' it would appear from here it has less to do with religion than it does with politics.

The theatre practice which gave rise to this book addressed this 'other' in practice, in the everyday life which neither could remove themselves from. The community arts movement in Britain has always taken this question of the 'other' as its *raison d'être*, whether reinforcing the role of the community, or the artist/animator's work within that community. Here the 'other' is often called 'the people' for reasons discussed earlier. The economy of the operation changes and is particular to each artist and audience. From the perspective of this study it would appear that the one way to conceal the logic of these operations would be to pretend that there are no producers and consumers, no makers and users, but a formless society of 'readers'. These readers are turned, for the purposes of aesthetic emancipation confused as political emancipation, into writers. This is the 'utopian' scenario outlined by George Steiner in his essay *Real Presences*, and one which might have ironic affiliation from its 'high art' intellectual ground with the 'enabling' aspect of a socially orientated community arts. But from the view of a theatre in a neighbourhood, this society of 'citizens of the immediate', this 'politics of the primary', looks more like a religiously inspired dystopia. It is the unwarranted dismantling of the reading room rather than its reinvention, where the fertile cacophony of secondary interpretation and commentary gives way to the idyllic yet uncritical communication of art work with art work.[44] The emphasis on the other which an ethics of performance entails, the residence of truth elsewhere, is therefore not to be taken as an argument for the response-ability of the artist, nor the excision of the artist. But rather an emphasis on the theatre's need to know, to begin to see the faces of its community of users.

In the last chapter I spoke of an aesthetics, an ethics and a politics of theatre and here the same terms reappear within the everyday. Michel de Certeau wishes to work out a science of relations between 'everyday pursuits' and 'particular circumstances'. In the local network of labour and recreation he will identify 'relational tactics (a struggle for life), artistic creations (an aesthetic) and autonomous initiatives (an ethic)'.[45] Everyday life is perceived as inventing itself 'by *poaching* in countless ways on the property of others',[46] and is thus concerned with the organisational 'logic' of this seemingly unproblematic and tedious domain. A study of everyday life, in the wake of Henri Lefebvre's work, is concerned with the socially abstracted individual not as an existentially fragmented being, but in a complex of social relations, the most particular of which is the 'making do' of consumption. 'To read everyday life, what Hegel called "the prose of the world" is therefore to become engaged in an act of *poiesis*.'[47] This is the *poiesis* that is eclipsed by the technology of production which has for so long been so much more accessible to scrutiny. As I have said before it is a question of how and where you look, and for de Certeau the place for scrutiny is the use that is made of representations: 'Only then can we gauge the difference or similarity between the production of the image and the secondary production hidden in the process of its utilization'.[48] This is the tract for critical investigations, a poetics of the image in theatre which does not wish to exclude the political context of its creation nor the ethical dimension of its relations with an 'other' in the audience. This enquiry is a 'scientific' one in as much as it looks for a 'logics' of operation in the art or way of making. Central to the practice of everyday life are discursive practices, stories and ruses that keep us on the material side of 'religion' without wholly excluding the metaphysical aspects of our everyday conduct.

Disciplines extract their documents of study from their historical context. Theatre 'uproots' the everyday, long the domain and subject matter of fiction, to a place where it can be better lit. As de Certeau tells us, only what can be transported can be treated, and what cannot be dug up in this way remains outside the language of knowledge, the interest of study, and hence bounded by the marginalisation of the 'trivia' and 'banality' of speech acts. These are central questions for the practice of everyday life which after all defines such division. This is a science quite distinct from a sociological analysis which 'cuts out', and through means such as statistical analysis, partitions that which is organisable in heterogeneous and everyday activities, returning it to the homogeneous foundation of an isolated and 'objective' discipline.[49]

Theatre is not immune from this tendency to 'cut out' its audience and transform its heterogeneity through architecture and other means. I will explore this proclivity in the next chapter. And yet, like the everyday life from which its audiences arrive, it has surprisingly little control over its audiences' imaginings, its making do. It would be an overestimation of theatre's power to believe it inscribes its participants and removes them from the everyday even if that were its ambition. Moments of theatre achieve this, but then so do moments of eating, everyday hobbies and tasks so it would be unwise to make claims for the value of theatre on these grounds. Theatre has often been thought of in a 'strategic' way separating it off from its natural environment in the everyday to a place that is 'proper' to it, and from this place it has been thought of as generating a set of relations which are in turn 'proper' to a convention called theatre. These if they are anything are the illusory, entertaining, mimetic qualities that Antonin Artaud wished to destroy. Here theatre is removed from the everyday and insists on its distinction in a set of codes and signs that has become the rationality of theatre and its pedagogy. That this theatre is unable to see outside its 'proper' place, is not to deny its specific powers and professionalism where it has found itself, but by definition that 'proper' place, according to de Certeau's analysis, can do no more than minister to the other from which it has been divorced. Again this is not an argument for totalised production and participation, the extreme of *Real Presences*, which is often proposed as the corollary to this argument. But rather a more detailed and specific analysis of the ways in which the theatre, almost always a *tactical* operation at its beginnings, becomes institutionalised, strategic and separated from the everyday. This has to be undertaken historically and I contribute to that work later. Here the power of the subject is not perceived as finally or 'fatally' removed from the everyday but in a state of temporary emergence which tactics of everyday analysis work upon.[50] Detailed studies of the formations of specific practices, such as Mass Observation's record of the Lambeth Walk, would trace a repetitive movement from the everyday to the fragmented domain of commerce. It is in the latter that a profitable writing begins to occur and it is therefore the latter which survives. But these are the strategies of performance that have overlaid and obscured the tactics which gave rise to them.

Michel de Certeau's idea of 'tactics' insinuates them in the space of the 'other', without a proper 'place' – they are 'ways of operating', in and on the everyday. The intelligences of living are evident in cooking, shopping, mending and reading. The 'knowledge' of strategies is different, it is concealed and separated from the everyday it is licensed to work upon. Without this separation there would be nothing in the way of expertise or specialism to 'buy'. This economy might account for the persistence of strategies over tactics, contrary to the arguments of people like Ivan Illich and Michel de Certeau, who announce, analyse and demonstrate the way knowledge operates and restricts. Where Illich connects these analyses with political parameters, de Certeau, usefully for our purposes, reconnects them with the practices of language. Tactics work spatially, in the context of 'reading' like a renter occupying an apartment and then moving on. Here texts are less interpreted, than made 'comfortable' and 'hospitable' in the terms of the renter who uses them, rather than on the terms of an external, strategic and institutionally validated operation. These diverse operations are not seen as isolated, to perpetuate the metaphor, like tenement blocks of flats, but contribute to the political dimension of the subject whose ecological activity reflects the ambition on a collective level to secure relations with the environment.[51] It is that 'position' from which I speak, an 'improper' intervention in a discourse situated between 'community arts' and the 'mainstream' both of which strategically validate their own claims to severely truncated resources at the expense of each other.

But what is a tactic? Tactics 'foil here and now' social hierarchisation and dismantle its powers over culture. Like Paul Feyerabend who addresses the 'here and now' with a dose of 'anarchist epistemology' in *Against Method*, so de Certeau looks for the point of purchase not in long-lost traditions, mythic constructs, or the rural alternative, but in the contemporary economy and provides us with the amusing if problematic example of '*la perruque*' in the contemporary French factory system. *La perruque*, 'the wig' of concealment, or 'parroting' is an anecdotal example typical of de Certeau which stands out for its poetic possibilities as much as for its political 'validity'. The factory worker using the time and waste materials of the company turns these elements to his or her own advantage, transforms the materials into something to 'take home'. It is a reminder that within oppression, from the 'extruder' to the executive suite, the worker conducts his or her 'own' work disguised as the work of the employer.[52] *La perruque* might, in London, be described as 'bunce' but that would only describe the part of the activity which is 'getting one over' the employer and getting one out of the work place. De Certeau is more interested in these tactics as a transformative project in their own right: 'the worker . . . diverts time (not goods since he uses only scraps) from the factory for work that is free, creative and precisely not directed toward profit'.[53] Here the praxis of the city becomes the *poiesis* of urbanism. This is just one example for de Certeau of a whole range of introductions of the improper into the proper, a time and a place from elsewhere being introduced into the industrial space. This analysis has significance for the way it guards against isolation of the separate domains of work and 'leisure' and encourages the perception of leisure and pleasure within work. From the perspective of the theatre operation this would appear to be a more enabling mode of analysis, and one on which theatre practice can be built. For the process of *la perruque* is itself a theatre in emergence, a small art of making do which can manifest itself more widely than the axis between work and home on which it initially operates. It is that will to subversion that often finishes up in the neighbourhood theatre 'set', constructed on company time with company tools, or in the lay theatre the carnival float mysteriously appearing around a corner on a brewer's dray, the alien arriving at a neighbourhood event on a river-police launch, or the occupation and transformation of a factory.[54] None of these activities could be tolerated by the highest authorities, but everyday life and theatre are more often, and usefully, in connection with those in the neighbourhood who are in their own way 'getting one over' the boss. If this operation sounds hopelessly marginal, living in the cracks as Howard Brenton once said, like the ruses of fishes and plants that de Certeau speaks of, there is to be admitted its guerrilla side. But that would not deny its place as the vast and threatening remainder to a mainstream theatre which nervously speaks in the name of what theatre can legitimately do.

Tactical operations of everyday life resist reactionary academicism, and allow theatre to remain 'true' to anecdotal or occasional experiences of practice without forgetting the theoretical formations that are necessary for it to move on. Thus the question is not 'this' or 'that' *perruque*, the brief examples will suffice, but the 'modalities of action' and the 'formalities of practices' which constitute these broader social manifestations of opposition and creation. There are countless models of theatre work of this kind beyond the parochial examples of the lay theatre: Armand Gatti's theatre in factories, Olivier Perrier's theatre with farm animals and Bobby Baker's domestic routines are three examples, but the credibility of each of these exemplary projects is theoretically undermined in the absence of an understanding of their contribution to a formality of practices, the relations between theatre and everyday life. They ironically remain outsiders to a theatre culture. In fact they are the few insiders working the most significant but elusive boundary for the theatre artist. Theatre can move through and beyond Jean Baudrillard's model of the enigma of the communications media, and the optimism of Umberto Eco's conception of a media guerrilla warfare, by tracing these 'modalities', or as de Certeau more specifically describes them, 'trajectories'. In the lay theatre these trajectories included a young man, working as a postman by day, writing for his neighbours to perform at night, an older woman cooking for functions providing food for audiences, another woman waiting at tables by day keeping the theatre accounts, her husband, a craftsman, building the theatre offices, a film set builder constructing the theatre sets, and the building itself in its last days decked with a sign borrowed from the South Bank arts complex turned inside out. Ironically, given the elevation of the 'people' and the pleasure in incongruity and candour both projects shared, on one side reading 'Rotherhithe Theatre Workshop 1978–1991', on the other 'In Our Time: The World as seen by Magnum Photographers'. It is not possible to transform these trajectories, their temporal articulation of places into a spatial sequence of points, as a mapping would do. This would substitute marks for operations. But in the absence of this writing it is necessary to value the tactical nature of those operations of the supposedly 'weak'. These tactics define a practical and intellectual activity that is 'as persistent as it is subtle, tireless, ready for every opportunity, scattered over the terrain of the dominant order and foreign to the rules laid down and imposed by a rationality founded on established rights and property'.[55] This is an activity of 'poaching', until it is recognised and formalised, by which time it has probably lost its usefulness for a lay theatre. The conjunction of an absence of power and place leads to a reorientation of their uses of time, and here 'play' is ironically often found in that time that is least obviously left for it.[56]

The language of everyday life analysis that de Certeau employs did not spring forth fully formed. It is derived from the analysis of 'discourse' and 'habitus' in Michel Foucault and Pierre Bourdieu. Contrary to Foucault's 'panopticism', the 'all seeing' pervasiveness of power and authority, de Certeau identifies a 'polytheism of scattered practices', as though working in the blind spot at the base of the panopticon. De Certeau points out that the very existence of panopticism relies on the 'place' of the panopticon, whereas the everyday is characterised as much by its placeless tactics, its using and consuming, as its strategic sites. Theatre here occurs not only in the shadow of everyday life but within a circumference drawn by the disciplines which tower over it. Once caught in their sight a multiplicity of tactics are turned into the 'proper' discourse that can no longer acknowledge incidental glories.

These practices of the everyday emerged with a vengeance in the nineteenth-century realist novel and reappeared in the 'kitchen sink drama' of the 1950s in Britain. From the perspective of everyday life the meaning of watershed dates such as that of 1956 will have to be reconsidered. The more useful genealogy is the very resistance to the everyday that theatre in Britain had maintained prior to its irruption in the subject matter of Arnold Wesker and John Osborne. Why did these revolutions of content, so long after Molly Bloom's stand for the quotidian in literature, not ultimately penetrate the forms of theatre in anything like the way the everyday entered its contents? It is as though what Michael Kustow ungraciously, but accurately, calls the 'tiny space that has traditionally been the British theatre's brain' could not accommodate two challenges, to its forms and contents, simultaneously. The longer and more interesting campaign of this period may turn out to be the formal questions provoked by communities and theatres rather than the presentation of the everyday by playwrights. The lay theatre is characterised by both, neither one nor the other in isolation – presenting an epic in a factory, a social realist statement in a proscenium arch, and the everyday in between.

There cannot be a polarity between these practices given that they all in the end are stories of a more or less sophisticated kind. As de Certeau is careful to maintain throughout his work: '*narration is indissociable from a theory of practices, as its condition as well as its production.*'[57] Here narrative is less interested in grasping the 'real', or in 'indicating something', than in producing *effects* rather than *objects*. Stories do not therefore insist on endings whether happy or not. This is apparent from the arts of speaking that have been mistaken for the 'reason' of Galileo, the tricks and ruses of speech gaining desired effects. From Aristotle's confession: 'The more solitary and isolated I became, the more I came to like stories,'[58] to Jean-François Lyotard's foregrounding of the narrative as a bonding process in the absence of metanarratives, there is a continual return in philosophy to the operations that stories *conduct* rather than describe. This is of course the means of the theatre, for theatre never describes an event but shows its operations. The stories it will draw upon will not just be those of history, although the temporal has always offered itself through historiography to the theatre for reaccentuation, but also of geography. The operations of theatre in and on neighbourhoods, in site-specific events and in the streets of the city and the lanes of the country are all topographical operations. These are not necessarily large-scale events but often micro-movements, pedestrian activity barely discernible from the 'everyday'. Here place becomes describable as something which has become invisible, an 'absence'. As Michel de Certeau says it is definable as a 'series of displacements and effects among the fragmented strata that form it and that it plays on these moving layers'.[59] It is these displacements and effects that are prevalent in the olfactory, an everyday sense which contributes to the restoration of memory against the emotional and political amnesia of forgetting. This is not a nostalgia, but the emergence of others' stories from other places, through which theatre might elucidate a political claim, a romantic gesture, or a metaphysical meaning. These topographical practices of theatre are indissociable from narrative, but why?

For de Certeau, all stories are 'travel stories', spatial practices. Space is 'practiced place' where the mobile elements of place break down the stability of the 'proper', by their direction and velocity. Moving on from the characterisation of theatre 'space' in the phenomenology of Maurice Merleau-Ponty, de Certeau emphasises the necessity of a place to speak from and a transformation of that place, once grounded, into the space of theatre. This three-way process moves beyond the polarity of place and space to give context to the coming to be of the theatre image. Characteristically de Certeau sees this transaction as a familiar one, it is hardly original, for stories 'carry out a labour that constantly transforms places into spaces and spaces into places'.[60] Where geography isolates and organises places so 'everyday stories tell us what we can do in it and make out of it'.[61] They are the 'treatments' of space which I identified in my introduction as distinctive to theatre now. The loss of Walter Benjamin's 'storyteller' from these places jeopardises the very spaces and places once described. In this sense stories are as *founding* of space as they are *founded* by it. Here the work of John Berger and Italo Calvino can be seen in distinct ways as a conscious narrative of space, and one which a theatre practice wishing to attune itself to its borders could do well to interrogate. The cutting out and inversion of this space is not simply the prerogative of the geographer. Its transformation into place by the architect speaks of the ambiguous relations between the theatre building and its neighbour-hood. The 'empty space' might have been claimed for the theatre but the narratives of either side of the fence continue until they are subordinated to those more strident tones parachuted from above into the place of the building. Where the stories of everyday life were already being exchanged over the fence and through its gaps, they are now transformed from elsewhere into the 'everyday' subject of the theatre. The economy here is an unequal one, however, when the correspondents in the original conver-sation are pre-empted from the theatre space by an 'other' audience, which is less familiar with these tales and therefore always interested in the exotic, in how the other half lives. Speakers become speechless onlookers.

But isn't this the point of education – to open a space in the fence and let everyone through? The possibility of a move being made from one realm to the other, from one side of the fence to the other, has been impoverished by the thought that it is a one-way traffic. If there is movement it is expected to come from the profanity of the 'other side', via education, to the sophistication of the arts. Meanwhile theatre maintains its sporadic interest in the other side just long enough to wrap up its juiciest stories. The uncritical thought that 'reading', the guiding activity of know-ledge, whether it be television, books or theatre, is necessarily an activity which makes the consumer 'similar' to it is fundamental to this unequal economy. The production is seen as the source of influence and denies the possibility that the 'user' might make something of it.[62] This is evi-dently more understandable in the terms of television, where the parental phrase 'you will get square eyes' sums up the expected direction of exchange. There is rarely heard the corollary that the 'box' will become organic if watched, or 'read' enough, and given my reticence as to the possibilities of a nonconformist television that is not perhaps surprising. This 'inertia of consumption' lies in the traditions of education and leaves the 'remainder' to the consumer after the producer has taken their stories, their place and their share. Given the debate in media as to whether television shapes us or we shape it, there perhaps could be reticence about romantically assigning any power to such a transaction in the face of massive odds. Yet this is not the task for de Certeau who wishes just to 'relativize the exorbitant claim that *a certain kind* of production (real enough, but not the only kind) can set out to produce history by "inform-ing the whole of the country" '.[63] It is after all against the postmodern extreme of atomised, asocial individualism that de Certeau, long before it reached its apotheosis in the 1980s, is positioning himself, taking the contrary line to the 'unsurveyable' by starting from positions which make the state of play seem quite surveyable and not unoptimistic. De Certeau recognises the very real division of labour that social abstraction has brought with it, and the ways in which such division has produced that abstraction. But he will not abdicate the role of the reader to one of passivity.

This is an important task for the theatre as well as for literature, for the reason de Certeau spells out: 'A politics of reading must thus be articulated on an analysis that, describing practices that have long been in effect, makes them politicizable.'[64] Against the orthodox view of the 'work' as surrounded by conformist consumers, reception theory has long since posited a complex presence, informed and formative of the work, in the manner in which I have described the theatre image. The question might be asked as to how this 'participation' looks alongside the models that already contribute techniques of participation to a lay theatre – the 'sing-along' of music hall, the shouts of warning in pantomime, the intervention of Augusto Boal's forum theatre, the involvement in the community play movement, the immersion in the Carnival for a licensed festival. But what is at issue here is a much more familiar and discernible trait, one that we know well and from which we might begin to theorise a more modest 'participatory' model. For de Certeau it starts with 'discovering the move-ments of this reading in the body itself', the audience of theatre appears, at first to be silent, but in time there inevitably emerge 'subconscious gestures, grumblings, tics, stretchings, rustlings, unexpected noises, in short a wild orchestration of the body.'[65] The site for de Certeau's observations is the 'reading room', a 'silent retreat' which is surprisingly noisy. But these cacophonies of witness are much more apparent in the theatre, and in the reading of a theatre event. This may not seem a very auspicious beginning to an ethical and political theatre but it as useful a place to start as an untheorised and utopian 'participation' which conceals the real 'structures of belonging' that a suppressed sneeze, a nervous cough, a premature departure, are likely to expose. For all the audience's adherence to a convention of theatre, the cacophony that occurs within it is a poignant reminder that there is often little direct attention being paid to the very procedures the analysis of theatre has given so much thought to understanding. The imbalance between what we know of audiences and constituencies and what we know of dramatic texts in theatre is indicative of its economy of exchange with that audience.[66] It is here that everyday observation becomes the precondition for interpreting and intervening in a theatre whose audience is politely covering up its distractions with after-show talk.

This talk rarely begins without a surreptitious dance of fear – the estimation of what others thought, often derived from the most oblique body language, before personal evaluation can be made. A shift has occurred historically from a time when seeing was the precondition of belief, to a time when what is seen *must* be believed. This process, once bounded by a fiction, which de Certeau describes as 'pointing to itself' in aesthetic and theatrical places, now is informed by that fiction. In this world beliefs are no longer expressed in direct convictions but 'only through the detour of what others are thought to believe'.[67] Here the referent is always an 'other', contradictory or supportive, legitimising that which is here and now. This was unfortunately never the dubious pleasure of the lay theatre, where immediately following and often during performances the question whether it was good or bad would be expressed very forcefully. The ability to state something's worth is surely the primary biological necessity before the sophistications of meaning are teased out and that returns us to the first question of this book.

Citation and quotation of Michel de Certeau make believe that a theatre of ethics and politics can be valued through a procedure called a poetics of theatre. The citation has to be coupled with a 'believable object', a theatre practice, if it is not to be another theoretical illusion, a cause for mistrust and suspicion. That object is historically and geographically constituted and it remains to show how everyday life is not just a phenomenon of today, but a means of exposing theatres of the past to closer scrutiny.

THE ART OF EVERYDAY LIFE

I have so far in this chapter traced the contemporary rediscovery of everyday life, its observation and interpretation, and its connection with a theatre practice. It is necessary finally to identify how it has informed a cultural practice that borders theatre which distinguishes itself from performance by its endemic revelation of the everyday. Echoing Vassily Meyerhold's discovery of the 'fantastic' in the everyday, Siegfried Krakauer writes: 'Film is the discovery of the miraculous in everyday life.'[68] This reference invites us to consider the essential 'everydayness' that is at the root of all film. However 'directed' the operation of cinema might appear, its characteristic tendency is to record the detail which in other art forms is edited out. The critic Yvette Biró states that if the social function of film is unique, it might be time to stop 'proving' its role as 'art' and begin to assert its true originality, that it is '*not* an art form'.[69] It is at once less and more, a medium with direct relations to the quotidian and therefore problematic to analysis, but very significant for everything said about theatre and its relation to these boundary conditions.

Film, primarily, and in its simplest sense, records detail from 'reality'. This was attested to by Sergei Eisenstein, and montage became the formal arrangement of this detail in juxtaposed composition. In writing about film in *Profane Mythology* Yvette Biró concentrates on this level of detail, to see what the everyday offers film prior to composition. Like Bachelard's concern for the sub-atomic nature of physics and human ignorance of the elements, Biró identifies what we take for granted in the recesses of film. For not only do the major movements of history appear here, but precisely the unnoticed, the incidental, that is inadvertently captured by the cinematic process.

When I speak of the cultural conception of the 'everyday' it is film that plays the key modern role in an ancestry which stretches beyond antiquity. Eisenstein's conception of 'actuality', the fragments of the real that montage works upon, follows the precedents of Surrealism and Dada, Duchamp's 'ready mades', the montage of everyday objects in the fine arts, in surprising and disconcerting circumstances, Rousseau and Pushkin's conception of a drama of public spaces. All of these cultural responses to the quotidian were predicated on a view of the 'everyday' as a quantifiable, if not *changeable* entity. Eisenstein's early theatrical work with Meyerhold attests to this enclosure of the quotidian, his plans for the annexation of a factory for their production of *Gas Masks* was an 'expansion' mirrored by all the arts. From the turn of the century, there had been relentless annexation of 'everyday life' by culture, an integration and violation of the borders of previously defined fields, the move from the stage into the factory and its swift return to the conventions of auditoria on the discovery of the competition it faced from everyday life. What was called 'kitchen sink' drama in Britain in the 1950s was the belated return of the everyday to the contents, rather than the forms of a theatre bound by the securities of the proscenium arch.[70] Biró describes this search for heterogeneity in the following way: 'Literature and theatre also show expansionist tendencies: raw and processed elements, whether lifted from life or from other forms of art, are appearing in them, well mixed, with increasing frequency.'[71]

So the expanded field of cultural practice is one of interdisciplinary borrowing as much as the extension of borders and the corral of domains outside artistic definition. In this climate an ethics of performance guides entry to the everyday where others live, work and play. Enquiring after an 'ethics' of the theatre and noting the eclipse of that category from discussions of the politics of art ironically replicates the call of the Surrealists, those notorious great annexers, who spoke of a 'new ethics'.[72] This demand was itself the recognition that the 'everyday' was no longer acceptable and its transformation the purpose of 'Surrealism'. I have already explained why this was more a retreat from the everyday than a transformation. Film was to enter into this domain more purposefully and securely than theatre because of its technical attributes for recording the unnoticed detail and the coincidental. Its technology literally allowed it to intervene in the quotidian. Normality led film into a realm that appeared distant from the conventional heightened subject matters of art:

> These are images of a new civilisation. This time, however, expansion is not toward some distant land of exotic and rare sights, but rather into the fantastic territory which happens to lie right in our midst: behind the scenes of our everyday life.[73]

This cultural history has not occurred in placeless abstract space – it has been precisely located in the city, the metropolis from which a critical art derives: the city that Marshall Berman describes to such effect in *All That Is Solid Melts Into Air*, the maelstrom that Charlie Chaplin walks into in *City Lights* and *Modern Times*, the Romanticism of nineteenth-century Soviet urban fiction, the 'mapping' of the city and its cool, rational control through the fictional detective. The technical developments of film, the emergence of a lightweight, hand-held camera, allowed for an enquiring cinema eye to record a new view of the interior of the city. With the increase in technical sophistication and sensitivity, so real life, unilluminated or decorated, became available to the film. In this and its equation to the city, film paralleled the simultaneous developments of modernism in photography and architecture, the imagery of one having a complex relationship with the other, indicating well before the articulation of such phenomena in postmodern theory the ways in which reality followed its representation.

Simultaneously the technology of theatre has removed performance as quickly as is decent *from* everyday life, has made the reciprocal trajectory to cinema's 'lightness of movement'. When Grotowski wrote *Towards a Poor Theatre*, he reacquainted the theatre with the possibility of a modesty of means, to get closer to the life that Artaud demanded it stop representing. Indeed there had been a continual presence between 1880 and 1930 in Britain of a politicised theatre that retained this directness of expression without losing its contact with the developing modernisms of the European avant-garde. But as Raphael Samuel points out this trajectory was lost, at least in Britain, with the formation of the Popular Front in 1935 and the incursion of socialist realism into theatre forms.[74] The work of Joan Littlewood stands out as the bridge between this unwritten tradition of experiment and the relief of the firm ground that the angry young men provided in the 1950s for a scholarship that could only tolerate improvisation within bounds.

Now theatre has attempted to subvert the opulence that characterises its mainstream by refitting the city's derelict sites, its factories and by animating its leisure grounds, its parks, gardens and swimming pools.[75] It has taken what might be considered the cinematic underside of the city, and made it at once familiar through the presence of people and theatre, and unfamiliar again by the transformation of the landscape through imagery. This is not just a process of reclaiming and conserving that which has fallen into disrepair, but animating those environments, with what has been variously described as 'environmental theatre' or 'site-specific work'. For the natural hinterland of these sites is often characterised by the anonymity of city life, punctuated by intense local affinities.

But not all environments, spaces in the city, are of course spaces of indiscriminate detail. Some are 'public places', clearly defined space as culturally defined as the drawing room of the interior play. The most obvious, as Biró points out is the street, which has 'a unique position just by belonging to everyone and no one all at the same time'.[76] Here there is the sense of location that Rousseau and Pushkin chose for their outdoor theatre, which is not nature, but nature in limits: 'These public places have become strange and chaste communal locations, which because of their heterogeneity, attempt in some sadly atrophied form and almost as if secretly, to take on the role of the old market place.'[77] The ordering principle of these places of 'culture' in nature lies, Biró believes, in their capacity to both group and disperse people. They are potential meeting places quite distinct from other parts of the country or the city.

Where cinema thrived on its distance and anonymity from the subjects of these places, the theatre made up of bodies turning places into spaces is too recognisable a circumstance, too close to 'the presentation of self in everyday life', to treat the 'public places' in which it operates innocently. The question here is not how to distance the theatre, like cinema from its subject, but how like Walter Benjamin's storyteller, to bring it back into contact with its subject and the everyday life of that subject. This passage, if not understood, will consign theatre to being never quite as 'incredible' as life, nor as 'credible' as life's communicating channels. Here theatre has to address precisely what Yvette Biró considers is its profound character-istic: 'Only the theater is forced to show the pure persona of its characters (individuals) – shutting out the resistance of live environment. Film returns man to his snail-house, be it a protective or a vulnerable shell.'[78] The theatre attempting to address this environment, as Sergei Eisenstein and Armand Gatti discovered in factory sites, is always threatened by the 'reality' from which it removes itself. Does this not consign theatre to a margin of the flexibility of film, so much more adaptable and appropriate to an age of panning and close-ups?

Theatre is wholly distinct from film yet cannot be seen in isolation from it. As I opened this study with a discussion of the prevalence of the image over the 'real', so our conception of the city in which theatre takes its place is profoundly altered by film memories. As Biró says: 'Perception and interpretation blend into an indivisible whole, since our comprehen-sion is no longer "virginal", it no longer contains any innocent parts – anything that could be separated from a predetermined meaning.'[79] This has always been true of the locality of the lay theatre and profoundly affected the terms on which theatre activity there could proceed. For in that dramatised environment theatre was squeezed between the filming of two very particular genres: the nostalgia industries of Charles Dickens and the criminal genre of 'cops and robbers'. In warehouse studios close to the theatre the minutest detail would be built to reconstitute a truer Dickensian world than Little Dorrit could have believed possible, and one which somewhere lost sight of the social tensions at the heart of this most local of literary works. The social tensions of gun-toting, respraying, and fencing dodgy goods were in the gangster fictions played for all they were worth with advisory nods and winks from those in the area who claimed they knew a thing or two about the realities. This analysis questions the very heart of the debate concerning the relative merits of theatre, cinema and television. For in reverse order in the West, each is perceived through an imagery wrought by the other. Any theatre which does not recognise that 'image block', as Paul Virilio calls it, will unwittingly confirm the power of such images and they will return as 'myth'.

For Biró the transition between a natural relationship and a social one is the substance of myth, and it presents the cinema with the possibility of an accurately defined role. In theatre terms this is problematic, for the term myth has often been used to justify a theatre practice loosely based on a vague understanding of ritual. Also for Biró, myth is an entity which raises as many questions as it resolves: 'Myth is a system that includes the whole network of ideals and values, taboos and rituals, and customs regulating social intercourse.'[80] Myth is an ideal, an informing principle and a socially unifying ethic. But the effects and constructs of myth are ones which I ascribe to cultural practices: the binding function of language and narrative, the consolidating function of tradition, and the identifying features of place. Modern myth for Biró is a 'going beyond' these particularities to a 'comprehensive universality'. It is another way of describing the 'something more' of the image and its facility for expressing the universal from the particular. Similarly Roland Barthes identified 'myth' as the 'awarding of the status of the absolute to the unwhole and the ephemeral'.[81] Here value is ascribed and laws determined that dictate our responses to the passing images of our society. And in the confusion over what is truly valuable we are divorced from the possibility of making distinctions between soap operas and tragedy. For the homogenising effects of electronic media, the levelling of difference to the mundane, has not only levelled all experience to 'everyday' experience but simultaneously raised that experience to the status previously ordained as the realm of the arts.[82] Biró puts her faith in cinema's intervention into this world. Its technical means will ensure it a place within and indeed formative of this world. Film might then not be an art but it has mythic qualities which operate in a domain once occupied by ethics: as an informing principle and a socially unifying construct. Can we say the same for theatre?

Biró points out that it has precisely been art's and science's project to identify and order the features of the everyday which it takes as its subject matter for transformation. It is these indiscriminate stimuli that in everyday life escape the frame of this ordering, and induce us to live with increasing familiarity and ease. Here dangers of passivity and acquiesence to habit prevail. But also here lie the securities that make everyday life bearable and pleasurable in the first place. So, the relations between passivity and consciousness are fraught and film intrudes upon them in ways that theatre might consider somewhat pushy. The 'explosion of the tenth of a second', as Walter Benjamin referred to the revolution of film, has opened up this milieu previously dissociated from the arts: 'the great gain, the newly conquered continent, film's dowry – all these faded habits, reflex like functions and vegetative processes'.[83] In an indiscriminate world of confused values, where seeing has become believing, film can enter and offer the quality of a 'concreteness of lifelike traits', where before there was lifeless abstract 'differentiation'. In this endeavour film brings us closer to the everyday and reacquaints us with the 'trivial'. This is the primary characteristic of cinema for Biró.[84]

Like the banal, the trivial is not just an irrelevance, but from the perspective of everyday life, the opposite. It is the implacable view of sameness and necessity. The individuation of the subject through their witness of the everyday on the screen occurs as a two-way process: first there is the film's recording of the everyday, the trivial, and then the spectator's imitation of that model. But in film these processes, pedestrian movement and habits do not stay on the level of the everyday. Actors take on the status of symbol, they become mythic, exemplary beings. Biró points out the *festive* character of this mythic quality, which is derived from its condonation of 'exaggeration'. Quoting Freud in *Totem and Taboo*: 'A festival is an authorized or organised exaggeration. People overstep boundaries not because they feel that some regulation permits it; exaggeration is part of the festivities.'[85] Biró equates this exaggeration with the transformation of the everyday in film, and here film itself is ascribed 'mythic' qualities through its 'hypnotic' effects. It is film's strength, for Biró, that it surrounds its audience from all sides, achieving what both Artaud and Meyerhold had striven for in their 'metaphysics of the stage' and 'perfect theatre'.

But what is the audience captured 'by' in the cinema? The audience is captured by light, by illumination, fragments of projected reality which resist the participation and rhythms of its audience's own 'inner speech'. It is eminently forgettable as an escape from the everyday. Theatre threatened by this escapism has perhaps reinforced its hereditary relations to the everyday in the wake of cinema. The implacable logic and rigour of a performance by Pina Bausch's *Tanztheater Wuppertal* simultaneously resists the participation of the audience while inviting it in moments of physical proximity.

Theatre transmits and transforms, cinema records and preserves.[86] There is a sophisticated though fundamentally limited relation between the spectator and the film, where the theatre image is at once more complex, intimate and ambivalent. Cinema channels spectacle, where theatre diversifies and multiplies it. In theatre there is a proliferation of the image from a singularity, the original audience and performer configuration, in cinema a concretisation from a multiplicity. In this 'proliferation' the theatre initiates multiplicities and possibilities, the way the city itself multiplies 'lines of flight', 'intensities' and 'deterritorializations'.[87] As Biró says: 'the big city has become the distinguished stage of dramatic contingency, where the accidental and the irretrievable are frequent guests'.[88] Where the 'accidental' in film appears effortlessly and therefore surprisingly, the theatre's technology cannot begin to compete. When Biró talks with enthusiasm of the ship's appearance in Antonioni's film *Red Desert*, I return sceptically to the mechanical excrescence of the train in David Edgar's *Maydays* for the Royal Shakespeare Company, the boat in Tom Stoppard's version of *Rough Crossing* for the National Theatre, and only rarely can we think of such technology achieving its aim; the ocean liner in Peter Stein's production of *The Hairy Ape*, the chariot of the gods in Ninagawa's *Medea* are exceptions. Technology in theatre fails to take on the 'anthropomorphic' character it achieves in film, except where it is wholly integral to the performance: the resuscitated barge of Bow Gamelan's *Offshore Rig*, the cars of La Fura dels Baus' *Accions* Royal Victoria Dock performance, the hay train and paper boat of George Wyllie's site-specific projects in Glasgow. And these last are exceptional for their return through technology to the simplest of media: hay and pulped wood. This does not limit the theatre so much as release it into more imaginative relations with its audience. The everyday threatens the scale of cinema and the import of technology to the theatre – a pair of shoes in Robert Lepage's *The Dragons' Trilogy*, a cake stand in Bobby Baker's *Kitchen Show*, a beach towel in Pina Bausch's *1980*, a pile of plates in Jan Fabre's *The Power of Theatrical Madness*, are the props of the everyday whose poetic potential confirms each event as a special art.

It was film's fortuitous accident that the flow of everyday life in its background provided the canvas against which the subjectivities of story and plot were set. Theatre has not, since its move indoors, allowed itself that panorama, and where in contemporary theatre it is suggested, some would say by Robert Lepage's work, others would cite Ken Campbell's, it is notable as an exception, not as a rule. The private and the public domain has long been a suspected coalition for theatre, split between the psychological and the epic. But where the gestation of performance has been given the same extended preparation as cinematic production, for instance Jan Fabre's quarantine of his actors in training, there is the recognition of the power of the everyday gesture. Fabre's *This Is Theatre* might well have been the object of Biró's description of a market when she said: 'the most profane human activities and everyday misery appear as extraordinary and comprehensive experiences, which, charged with the emotional content of ceremonies, present to us the malevolence as well as the benevolent pathos of labor.'[89]

The 'archetypal' circumstances of the city and its markets also occasionally, in Biró's view, give way to something that appears more 'natural' – an experience of 'continuity' and 'certainty' that traces back to the source of the market's produce. The village and its pastoral setting is seen as the embodiment of the archaic-romantic ethos. But the smooth space of the countryside can become striated by the life lines of people living through that world, their psychology at odds with its calm exterior. The time spans of nature are here at odds with the mortality of the individual whose life is circumscribed by more modest limits. In theatre, the work of John Berger has reflected this relationship while more specifically, Olivier Perrier, the French performer, has transformed its relations into a theatre life.[90]

Where film from its beginnings made the city its natural landscape, the interior scene, the drawing room which was the natural landscape of the Edwardian theatre, was challenged by a new generation of writers after Brecht. All reintroduced theatre to the outdoors, whether in its own right, as in Edward Bond's plays, or as a reorientation of previous city bound scenes. Howard Brenton has used the latter device to considerable effect, such as the last scene of *Magnificence* in the English Country Garden, or *Weapons of Happiness* in a winter orchard in Wales.[91] There is a lyricism in the latter which Eisenstein spoke of in connection with Ostrovsky, which arises from its juxtaposition with the factory scenes and episodes that form the major part of the work.

Biró returns us to the lyricists of the cinema, and reminds us of the call from Meyerhold for a lyricism in the theatre. The lyricist is able to communicate the transforming qualities of nature and landscape – not the social realism of Shishkin's landscapes, but the monumental nature of Ostrovsky's *Forest*. This is not a romantic pastoral attitude to the 'other', outside the city, but is integral to the post-industrial transformation of society within which the individual lives: 'Nature is no less a struggling organism than our man-made social existence, and therefore it is not surprising to find clashes, battles and death, destruction and devastation among its elements.'[92] As Raymond Williams warns in *The Country and the City*, the classical dualism of Nature and Society is one to be wary of for the ways in which it polarises and leaves uncriticised a set of changing entities. As Biró points out, such a 'romantic act' of confrontation leaves the outside world undifferentiated and unthought. In that state it cannot be acted upon, nor in, and as the purpose of theatre is to do both, the perpetuation of such dualisms will deny the theatre its specific role in everyday life.

While the landscape of the preceding pages has been the urban I can therefore no longer artificially deny the contingency of this realm, dependent as it is on the country and defined by that country as suggested in the root of the word itself, *contra*. It remains to locate theatre again within an understanding of the relations between nature and culture, for it is this tract which defines what everyday life can be in the first place. This conclusion to a cultural question is simply the premature emergence into the realm where theatre does what I have claimed it does. It is premature because without a critical history of theatre we run the risk of being definitively lost in that most familiar place, which, for all its habit, requires the most careful mapping. The achievement of cinema in allowing us to 'travel through this debris', to wander in the realm of the everyday, reasserts the possibilities as well as the problems of everyday life. Theatre might now decide whether it is a place it wishes to be.

Part II

NATURE THEATRE CULTURE

This book has so far followed a path between the given and the created. For my purposes everyday life is the given, theatre the created. This distinction rests, however, on an exclusion which if admitted threatens everything said so far. For in broader terms nature is the given and culture the created. Everyday life is not nature, though it is shaped by natural phenomena. Everyday life is human, and as Maurice Blanchot says: 'The earth, the sea, forest, light, night, do not represent everydayness . . .'. But the relations between the everyday and nature, and humanity's place within that frame are often in political urgency overridden for abstract ideals of progress and universal emancipation. The theatre is in no position to deny local imperatives for such universal ambitions, its political aspirations remain in the everyday. Being centrally concerned with the body, theatre is behoven to the question of the body's well-being, and sickness, old age and infirmity are natural boundaries of theatrical creativity as well as life. Like the boundaries of a neighbourhood they are there to be crossed, reinvented and imagined, and theatre provides an enduring means by which this revisioning of limits can be conducted. Nevertheless a philosophy of theatre which does not think through these relations between natural limits to action is an idealism.

Theatre does not exist on a pin-head removed fom these natural limits. But just such an absence would appear to jeopardise political thought since Marx, little heed being paid to the inevitable biological specificities at the heart of everyday life. The sober truism is that there is an element of passivity in experience: the acknowledgement must be made of the external situation which I do not create but which imposes itself on me. Theatre might wish in its headlong rush to escapism to provide an exit from this world, but the wires and traps are always visible and provoke the most down-to-earth laughter. There is a passive relationship to gravity and light which is marked by astonishment when these most everyday conditions are suspended – for instance watching astronauts float in space or, more mundanely, when power cuts plunge cities into darkness. These elements are part of the human's constitutional make-up, there is expectation of them and when they are disrupted there is disorientation and unhappiness. When they are suspended through theatre, when the lights go down, when the rain holds off, when the wind drops or someone turns up the heat, there is reorientation to the conventions of theatre and more or less pleasure. These are the inherent physical conditions in which theatre action occurs – a specific universe, planet, evolutionary system and lives from which practices of creativity and consciousness have arisen. In this sense, nature, while being transformed in the social of which theatre is a part, precedes the social and the theatre. The terrain of theatre is marked out by a set of associations and presumptions about the natural world which bear reformulation before they reimpose themselves on an unsuspecting audience.

Rethinking socialist categories and the relations between theory and practice is not unusual for a theatre whose practices require constant attention to these concerns. But to do this with any claims for a materialism, that is, a science of these operations, and to aspire to a theory of needs which takes due account of the relations between society and nature, is by no means a common enough procedure. The work of Raymond Williams whose concept of 'structures of feeling' was unusually sensitive to these issues, and Sebastiano Timpanaro's tone of 'hedonistic pessimism' about life's enduring limits, demonstrate the possibility of moving beyond the compromises between Marx and Freud that have given rise to the mutations of existential Marxism during the twentieth century. There is also here the chance to move beyond any number of 'absurd theatres' and their relations to a single philosophical disposition. The first requirement in this rethinking of being human is not to reduce the social to the biological, or to 'biologism'. But this cannot imply the denial of conditioning which nature continues to exercise on people, the relations between biological phenomena and happiness. Nature would of course continue to exert its force and cause profound unhappiness in any society whatever its political make-up or hue. No socialist revolution, however unlikely that might appear anyway, can have any direct influence on this fact, rather, and more modestly, on the constituents of being older than average and what it means to be that age. It will mean for many an unpleasant experience of retarded horizons and possibilities, but it need not necessarily be so, and this will be one of the undercurrents of the following. Like everyday life, nature is so problematic to cultural disciplines it has to be ignored for fear of its effects on the status quo between powerful and subservient fields of enquiry. What is needed is not the ignorance of nature but more acute definition of the links between political, ethical and creative progress and living within nature, which inevitably is a transformation of nature.

The dangers of a reactionary biologism are clear and I wish to dispose of this first so as not to be mistaken in what I am introducing to this argument. The continuing presence of racist activity and perceptions and theories to back up these oppressions drawn from spurious biological stereotypes is all too evident. Throughout the work described as a lay theatre these tensions were ones which served as a reminder to participants that there were continual exclusions and prejudices operating between the most apparent distinctions within the community, and between insiders to certain groups and those outside such groups. In the wider sense an inverted prejudice towards other peoples and their 'exotic' cultures can be identified in theatre thought, from Artaud's considerations of Balinese dance, subtly criticised by Grotowski, to the wholesale adoption of ideologies such as Orientalism, through to the fawning subservience to the 'cheeky Cockney' that embraces the complex genealogy of the London East-Ender. No less disturbing than, and not unlinked to, these racial issues are the behavioural tendencies of educational psychology and the use made of biology to support a spurious and reactionary ideology of the human's innate aggressiveness. The latter has been widely, and within theatre, notoriously, discussed in Edward Bond's prefaces to his plays, views which when they appeared were thought to be somehow separate from the plays themselves. But these prefaces introduced to theatre already well established arguments between anthropologists, such as Ashley Montague and Desmond Morris, who fundamentally disagree about the sources of violence. Edward Bond's critical optimism that people are not inherently or necessarily violent beings but conditioned to become so, draws from Montague and against Morris. If as Raymond Williams has made clear such materialism provides a way of looking, the need to reject received hypotheses and define one's own categories in terms of demonstrable physical investigations, there is always the problem that initial and successive categories are inherently subject to revision and here 'the' materialism becomes 'a' materialism. Morris's materialism, his view of the world, gains ascendancy over Montague's, inadvertently justifying as it does people's violence as genetic and in so doing neatly promoting the conservative shibboleths of competition and self-help. There is no support or justification for these three areas of mystification and the following does not wish to propagate their claims in any way whatsoever.

To move beyond romantic and existentialist categories of pessimism is not to ignore physical ills and the inevitability of death. As Timpanaro says, these are not just 'bad social arrangements', and to recognise the revivifying power of illusions which imaginatively revision these limits is not to have to accept or rely on them as an escape from harsh human reality. Old age might be a 'sad reality' but theatre suggests it need not necessarily be so. Hence theatre is a return to the reality of the everyday not an escape from it. Between voluntarism and pragmatism there is then a position to take up regarding the way in which nature, theatre and culture interrelate. I place theatre in the middle of this triumvirate not wishing to consign it finally to one or other realm. Culture is after all simply the remainder that science left over from its partitioning of knowledge in the seventeenth and eighteenth centuries. This remainder, constituted by the part of human experience not tamed and symbolised in language, has been strip-mined by the disciplines which make up cultural theory, the detritus of this operation providing rich pickings for the cultural interpreter as scavenger. While the sciences have succeeded in resisting the claims for attention from this vast remainder, via definition of their terms of operation and displacement of threatening border disciplines such as psychology, the arts of theory have continually to return to this field to constitute a place for themselves and their practices. And nature, in the sense that biological phenomena are thought 'natural' to being human, is precisely what would appear to make theatre a fundamental human activity. Theatre is after all the only art which requires the presence of two organisms in the same place, bodies of the same species, one as a performer the other as an audience. This is so obvious a precondition for theatre that it remained largely taken for granted, unremarked and unthought until the relatively recent work of theatre anthropology and biology. This fact is only as obvious, in other words disregarded as a commonplace not worth consideration, as the everyday, and it poses first principle questions about theatre as foundational to human nature.

It is worth reiterating that it is not here the division of practice and theory that represents the central problematic, but rather the tract between those practices which are articulated by discourse and those which are not, or not yet. There has been a proliferation of debate in the West concerned with recognised genres such as Greek and Roman theatre, or Restoration theatre, and familiar individuals such as Shakespeare, Stanislavsky and Brecht. Adjacent to this tradition of 'dramatic scholarship' which often derives from the literary aspects of theatre, there has developed through the auspices of groups such as the International School of Theatre Anthropology and journals such as the *Drama Review* the discourse of anthropology and theatre and deepening and widening studies on a plurality of practices. Here the East has provided the West with a Burgess Shale, brought to life, documenting and interpreting the myriad forms of performance, expression and pre-expressivity that constitute a Eurasian Theatre. What is visible is recorded and analysed and what is not visible is imagined and analysed. The status of these techniques pursued by occidental theorists points to a plurality of scattered practices but also, ironically, as with all such endeavours, to the different developments which have been disregarded. It is these shadowlands closer to home which are worth poaching on now, not simply in the absence of generous travel grants, though the academic geography of knowledge is another determinant which shapes the spread of known theatres, but as a political commitment to minority theatres which in innumerable ways make use of the

154

majority culture here and now. Thus the cosmopolitan must, if at least temporarily, continue to give way to the local and the particular for there to be a language of theatre that is not a transnational Esperanto of the arts. This does not mean a parochialism where there was an international-ism, realism where there was abstraction, but a return to some of the first principles which govern the conditions of theatre wherever you are as distinct from where you happen to be.

In the second part of this book I will therefore focus on four natural phenomena and see how in different ways they are transformed from one domain to another, from the given to the created. There would appear to be nothing more natural than the four elements: earth, water, air and fire. As a set and individually they have throughout history been the stimulus for the most profound imagery and poetic expressions. It was, after all, the elements which allowed humans to place themselves in the world and thereby define their relationship to the gods. It is not these inevitable inflections of their existence and importance for human life that I am primarily interested in, though all these influence their profound habitual dimension. Nor am I particularly concerned to rehearse their 'romantic' associations, with one-world philosophies or ecological politics. Rather I am interested in a more mundane and local problematic: the way that such elements are cut out from the fabric of everyday life, turned over and reinterpreted through the mediation of a middle term between nature and culture: theatre. Further I have chosen from the infinite possible approaches to such elements a particular perspective which seems to throw a strong partial light on the relations between the mediating disciplines in this process: geography and historiography. I have done this to elucidate perhaps new ways in which these disciplines can make theatre a theorised practice as distinct from say a 'history' of theatre, or a 'geography' of theatre, however welcome such disciplines are.

So while this part of the book follows a boundary between nature and culture it is also traversed by the interstices of space and time as conceptu-alised by geography and history. This is only proper given the significance both phenomena have for theatre. Not wishing to forget the place of the human species within this frame the mediation in each case is conducted by an individual whose work marks the border between the natural and the cultural – for earth I look at the miner, for air the prompter, for water the hygienist and for fire the fireman. In this way the mental and the material are reassociated through the operation of turning natural elements into a cultural environment and it is my aim to locate the terrain where such operations occur and to examine how they occur. Each of these operations involves ethical, poetic and political dimensions and in that sense the earlier discussion of these themes is tried out again with new empirical objects. This begins inevitably with a look at the ways in which the most fundamental phenomena of space and time are to be considered from theatre's perspective. Given the predominance of time over space, a history of theatre over its geography, I will first look in some detail at the spatial determinants of theatre and then, having worked through the elements, complete the set by indicating ways in which history turns natural elements into culture.

4

ORIENTATION
Space and place

To be in one's element is to be in one's preferred or accustomed surroundings. This is a derivation of the medieval conception of the relations between the body and its humours and is drawn from the four elements to which individuals were thought to have a propensity. The relation immediately established between biology and context is a central one for theatre, and a place to start reviewing the unwritten again. The persistence of the biological within social beings, despite the inauguration of a new autonomy from the animal base that work and labour wrought, is one salient reminder to any progressive politics which seeks universal emancipation from oppression. The places where people live is therefore a pressing problematic for political theory, as it was for the conduct of a lay theatre described earlier. Marx's acquaintance with the oppressions of a feudal system wished to untether the process of emancipation from the local and the particular, seeking instead a universal class consciousness. Despite the associated aesthetic gains of modernism these abstractions are not helpful ones for a theatre seeking the importance of place within a socialist perspective. The aura of theatre as described by Walter Benjamin appears to depend upon this unique place and time of its occurrence for its effects, and it is this that distinguishes it from mechanically and electronically reproducible media. It is this 'aura', an apparently vague and metaphysical concept, which this part of the book attempts to reveal by looking more closely at the relations between space, place and cultural practices.

The excision of the 'urban', the privileged site of postmodern theory, as distinct from other inhabited environments, is only the most recent manifestation of studies concerned with an interest in geography and the relations of people to the earth. These studies have in the contemporary period replaced the vague and problematic notion of humanism with a highly specific set of genealogies and technologies of the body, histories of sexuality, the institutions designed to accommodate the mind and its mutations. While historians have long been filtering through the wastes, artefacts and natural phenomena of the landscape, turning it into the artifice of their work, geographers have only in the recent period been theorising a politicised spatial practice. This problematic has been almost wholly absent from analyses of theatre despite its formative and enduring influence. The Greek theatre would have been something else if it had not been for the terrain and climate in which it occurred, and yet poetry which makes constant allusion to these conditions of production is removed from its specific geographic context to be universalised through criticism which diminishes the significance of place. The works of scholarship by Margarete Bieber into the conditions of production of such works remain to be reacquainted to the practical consideration of the work today. Marx called human geography an 'unnecessary complication', and until the work of Henri Lefebvre, the journal *Antipode*, the radical feminist geography of the 1980s, and David Harvey and Edward Soja's spatial criticism, there has been little direction from this field, little need to ask the pressing question why no geography of theatre when there is so active a history of theatre?[1]

What do I mean here by proposing a 'spatial problematic'? There are three aspects to this question, which Edward Soja summarises for us. First that human spatiality is a 'social product'. Second that social space is here distinguished from 'mental space', such as the abstract forms of geometry. And third that it is also distinguished from 'material space' – the sensory perception of concrete form in nature. Walter Benjamin provides searching analyses of all three manifestations of space through his writings on the 'aura', the image theory of Paul Klee and the fictions of Franz Kafka. The interest of this comparative discussion across cultural fields is the dialectical nature of the perception of material and mental space. Theatre, being composed of images of a material and mental kind, is continually in the process of refashioning this dialectic in inevitably political, though wholly undogmatic ways: 'Social space is both real and abstract, what Marxists would call a "concrete abstraction".'[2] Theatre occurring as it does through images which are equally a concrete abstraction, cannot occur in an empty space. From this perspective socially transformed space is understood to be a 'container', but as with the image not simply a container of 'things'. It is argued by Henri Lefebvre that what it contains is its 'relations of production' and 'relations of reproduction'. Here the social space in which the image occurs is itself a conjunction of political relations. It is not innocent space, neutral space, nor utopian space, but manifestly organised by the dominant relations of production. Thus the word 'occupation' brings with it a challenge to that organisation of space by presence and 'trespass'. It is the demystification of this space which is seen by Lefebvre to be the goal of a spatial praxis, a revolutionary spatial consciousness, and it is this political dimension which will demand attention in conclusion to other imaginative ways in which space can be considered.[3] When Soja describes social space as 'in part a projection of mental space, a "design" imposed on material reality and given symbolic/ideological meaning', there is a return to the 'imagined communities' considered earlier, though now in a critical and reformulated light. It is these imagined possibilities that theatre produces and they have very specific relations to the other forms of space which contain and jeopardise their effects.

A spatial analysis is important to begin to take the specifics of place, rather than the idealised empty space, seriously. It is place after all which allows this discussion to occur, that makes what I say neither legendary nor a-topical. To be 'topical' is to be aware of *topos*, place, and its current and local commonplaces. The obverse of this condition, the denial of specificity of place, is the condition for ideology to flourish and theory to be driven out. Legends and rumours abound in space, untethered from the specific nature of discursive practices which root histories and stories in places. The renaming of delinquent areas follows this path – between the words Surrey Docks and Surrey Quays, in a neighbourhood close to where the lay theatre occurred, there is a curious feint between history and elision. The former, a traditional name for an area and a station, succumbs to the latter, an invention of commerce. The rhyming slang 'Docks' for 'Pox' gives way to a more wholesome thematic interest for a regenerated docklands – not a workplace and ghetto for the disadvantaged, but a leisure centre and a chance to buy, a landing place more than an enclosed and stagnant water, and a key to the outside world of markets and goods. Renaming is meant to inaugurate a flourishing, befountained, a-topical place that derives its power from architectural and sculptural allusions to buccaneers and other seafaring types. But delinquencies, like pirates, are never far away and refuse to be contained in their jolly rogered sandpit. At the opening of the locally notorious, and renamed station, the word is that Surrey Quays said with a silver spoon in the mouth bears more than a passing resemblance to the ex-mistress of the transport minister whose job it is to cut ribbons. Changing names, as Brian Friel made theatrically enduring in *Translations*, is never that simple or totalising an endeavour, and as one slang is replaced and flushed away so another emerges more resilient than the last. Here language and place share microbe-like interests. The shortest sentence inserted at just the right point transforms the alien landscape of conversation into the known, just as a loved one's window lights up a neighbourhood for the stranger visiting unknown parts. The arts of making do or turning a trick are never more acute than when they are to do with a place you call your own. Name changes in urban regeneration are not alone – they are accompanied by the work of the historian who transforms the environment and reorganises its boundaries before your very eyes. The theatre and the geographer might look closely at this constant reinvention to establish a place for themselves. Name changing is hardly a new affair, it has been going on as long as space became place, proper to one person or group and then the next. It is rather the relations between changes and the demands of commerce over the narratives of those who live there that invites interpretation and intervention.

It is money which governs the buying and selling of space (as well as time) and it is commodity-exchange and commerce which substitute relative value between places in opposition to the unique and irreducible topicality that exists for people within those spaces. Space after all is only valuable once it has been divided. There are exceptions which illuminate all rules and the impossibility of 'fixing a price' on the only Charles Rennie Mackintosh house in private ownership speaks to the inevitable breakdown of a system where nonconformist creativity is concerned. Despite these aberrations it is clear that it is in a world market, within Western economics, that space becomes both a real but nevertheless abstract condition through which practices become placed.

The processes by which power governs space and the genealogy of that power are finely traced by the geographer David Harvey.[4] Space to be conquered must first be thought of as useful, usable and able to be appropriated. It is not necessary that space be 'available' but rather 'achievable'. The successive remonstrations as another beloved theatre goes to the developer, or is saved from development, is simply the theatrical manifestation of these broader processes of development. Those fighting the corner of their specialism often appear somewhat unaware of the developments occurring next door to the Rose, the Globe or other remains. While 'saving theatres' generates cultural capital it is an economy predicated on the bankability of its most prominent supporters and always demands a Shakespeare or equivalent sign of prestige at its foundations. Theatres that are saved perpetuate an identity for other theatres, they submerge those that are ignored, unwritten and lost.

The historic development of map-making, navigation and surveying provided, as Brian Friel has shown for Ireland, not just abstract representation of real sites with real stories and histories, but the objective, homogeneous and therefore usable qualities that developments and colonialism require of space. These conceptual 'nets' as Harvey refers to them, simply provided the conditions necessary for the buying and selling of space. They can be turned to other more progressive purposes, as Paul Klee showed. But it was in the real world of rents and ownership that the traditional orders of distinction and differentiation were confused by a parallel but connected global economy – a palace and a slum can both now be bought and developed, but it is the latter which remains the likely candidate for rough treatment. Fragmentation of cities occurred at the moment that homogenising urban landscapes was deemed central to the conduct of ordinary business. It was as an antidote to this fragmentation that the professions of urban conceptualism – planners and designers assisted by the intellectuals of the city as 'concept', sociologists – were recruited for the rationale they could provide that would bind the unruly body of the city populous. The measurement of time that had dominated the late nineteenth century and its literature was joined by the measurement and quantification of space – the condition described at the starting point of this chapter.

What is important to stress here is that this network which joins money and space is not somehow beyond the everyday awareness of those it most affects. It is precisely noticed and challenged and the lay theatre takes this as one of its recurrent concerns. For the tactics and resistances of everyday life require not rationalisation in political dogmatism but the resources of imagination linked to solidarity that knowledge of a place and its histories begets. This is no utopian gesture, alternative solution or abstract community of interest, but specific, deep and lasting work. It is not only the most obvious traditional allegiances that bear this out, but all manner of local resistances to subjugation to values from elsewhere – theatre this century has played a central part in this history and one worth reminding ourselves of in the following chapter. But to avoid the claim that such analysis unduly emphasises the local, the documentary and the social over the abstract, fragmented and modernist, it is important to say that the most avant-garde forms of each moment are ones which can speak as well to these concerns as other more traditional forms of storytelling. These forms after all have been riven from the period and places in question, where fragmentation and anomie appear to be the order of the day. Theatre, like the novel and all other forms of cultural expression, has inflected these tensions in revealing ways and there is no *a priori* need to separate one theatre from another simply because the analysis of space throws up a series of apparently political questions. It is bringing theatres previously divided back into the same social space for consideration that is important now to ascertain what it is about them that contributes to the revisioning of places in which people wish to live and protects those places from those who have no regard for their wishes and needs.

So theatre only 'in all innocence' can occur in an empty space. A critical theatre that can make any claims to be post-colonial, in a most local or international sense, requires a fully theorised, but not fetishised, understanding of the differential developments of the space, as well as time, in which this theatre occurs. Space is a socially constructed phenomenon and theatre inevitably operates within and across its borders, just as time inscribes its occurrence in history. Sources from which such a geography might be developed derive not only from the theoretical spatial analysis of David Harvey and Edward Soja, but also perhaps surprisingly from the composition theory of Paul Klee, and the fictions of Franz Kafka. The latter two are discussed in detail in Walter Benjamin's work, and are directly connected with a clearer understanding of what Benjamin meant by the term, the 'aura' of the work of art. It is useful to return to

Benjamin's work, as not only was his criticism assiduously placed, no less attuned to the everyday than de Certeau and Lefebvre, it was an art of theory which derived from walking and looking, articulating the observations of the one-way streets that made up his writing life.[5] It is these mental manifestations of space which provide me with three geometries of performance, what Lorca called 'the fundamental basic measure of the spectacle'.

Aura storyteller distance

An acknowledgement of the unique resistance of theatre to 'reproduction', and the loss of its aura, in Benjamin's essay 'The work of art in the age of mechanical reproduction' is to say the least, discreet. It occurs in a footnote to the second thesis of this celebrated though not unproblematic essay. Here Benjamin compares a modest staging of *Faust* with the film of the same subject.[6] The resonance of the staging, however poor, lies for Benjamin in the resonance the live production has with the tradition of that play, its 'competition' with the first staging at Weimar. The performance acts as a conduit of these relations in time and space whereas its authenticity is jeopardised by cinematic reproduction. Here it could be said that Benjamin recognises the particular qualities of the theatre as distinct from other art forms, its original and 'auratic' quality. Though this serves my purposes it is precisely this challenge to 'authenticity' that breaks the ambivalence of Benjamin's essay. The processes that Benjamin is describing, the technical reproducibility of Art, will he believes lead to 'a tremendous shattering of tradition'. And it is this 'tradition' that has given rise to the politics that provide the context of the writing, and Benjamin has already in the preface to the essay established his opposition to that regime. This break, Benjamin believes, will be linked to the contemporary mass movements whose inspiration will come from the film: 'Their most powerful agent is the film. Its social significance . . . is inconceivable without its destructive, cathartic aspect, that is the liquidation of the traditional value of the cultural heritage.'[7] Such an optimism was evidently driven by the work of Abel Gance, Eisenstein and the revolutionary role of film in Russia where Benjamin had spent time in the 1920s.[8] Benjamin sought not only to trace the decline of the 'aura' historically, but also subjectively through the contemporary transformations in human sense perception. The aura of art is here equated with the aura of nature, and in this respect Benjamin ascertains that the urge of the masses is to bring things 'closer', spatially and humanly, and in doing so deconstruct the 'distance' on which aura depends. This 'distance' underlies the 'uniqueness' of reality, and the overcoming of one will lead to an overcoming of the other through reproduction. In this transformation the masses, whose sense of the universal equality of things has developed to the point where it can be extracted from the unique object via reproduction, will 'destroy an aura', in Benjamin's memorable phrase, like prying an object from a shell.

The concept of 'distance' was central to this essay and was a recurring motif in Benjamin's other writings. Aura was defined as 'a unique phenomenon of a distance however close it may be',[9] and distance was equated with unapproachability and the status of a cult object. This distance was increased, Benjamin believed, in the rearguard action of the doctrine of *l'art pour l'art* which countered the development of the means of technical reproduction such as photography. This 'theology of art' would be met by a removal of art from dependence on ritual, and its movement into the domain of politics. Thus Benjamin refers back to the idea of technical reproduction bringing the art object closer to the beholder, meeting the beholder halfway. The concept of distance is one which is central to a spatial and cultural analysis. It lies, discreet but powerful, behind notions of accessibility and the manner in which all representational forms work. To look at something closely is to imply a thorough analysis, to take a step back is to get an overview of the infinite positions in between. If spatial practices are experienced, perceived and imagined, distance could be said to speak of flows and conurbations, the quantification of space through map-making and the mental operations associated with near and far such as attraction and repulsion. These are the mental manifestations of being human in a spatial world and it is these associations that impinge on the language of aesthetic responses.

In another text written in 1936, 'The storyteller', Benjamin spoke of the work of Nikolai Leskov and the disappearing tradition of the storytelling art.[10] Benjamin believed the best way to view this phenomenon was from a distance, the storyteller already being something remote, and something getting more distant. Viewed in this way 'perspective' would reveal that the art of storytelling was coming to an end, and by this Benjamin means the 'ability to exchange experiences'. Storytelling is seen here as a fundamental part of subjectivity. There could not be a greater contrast with the faith in the technical means of reproduction than this poignant celebration of the role of the individual experience in *communitas*, the simplicity of dialogue. And it is this seeming contradiction, 'the celebration of the aura that he has dismantled with his other hand', that reinforces the dialectical nature of Benjamin's world view.[11] This is a complex genealogy influenced by contrasting intellectual movements and religious/philosophical contexts. Dialectic is inscribed, for Benjamin, in the art of storytelling itself. The figure of the storyteller derives its corporeality from two urges or dispositions, the one who has travelled and returns with stories from afar, the other who has stayed at home speaking of the local and the particular: 'If one wants to picture these two groups through their archaic representatives,' Benjamin says, ' . . . one is embodied in the resident tiller of the soil, and the other in the trading seaman.'[12] The complex overlapping of these traditions is what gives rise to the historical breadth of the storyteller.

The demise of storytelling is equated for Benjamin with the proliferation of information which has gained precedence over intelligence. Benjamin touches on the inevitable outcome of the 'age of mechanical reproduction' when he identifies the control of the means of this proliferation, the press, being in the hands of the middle class, providing that class with its most important instruments in developed capitalism. The qualities that Benjamin ascribes to the story, and celebrates over information, are again strangely at odds with the loss of the aura, the destruction of the aura ascribed to the masses in 'The work of art in the age of mechanical reproduction'. Benjamin distinguishes between 'information' and the 'story' in terms that are reminiscent of criticisms of the contemporary press: 'The value of information does not survive the moment in which it was new. It lives only at that moment; it has to surrender to it completely and explain itself to it without losing any time. A story is different. It does not expend itself. It preserves and concentrates its strength and is capable of releasing it even after a long time.'[13] There is more than a hint of the aura of the work of art about the true art of the storyteller, and this is an art whose disappearance he is unwilling finally to accept.

Distance, reduced to 'proximity', returns to the analysis when Benjamin differentiates the storyteller from the novel reader, the one in close contact with the hearer of the story, the latter devouring the text in isolation. Thus an act of companionship is replaced by one in the novel of 'the hope of warming his shivering life with a death he reads about'.[14] The storyteller is a craftsman, far from the means of mechanical reproduction, his coordination of eye and hand in gesture is that of the artisan, fashioning the raw material of experience 'in a solid, useful and unique way'.[15] The narrative container which the story provides is decorated by the storyteller, whose craft is the intersection of a practice and a theory – the intuition and doxa of the storyteller is precisely a 'know how', a primary knowledge which has close links with the fable. In Kantian terms the storyteller is in receipt of a tact, an ability to judge the momentary and changing relations between a creation and its ethical purpose. The complexity of Benjamin's dialectic, the problematic relations between the claims of progress through technical revolution, and the utopian strain of thought that underwrites other elements of his work, owes more to the Romantic tradition than to historical materialism. The enforcement of this political perspective by the conditions in which he wrote provoked the tension between these two strains of thought.[16]

With this dialectic in mind, we can see that Benjamin noted how works of art were beginning to be designed for their reproducibility, the logical consequence of their changing status, and how the increased role of the exhibition of the work of art gained precedence over its previous function as a cult object. The 'being in view' of the art object, through exhibition, superseded the importance of the work of art to exist as an instrument of magic. Benjamin qualified his analysis of the loss of the cult value of the work of art, pointing out that this value retreats into the portraiture of photography, the cult of remembrance of the human countenance. This qualification could have been equally relevant to film and theatre with the cult of the individual, the face, in film, the star, in theatre, growing to disabling proportions through the Hollywood and Broadway system.

The disappearance of 'The Storyteller' is, for a book espousing a lay theatre, the precondition for the recognition of 'storytellers'. Yet this disappearance precisely threatens the existence of a social space where stories are heard. Space, I have shown, is more than an empty vessel in which the everyday takes its place. The disappearance of the storyteller leaves a space in which rumour can flourish. The narration of the practices of the everyday are held within decorated containers called stories but these containers are themselves socially and culturally constructed. Theatre is one important means through which these containers are expanded within everyday life. Stories are for Michel de Certeau a form of knowledge that is 'not known', a space between practice and theory where forms of intuition come into play, a rented form of knowledge, not owned, academically controlled or institutionally enclosed. Storytelling is a practical act like that of the equilibrists of the Victorian stage, where balance is contingent on all things being equal, never quite complete, and where judgement is the mediating skill derived from experience. Where theatre fails in judgement it looks like the tightrope walker from the same show, but now with a ventriloquist's dummy clinging to its back – a famous and top-heavy act literally taking theatre into the realm of the never-never land.

It is apparent that discourse of all kinds, scientific and poetic, is composed of stories, that sciences, like the acts of dwelling, eating and walking, are in a social sense brought into being by the narratives that are told of them. I have already indicated the formative part that metaphor and imagery played in the conceptual advances of science and Bachelard's examination of the scientists' stories of the sub-space of micro-physics. If that reflects a boundary between culture and nature at the frontier of science then there are tales from the other end of the spectrum where myth and nature meet. The Pintubi elder in Australia who told Gary Snyder stories in the bed of a pick-up truck had to recount his tales with great rapidity. The story of the mountain there, the wallabies here, the hill in the distance were all tales to be told while walking, and Snyder was hearing their accelerated, motorised recitation. But these maps and dreams of wilderness elsewhere whether micro-physical or not, are well known as models of 'another life' and more modest work is yet to be done. It remains to locate the urban texts where narration is the condition for the operations of everyday life, here and now.

The story does not express, describe or illustrate a practice, it makes movement and practice possible in the first place. To move into a place there is the need for a story about it. This goes for the most adventurous voyages into space, oceans and the earth as it does for the most mundane trips to the bathroom in an unknown house. The difference between the house for the estate agent or realtor and the dweller is that one maps and the other tours, not 'the bathroom is to the left of the hallway', but 'you go along the hallway and the bathroom is on your left'. Michel de Certeau distinguishes between these maps and tours and indicates a history of human excision from space. From the earliest itinerary maps of pilgrimage, such as those of Matthew Paris where the story of the individual founded the places visited *en route* to a shrine, to the abstract space of the contemporary map divorced from the stories that found and founded the places indicated, there is a disturbing and increasing propensity to trust not so much those who undertake the journey as those who make the maps. In a long address to his reader the Mediterranean chart-maker Francesco Beccari gives an unusual insight into how dependent on the everyday seafarer was the compilation of knowledge in the fifteenth century:

> It was several times reported to me . . . by many owners, skippers and sailors proficient in the navigational art, that the island of Sardinia which is in the Sea, was not placed on the charts in the proper place by the above mentioned masters. Therefore, in Christ's name, having listened to the aforesaid persons, I placed the said island in the present chart in its proper place where it ought to be.[17]

The distinction between sailors and masters is an important one for a theatre that seeks the everyday. For in that world it is pedestrians, not surveyors, who form the majority, whose own bodies in their multifarious and unsurveyable movements literally write an urban text that they themselves will rarely read. Only when the lift is taken up the Eiffel Tower or the Empire State Building does this chaotic pattern take on any wider meaning, and this is dependent on removal from its texture. From the bar overlooking Grand Central Station in Manhattan the rail lines out of the city are criss-crossed by the entrances and exits of those coming and going with different stories to tell. Here the concept city of the sociologists and modernists breaks down into a proliferation of discreet identities going about their business and making do. In the concourse of the station there is a single immobile figure whose stationary gesture is unique in this labile terminal. Like any story told on the hoof he sees a chance to insert himself in an otherwise seamless text of activity, he is on the ground of the 'other' but contrary to Michel Foucault he is not just watched, he watches at the base of the panopticon for the main chance. He has a sharp eye for the

166

detail that will reverse bad luck to good fortune – in this case a discarded copy of the *New York Times*, picked up, the inclement weather report declaimed to the bemused passengers, and ceremonially fashioned into a rain hat. The urban system was invented to obviate these stories and improvisations but it has done nothing of the sort – and a theatre of the homeless 'inspecting London, Amsterdam or Los Angeles', is only the most opportunistic manifestation of the importance of narrative to the diverting quality of these streets. None of this occurs outside the discipline of the system, the urban frame in this case, but thrives within it under constant duress and pressure of the extinction of stories from the fabric by rumour. Theatre exists to deny such rumours by introducing stories to places they have departed: 'stories differ from rumours in that the latter are always injunctions, initiators and results of a levelling of space, creators of common movements that reinforce an order by adding an activity of making people believe things to that of making people do things. Stories diversify, rumours totalise.'[18] The marvellous problem for theatre is that pedestrians are all too familiar with making stories their own – theatre looks parochial and local compared with the spatialising of walks. Theatre might reinsert itself where the yellow pages have substituted fingertips for feet and travelling distances has become the essential concomitant to walking nowhere the rest of the time. It is only at a distance, it would appear, that legends are available to replace what the locality lacks. Walking behind someone who has just picked up their holiday snaps speaks through giggles and exclamations of this private lore from elsewhere reintroduced to the locality by way of photographic reproduction. The barely concealable boredom of others in these images, like the recitation of someone else's dream, points to how inadequate mechanical reproduction as a means of imaginative communication can be. Theatre preserves us from its platitudes.

Point line plane

Are there ways of tracking these walks without becoming a master map-maker? The artist and theorist Paul Klee in both his *Pedagogical Sketchbook* and *On Modern Art*, presents us with a theory of the image which has resonance not only for the visual arts but also for the relations between theatre and the mental production of space through geometry.[19] If phenomenology was resistant to the idea of considering the complementary nature of images it is this complementary nature, the part–whole relation in composition which is of primary interest for Klee. Walter Benjamin emphasises this aspect of Klee's work, evident equally in his practice and theory, which recommends it to a study which begins from the association of these two activities. A geography of theatre would enhance this part–whole relation as it would allow the differential temporal development of theatre to be deepened by an understanding of the differential spatial dimension of where it takes place. Such 'places' would not be disconnected but, like images in Klee's composition theory, be given precise meaning through their connection. The question of the part–whole relation is of course the crux of dialectical philosophy and however surreptitiously provides the matrix for aesthetic enquiry in the theatre.

My interest in Klee's work is not in the theatre connections of the Bauhaus but in the conceptual frameworks he provided for a theory of imagery through his writings. It is characteristic that as in the Expressionism of Franz Kafka, a form where the logic of disintegration is pursued to its rational conclusions around the primacy of the human or human in animal form, the figure for Klee is never lost in the move towards abstraction. It is this enduring place for the human, on the edge of abstraction, that is of interest. For it would perhaps be possible to ascribe to this relation the moment when, and interface where, space becomes place in the creation of the image. Where space is made up of mobile elements, place is for Michel de Certeau the 'order in accord with which elements are distributed in relationships of coexistence'. And this order is in the end a human affair. In this sense place speaks of stability and space of velocities and variables. In contrast to Malevitch and Kandinsky, contemporaries of Klee, who took the form beyond the human bearings in abstract composition, Klee retains the seeing eye within the work. It is this dialectic of the rational and the non-rational that is provided by his practice, of the part in its relation to the whole in flux. Klee's language in the *Pedagogical Sketchbook* and *On Modern Art* takes us to the elemental nature of this project – the need to find straightforward ways of talking about complex things: 'there is bound to be some common ground between layman and artist where a mutual approach is possible and whence the artist no longer appears as a being totally apart.'[20] Thus what is sought is not correspondence between the arts but between art and layman.

The remainder that threatens theatre and everyday life equally inflects on art. Klee believed: 'For the artist communication with nature remains the most essential condition.'[21] Laconic statements threaded through each of the four sections of the *Sketchbook* provide us with ways of thinking and seeing the relations between abstract form and nature in contemporary performance and show that the question of space, place and theatre is not one which rests solely in the important but limited domain of known material worlds.

In the first section Klee summarises his position by describing 'vertical structure' as the 'repetitive accumulation of like units'. Klee here distils the central tenet of a history of performance to come, whose apotheosis might have been the gesturing themes and variations of Pina Bausch's dancers in *1980*. 'Purely repetitive and therefore structural,'[22] could be said to characterise systems music and elements of the classical tradition of Bach, which influenced any number of performances from countless groups endlessly replayed in the succession of avant-gardes predicated on circularity and refrain. But it is Pina Bausch's choreographic forms that carry the intensity of repetition to deeper levels and enduring influence, the whole of each of her works being greater and deeper in emotion than the parts they are so apparently built from. It looked at first sight like a miniature hand jive, or a disturbing psychotic tic, a constant brushing away of imaginary dust or a signal of distress. The performances of Tanztheater Wuppertal in Europe and North America in the 1980s are still being felt for their influence as they have been in their specific locality since the inception of this most local and simultaneously international company by Bausch. They have been the source of derivation and creative influence and widely influential they remain. Theirs is a theatre of dance imagery which is geographically distinct and internationally recognisable. Indeed Wuppertal, while being close to the industrial heartland of the Ruhr, is characterised by its combination of the rural and the industrial, a combination which is clearly evident in Bausch's work. Without labouring geographical determinism it is important to make the local connection between performance and place given the cosmopolitan hopes placed upon it by the international cultural industry: the turf covered place of *1980*, or the petals of *Blaubart*, the leaves of *Kontakthof* speak of local landscape as much as an amorphous nature.

In this work Bausch seemed, in her own words, less concerned with how people move as with what moves them. Here is a self-reflexive dance which tells a history of the body, a montage of the everyday social experiences of bodies which demands the audience's questioning of its own everyday experience. The whole apparatus of theatrical technique is placed into question as the dancers run to the lip of the stage threatening to topple into the auditorium, or simply appear to serve tea in the aisles to unsettled spectators. Bausch brings the outside inside, in the case of *1980*, with real turf which permeates the auditorium with a characteristic odour, with a stuffed deer, childhood games and social rituals combining to form an archaeology of the everyday. That Bausch also reflects and reaccentuates a German modernism – the work of Kurt Jooss is one influence on her work – is to perpetuate the geographical setting of this debate in and around the texts of Benjamin, Kafka and Klee.

The second part of the *Sketchbook* on 'Dimension and balance', analyses the humanism of the activity of seeing line, from a perspective. Here for Klee lies the possibility of 'non-symmetrical balance'.[23] Moholy-Nagy points out that there is a supersession here of the old idea of symmetry as 'the bilateral conformity of two parts', by the 'equalization of unequal but equivalent parts'.[24] The subject, through the medium of the eye, governs the movement of the object into height, width, depth and time, that is the 'dimension' of the object. When Theodor Adorno speaks of the debate between the polarities of the avant-garde and the popular as 'two halves of an integral freedom, to which however they do not add up', there is a sense of the possibility, necessity, of a 'non-symmetrical' balance.[25] But this balance, this dimension, will be governed by the individual eye and will appear differently to each perspective. What is popular for one will be avant-garde for another. Equilibrium and harmony might come to the individual but the question remains how such a view can be 'complementary' to other views.

The third section of the *Sketchbook* moves us from observation to intuition, the limitation of gravitational pull on humans' ability to project themselves into space. When Klee speaks of 'regions with different laws and new symbols', where there may be freer movement, the metaphysical dimension of his work cannot be ignored. There is a 'spiritual dynamism' within which the simplest of directions appears: 'To stand despite all possibilities to fall.'[26] Where choreography becomes named and institutionalised it suffers the same fate as other theatre forms. One such movement, New Dance, whose dicta seemed to be for a decade to fall despite all possibilities to stand, demonstrated this consistency principle to its own ultimate disadvantage. The work of Bausch on the contrary foregrounds for us the tension between the inevitability of gravity and the urge to escape its power. Where contact improvisation mediated between these energies, proposing a movement mechanics where the flow is followed not resisted, the work of contemporary groups increasingly explores the problematics of tension and stress, conflict and disjuncture. Here the idyllic alternatives of the passive space of New Dance gives way, not uncritically, to the contemporary urgencies to explore forms that reflect the heterogeneous places performance has arrived at.[27] The tensions of ballet are transformed and superseded not by the same tensions but by new and inclusive ones of that history. Thus the image of a ballet dancer repeating for an hour a *pas de seul* in Jan Fabre's *The Power of Theatrical Madness*, is resolved as an image, not in tearful acquiescence, but in the power of the dancer lifting a prostrate male body from the back of the stage. Criticism of the image described, of the cruelty of the ballet dancer's exercise, are misplaced if projected as they were at the director, rather than the tradition under examination through the image. It remains to assess whether the connections between issues of sexuality and New Dance which sought to foreground formal concerns, often at the expense of content, will have any more lasting effect as a movement than that image of the ballet dancer repeating her routine *ad infinitum*.

The single, isolated 'dot' that begins Paul Klee's *Sketchbook*, through activity becomes a line, and through the medial line becomes both ' point progression' and 'planar effect'. It is this planar effect that provides the abstract conceptualisation of the geography of theatre. The individual through the motion of theatre joins other individuals and forms, in the medial relationship of joining the circuit of audience and performer, a community within, a planar effect of common interest. By its passage through the *Sketchbook* these elements of composition 'transformed by the counter forces of earth and world, of mechanical law and imaginative vision' find an equilibrium, a rest within 'unified diversity'.[28] And here we gain a sense of the complementarity spoken of above. The total effect of this conception Klee calls '*Resonanzverhältnis*', meaning: 'a reverberation of the finite in the infinite, of outer perception and inner vista'.[29] It is this reverberation, like the reverberation of the forest that I spoke of earlier, or the image of the stream of golden sand, that creates the possibility of the image that Klee pursues in *On Modern Art*. Klee resists the binary form of the image of the tree, the determinist balance of cause and effect, that is such a problematic to aesthetics. Where Pierre Macherey speaks of relations of refraction rather than reflection between literature and societal forces, moving beyond the vulgar Marxist base–superstructure model of analysis, so Klee seeks to establish the complexity and possibility of a non-symmetrical balance: 'Nobody would affirm that the tree grows its crown in the image of its root. Between above and below can be no mirrored reflection. It is obvious that different functions expanding in different elements must produce vital divergencies.'[30] Theatre is a process of vital divergence from everyday life: it does not simply reflect the everyday but as with the simplest pedestrian dance diversifies its habitual patterns and opens its place of occurrence to the imagination.

The very project of attempting to conceive of this 'whole', which is formulated from parts belonging to different dimensions, is jeopardised for Klee by the deficiencies of the spoken word: 'For with such a medium of expression, we lack the means of discussing in its constituent parts, an image which possesses simultaneously a number of dimensions.'[31] In this 'lack' is focused the dilemma of a study seeking a 'language' of theatre. Kafka himself reiterated this when his disillusionment with language as a means of conceptual communication led him to make the analogy of words to 'bad mountaineers' and 'bad miners' of the soul.[32] Even so music is characterised by Klee as polyphony, as are the simultaneous dimensions of 'drama'. The *Pedagogical Sketchbook* provides us with a way of both looking at the nature of images in composition and a technology for advancing the thought of theatre beyond 'simultaneity'. Klee's 'visions' and 'illustrations' evoke what is literally 'virtual' about imagery – that which is 'beyond' language, not religious but metaphysical, and to be understood, materially, beyond its immediate physical appearance. Here we are working towards a concrete abstraction, the material and the mental, the energy of the symbolic arrow, that takes us beyond the arc of the 'actual arrow': 'a bit farther than customary – father than possible!'[33] Nothing that has a start, in Klee's world the dot, can have infinity, and we are constantly reminded of the limits to the activity, a time and place to rest, the continuing restraints of the limits of nature on theatre.

Nature theatre Oklahoma

Franz Kafka's fiction concentrates a number of the themes which have arisen in this chapter, and his name has woven through it.[34] For Benjamin: 'Kafka touches the ground . . . the core of the folk tradition, the German as well as the Jewish.'[35] In two texts written either side of the 'Work of art in the age of mechanical reproduction', in 1934 and 1938, Benjamin wrote at length about Kafka. Kafka is the quintessential 'storyteller' for Benjamin, the descendant of Leskov: 'In the stories which Kafka left us, narrative art regains the significance it had in the mouth of Scheherazade: to postpone the future.'[36] In the first of these texts, 'Franz Kafka', Benjamin quotes at length the opening of the final chapter of Kafka's unfinished novel *Amerika*. Karl Rossman the picaresque anti-hero of the novel, has finally, from the arrival in a new country and the loss of his friend the stoker in the hold of a ship, discovered an opportunity in life. The placard he sees before him says that all are welcome in The Theatre of Oklahoma. There is employment for everyone, a place for everyone, and this to Karl, whose every action so far has been ignored, is too good a chance to miss. This opening of one of Kafka's favourite chapters, 'The Nature Theatre of Oklahoma', a passage which he liked to read aloud, is a fictional evocation of a theatre of everyday life.

The Theatre of Oklahoma is recruiting at Clayton, a racetrack, presenting a dilemma for Walter Benjamin: 'This racetrack is at the same time a theater, and this poses a puzzle. The mysterious place and the entirely unmysterious, transparent figure of Karl Rossman are congruous, however. For Karl Rossman is transparent, pure, without character . . .'.[37] When Karl arrives at the racetrack he finds his way to an abundantly laid table, where for those not taking part in the conversation there are views being passed around of the Theatre of Oklahoma. The one which Karl gets to see is of the president's box in the Theatre, and it is so grand that it might be mistaken for the Theatre itself. And Benjamin, as though taking up these views himself, suggests we see Kafka's stories as 'acts in the Nature Theatre of Oklahoma'. Here Benjamin connects his analysis of the gestural qualities of the fictional work, which hark back to the gestic qualities of the Chinese Theatre, with the appropriate context for such physical writing: 'Kafka's entire work constitutes a code of gestures which surely had no symbolic meaning for the author from the outset; rather the author tried to derive such a meaning from them in ever changing contexts and experimental groupings. The theater is the logical place for such groupings . . .'.[38]

Benjamin's analysis of Kafka locates the theatricality of his fiction, influenced by the Yiddish theatre and the gestural qualities of his work which 'dissolve happenings into their gestic components'.[39] It is reminiscent of the analyses Artaud brings to bear on the theatre in *The Theatre and its Double*.[40] Indeed Benjamin's summary of Kafka's vision makes the connection explicit, combining as it does the implacable necessity of everyday life coupled with the dismissal of the criteria of 'dramatic talent':

> Kafka's world is a world theater. For him man is on the stage from the very beginning. The proof of the pudding is the fact that everyone is accepted by the Nature Theater of Oklahoma. What the standards for admission are cannot be determined. Dramatic talent, the most obvious criterion, seems to be of no importance. But this can be expressed in another way: all that is expected of the applicants is the ability to play themselves.[41]

To be present to the Theatre of Oklahoma is at once to recognise the gestic quality of life and yet to continue living that life. Karl Rossman gains membership of the group, and begins to see the expanses of America, its space, for the first time. It is a 'care free' journey which to that point in his life he has never known, and we are left in Kafka's unfinished manuscript, on a train, far away from the hold of the boat where we began with Karl, rushing through this new land. It is a land which Kafka imagined from the travel books and memoirs which he loved to read, for he had never travelled further than France and Italy.[42] But his travel is not unlike that of Walter Abish's 'Germany', an imagined landscape in which the transparent Karl acts as a glass for seeing the contours and humour of our own solitary lives, our isolation in *communitas*. The dialectic that Benjamin sees at work in Kafka's fiction is that of the individual in the crowd, the part–whole relation that gives the image its qualities: 'Kafka lives in a *complementary* world. (In this he is closely related to Klee, whose work in painting is just as essentially *solitary* as Kafka's work is in literature).'[43]

But what of this fictional place where our stories of the everyday have ended up? It would appear, if Benjamin's sketch of the isolation of the novel reader is accepted, to be as far away from the practical actions of theatre as a cultural spectrum could include. The novel is not only the zoo of the everyday, its stories if read aloud, as Kafka was wont to do, are a way of operating, a form of narration which is founding of fictional space and opens the theatre for practical actions. Stories are not limited to describing actions, movements and practices but make these operations possible in theatre forms. The community is clearly both imagined and material, it has symbolic determinants as well as concrete spatial dimensions and these reverberate through the stories people tell. These narrations are not solely for the purpose of aesthetic edification but occur for political reasons which escape notice if the determinants of space, both visible and covert, are not assessed. In his short story 'The English garden' the American novelist Walter Abish asks the question 'How German is it?', and in so doing reminds us how important it is that these questions of space and its history be asked. In that story, and in the novel that followed extending its themes, Abish asks from America, no more having seen Germany than Kafka saw America, what we imagine the German-ness of Germany to be. To this point the symbolic nature of identity is apparent. The problem is to determine the lifelikeness of everything one encounters in another culture with another name. For Abish it is a question of language and philosophy, the ways in which we familiarise places and the past in which traditions persist, and to this point there is accord with much that has been said in this chapter. But the pervasive historical image of this story is a concentration camp onto which a new town has been built. It is here, quoting John Ashbery, that: 'Remnants of the old atrocity subsist, but they are converted into ingenious shifts in scenery, a sort of 'English Garden' effect, to give the required air of naturalness, pathos and hope.'[44] The town which Abish describes, trying to forget its past, its image and its historic reality, covers these traces with language, yet is undone and exposed by language, by the arrival of a character in search of a past; a character who in the first person narrative tells a story of the writer in search of the atrocity of an age. The English Garden effect is an anti-ethic, a will to obstruct the eye of history. The storyteller here is driven by the need to expose the monumental denial not just of place but of race, a denial that follows other genocides and the reinvention of these acts through spurious histories.

John Berger, the novelist and art critic, might well have been responding to Abish's writing when he summarised many points already raised in this chapter, the dialectic between technological process and the narrative art, the relations between power and space and the ethical importance of acting within an understanding of these parameters:

It is scarcely any longer possible to tell a straight story sequentially unfolding in time. And this is because we are too aware of what is continually traversing the story-line laterally. That is to say, instead of being aware of a point as an infinitely small part of a straight line, we are aware of it as an infinitely small part of an infinite number of lines, as the center of a star of lines. Such awareness is the result of our consistently having to take into account the simul-taneity and extension of events and possibilities. There are many reasons why this should be so: the range of modern means of com-munication: the scale of modern power: the degree of personal politi-cal responsibility that must be accepted for events all over the world: the fact that the world has become indivisible: the unevenness of economic development within that world: the scale of the exploita-tion. All these play a part. Prophesy now involves a geographical rather than historical projection; it is space, not time that hides consequences from us. To prophesy today it is only necessary to know men as they are throughout the whole world in all their inequality. Any contemporary narrative which ignores the urgency of this dimension is incomplete and acquires the oversimplified character of a fable.[45]

As with Walter Benjamin's 'archaic' representatives of the storyteller, the one who travels the other who stays at home, Berger describes the importance of an understanding of human spatiality, the deep relations between geography and the history which tells us what occurred there. As Edward Soja says: 'Synchronic spatiality continually intrudes upon the diachronic, the "simultaneity and extension of events and possibilities" overlays the historical narrative.'[46] What is at issue between geography and geometric abstraction is the question of power, the need for stories rather than fables to reveal these power relations and to exile rumour. These stories derive from everyday life, but take important and distinct form in cultural practices which border theatre and define theatre's domain. These include novels and film, but also criticism and art theory where maps of the everyday are to be derived. For de Certeau: 'What the map cuts up, the story cuts across.'[47] Criticism and narratives are part of an indivisible whole which question official views of reality. But despite the innumerable tactics, ruses and delinquencies that form this system every power works by a process of naming and initiates order through that nomenclature. An official view of reality is often barely discernible from the words that resist that power. This is an important reminder, for the places of performance are like other social spaces governed by an economy controlled from elsewhere. This is an economy which is both symbolic (as we have seen) but also overtly material and practical in its associations with money. Location, place and the economics of spatiality are important reminders that theatre does not occur in a never-never land, and never will.

Like Walter Benjamin's characterisation of the 'Collector', theatre criticism begins from an accumulation of objects, lists and inventories. In this chapter, the aura of the theatre has been placed alongside the image theory of Klee and the fiction of Kafka, to ascertain whether a complementary criticism can approach a complementary form such as theatre with any more subtlety than single disciplines of analysis can marshall. Postmodern theory has already undertaken this role in the name of radical eclecticism but to accept its choices is to accept its positions uncritically. Returning to its predecessor texts does not protect the analytic process, for in turn the texts of modernism were, as I have said, in part a response to realist perspectives. Further we are in this activity reminded that postmodernism is an involutionary, rather than evolutionary process. It is already inscribed in the texts which immediately 'precede' it. Yet it reminds us of the complex and often contradictory relations between texts from the same period, and the necessity for a rigorous and continuing examination of their resonance for theatre. Attempting to couple this analysis with an elucidation of theatre imagery may appear to be an ambitious conjunction, but it is a project which Benjamin was himself concerned to define: 'explication of iconography not only proves indispensable for the study of reception and mass art; above all it guards against excesses to which any formalism soon beckons'.[48] It is against such a formalism that the preceding analysis wishes to assert itself in the name of theatre.

5

ACCRETION
Earth and depth

The theatre speaks continually of the 'world', but what can the earth tell us about the theatre? It is the place it occurs, and its ecological deterioration has become in recent times theatre's concern and contents. There is of course an ethical dimension to this state of the world, the traditional relationship between morals and societal behaviour now being extended to include relations with nature and the earth itself. This ethical expansion brings with it considerable problems for politics, reviving as it does romantic notions of conservation and traditionalism, of rural retreaters and utopian perspectives. Nature is a system of which the human is a part, an element one might say. Stability of this system and its complementary nature takes on deeper relevance than these concepts provoked earlier for here they are literally a cause of life and death. Care for nature implies, and is tantamount to, care for the human, as it is the value of nature for the human as a necessary condition for harmonious life that is at stake. It is impossible to avoid the anthropocentric in these issues, which makes them particularly relevant to a species-specific form like theatre. Unlike the splitting of imagination and production traced through Humphrey Jennings' *Pandaemonium*, there is now a growing perception that there should be neither a predatory nor a passive approach to nature, but a balance of extraction and transformation that protects both human and natural interests. Here is a ground where aims and practical actions are inevitably and continually at odds. It is clear from its inadequacies that science cannot be left to negotiate this responsibility, but the network of conflicting interests that would make up public discussion are disconcerting.

These are not responsibilities which theatre has wholly ignored and they are ones which should, if the ethical purposes of theatre are accepted, be central to theatre's place in the world. This is not an argument for a 'theatre of ecology'. It is important to emphasise that these arguments are not gender specific and to avoid facile relations being drawn between a rational, cultural 'maleness' and an emotional, natural 'femaleness'. The historic hierarchies which these presumptions and polarities imply, the

177

valuing of the rational over the emotional, the mind over the body, never mind the male over the female, are too obvious and deleterious to spend time on. This is not to say that certain features of both might not be fought for by one or other sex at different times. It is clear that currently the associations of sexual role are fragmenting and it is these contingent, culturally changeable circumstances applied to men and women within nature and society that demand constant reformulation. I do not therefore endorse here a vague eco-theatre unhinged from pressing material concerns but suspect there is room for closer analyses of the way the deep structures of everyday life, literally its geology, inflect on theatre processes.

Theatre accumulates expressive powers through a process of accretion. In this it metaphorically shares something with the earth itself. Images, theatres, and the identity of people within places share regard for such gradual and critical accumulation of meaning. Events are taken seriously when they incorporate this historic plenitude – a gardener knows not just about their own garden but about others, a jazz drummer about other drummers and their instruments, and football supporters about a complex inventory of personal histories and grounds. These 'popular' manifestations of historical lineage become problematic for all that is new in the arts, threatening each avant-garde with the taint of precedent and perspective. But simply ignoring these perspectives is to minimise the deeper meanings that theatre already holds for neighbourhoods irrespective of what is presented as the 'new' and the 'innovative'. The empty space assists in the artificial concealment of 'what went before' in the same place. This is not an appeal for the traditional over the new, for the new is nothing but the transgression of a boundary set by tradition's most recent workings. Accretion is not another term for the postmodern taste for eclecticism, though this bricolage often leaches for cultural capital on the power that accretion already holds within neighbourhoods. It is not inevitable, commercial, or professionally or institutionally bound, but on the contrary originates in and derives its accumulative power from, the lay remainder to these separated domains. A generation of artists, performers, composers and choreographers whose intent was to strip down this accretion, is coming to an end. John Cage and Merce Cunningham were the centre of a welcome movement to return performance and composition to their elemental parts – not the 'meaning' of movement but the movement itself, as you or I might be seen to move. This anti-accretion was necessary to remove otherwise sclerotic forms from their fossilised state, to challenge the classical traditions of ballet and the split between the upper and lower halves of the body. This return to the forms of the everyday was conducted outside the everyday realm, like other avant-gardes before it, in a heightened state of separation from everyday realities. The elemental was clearly most interesting to those whose lives were already cluttered with a profusion of *objets d'art*. But for all the gains of this period of minimalism the human need to accumulate has reasserted itself and it is perhaps time to mine this 'richer' field of complexity. Cultural accumulation and accretion must be seen as the obverse of a cultural capital, named and institutionally stored, driving the flagships of national cultural entities. It does not deny the existence of this economy but neither does it consider it the only market place for theatre to work within.

Articulation

The cultural as well as the natural understanding of the earth provides the ground on which subtle analyses of theatre can take their place. For mixing the themes alluded to above, the earthly and the human, or geology and biology, the earth can be perceived as an immense body without organs, a vessel of flows and compressions, junctures and releases forming and reforming a stratification, the earth's strata made of layers and belts. Geology shows these layers to be in the form of pairs, one serving as the substratum to another. Each stratum faces both out and in and is doubly articulated: in geological terms the first process of articulation is sedimentation, the second articulation is folding. This put simply is the structural basis for sediment to become sedimentary rock. The interest of philosophers such as Gilles Deleuze and Félix Guattari in these processes is not because they bolster a creaking structuralist system, but because they establish a more complex position from which to question the simplicities of analysis based on binary opposition. With a view to redefining these conventions of analysis they make an equation between the first articulation and 'content' and the second articulation and 'expression'.[1] They do not speak of the old binary pair of aesthetic analysis, 'form' and 'content', wishing rather to emphasise the possibility that expression has as much substance as content and content as much form as expression. This is helpful when thinking about the composition of images and a language to speak about them. It would appear from what Paul Klee has said about images that it is often the language of aesthetics which has hindered discussion and understanding of art. Despite the obscurity of certain post-structuralist critics there is a helpful reorientation here of otherwise habitual terms within which theatre has been thought. There is a double articulation, like strata themselves, between content and expression: both look into each other in that they are relative terms, and out to referential objects. A formless substance is after all unthinkable, the relations between the two are always shifting but present, like the sand that forms the golden cloud in Faraday's observation of the balloon. Each articulation is double because the relations between contents and expression are continually negotiated: 'What varies from one stratum to another is the nature of this real distinction and the nature and respective positions of the terms distinguished.'[2]

179

To think of these strata as inviolate would be inadequate, both metaphorically and literally, given the regularity in nature with which they are
shaken by phenomena of cracking and rupture. To see Mount St Helen's
one day and to see it differently the next is the least subtle reminder of
what the earth has in store. The relation between theatre and these
phenomena is not the installation, theme park or education centre built at
the base of natural 'disaster', telling us what to look at by showing it to
us in dramatised, videoed or photographed form, but the perspectives that
are placed around theatre where the threat of nature to the everyday
reasserts itself. The obverse of the order of the strata is of course these
fissures and ruptures, and it is in these strata that bacteria and germs as
well as insects thrive. These surrogate, delinquent forms are the natural
microcosm of the pedestrian in the stratum of the urban plateau, who in
common parlance is described as having disappeared down the cracks.

It is not so much a question of whether there are signs at all strata of
the work but whether signs are endowed with significance. Here structuralism breaks down, unable pliantly enough to follow the undulating economy of theatre, the relations between word, gesture and thing. The
expression of content is reducible not to a single thing but to a complex
state of things, a plane where consistency prevails for just long enough to
make itself known to the observer. A double articulation is required to
bring these elements together, in Deleuze and Guattari's terms, not signi-
fier or signified, not base and superstructure, but stratified. The theatre is
just such a stratification, the image is a plane of consistency where all
manner of incommensurable phenomena abound and clash: people, par-
ticles, furniture, disease and love. This is not a meaningless chaos as we
know and can demonstrate, but it constructs continuities of differing
intensities. The image could be said to create continuity for intensities that
conjoin and separate from distinct forms and substances. The seemingly
random process has a logic which is worth taking beyond the theoretical
positions explored earlier.

The following analysis could be conducted with a myriad images from
the contemporary theatre, from more and more work at the end of a
century when imagery combining gesture and speech have in welcome
ways been rediscovered. Not all of this work is 'new' work, whatever that
term might mean, it is international in origin, and has come from theatres
where words and actions have not been so persistently divided by literary
traditions. My choice of image might serve to concentrate the geological
theme of this chapter, but to this image others could be added which
would be no less resonant. What I have chosen is linked to a single image
in the spirit that Roland Barthes speaks of the 'third meaning' of images.
That is not primarily the image's informational or symbolic qualities,
although they inform the analysis, but its 'significance', its 'erratic' and
'obstinate' dimension.[3] In short: *a line of men, shovelling coal, into a row*

of furnaces. The bare description, as with all images, cannot begin to convey the experience of witness. A German production of an American play in the National Theatre of Great Britain is immediately to establish certain parameters to this discussion of theatre in Britain. This is the opposite of an unwritten theatre, yet despite its wide exposure, its capacity for images remains concealed behind biographies of producers which take little account of users. The visit of Peter Stein's Schaubühne company from Berlin, with *The Hairy Ape*, was one event in a series of international theatre productions which occurred at the National Theatre in 1986–7. The response was considerable, with long queues marking each night of the performance – and this was a production in which scene changes took almost as long as the scenes being played and the language spoken was alien to most of the audience.

The International Season in which this event occurred was one in a number of large-scale festivals bringing 'International Theatre' to London, Edinburgh, Glasgow, Cardiff and Dublin. When Gramsci speaks of Esperanto being a 'cosmopolitan' language, not one related to the 'stable productive citizen', I wonder to what extent such festivals have promoted an Esperanto of the image, a touring, placeless, image-orientated theatre without reliance on the specifics of a language beyond that of gesture, coherent for theatre-going audiences around the world. This would be theatre's anti-geography, and could, though often compromised, be used to radical effect. Whether it be the 'Olympic Arts Festival' (an unlikely alliance between physical dictatorship and liberation), or the Sant Archangelo Street Festival, the locality of the event is superseded by the internationalism of its participants. I would suggest that it is precisely through the power of the image, and a basis from which to judge the value of the image, that the specifics of time and place are revealed anew for each audience in each place and according to their own preoccupations. This is not an Esperanto but the equivalent of an intense dialect which by its very specificity speaks on a wider level than its own important but parochial community. Presumptions about appropriate forms and expressions are to be resisted if the coincidental and idiosyncratic aspects of the following examples are taken seriously. Although each that follows has a certain relation to something German, the question 'How German is it?' is a perplexing one. Here geographical materialism is reacquainted with the symbolic dimension of the construction of communities. Good theatre often arises from the process of accretion within a specific place and the revealing of that accumulated identity in other places where quite other meanings might be read off, and pleasures gained from, it.

Eugene O'Neill's play of 1923, *The Hairy Ape*, is considered a classic of Expressionism and it is no coincidence that Peter Stein should wish to produce such a play, whose very corporeality coupled with a *Realpolitik* distils so many of his aspirations for the theatre. Stein's work at the

Schaubühne is known directly or by reputation throughout the theatre-going world and has become a measure, a standard against which European 'Directors' Theatre' is assessed.[4] Stein is clearly placed within a tradition of theatre direction inaugurated by Max Reinhardt and is seminal to the recent history of a German theatre. Equally his theatre is influenced by the existence of a dramaturgical tradition since Gotthold Lessing wrote his *Hamburgische Dramaturgie* which provides a historical context to Stein's long partnership with dramaturge Dieter Sturm, and an intense collaboration with the concerns of design, as characterised by his relationship with Lucio Fanti who designed *The Hairy Ape*. The triumvirate dramaturgy/design/direction is central to what I understand by the theatre of Peter Stein and they have been the essential ingredients of a radical tradition of provincial, proscenium-arched theatres throughout Germany in the last three decades. That the Schaubühne am Lehniner Platz, a converted art deco garage from the 1930s, should differ so markedly as a space from this tradition is simply notice of the peculiar relations between Stein, and the authorities of West Berlin for whom Stein's theatre became an unlikely ambassador before reunification.[5]

It is then, from this tradition, a tradition specific to a place and its own historic continuities, that the stokers at the beginning of scene three are presented to the audience. Eugene O'Neill's stage directions give a sense of the Expressionist milieu from which the play derives, and the material elements which will contribute to the image as perceived by the audience. The original stage directions of O'Neill remain a literary device to project a possibility through time. They are in themselves an unusual example of the stage direction as 'poetic image', a literary image in their own right, but one which can only provoke our expectations from the distance of a reading room or the back door of the theatre waiting for a return ticket:

> SCENE. The stokehole. In the rear, the dimly outlined bulks of the furnaces and boilers. High overhead one hanging electric bulb sheds just enough light through the murky air laden with coal-dust to pile up masses of shadows everywhere. A line of men, stripped to the waist, is before the furnace doors. They bend over, looking neither to right nor left, handling their shovels as if they were part of their bodies, with a strange, awkward, swinging rhythm. They use the shovels to throw open the furnace doors. Then from these fiery round holes in the back a flood of terrific light and heat pours full upon the men who are outlined in silhouette in the crouching, inhuman attitudes of chained gorillas. The men shovel with a rhythmic motion, swinging as on a pivot from the coal which lies in heaps on the floor behind to hurl it into the flaming mouths before them. There is a tumult of noise – the brazen clang of the furnace doors as they are flung open or slammed shut, the grating, teeth-gritting

grind of steel against steel, of crunching coal. This clash of sounds stuns one's ears with its rending dissonance. But there is order in it, rhythm, a mechanical, regulated recurrence, a tempo. And rising above all, making the air hum with the quiver of liberated energy, the roar of leaping flames in the furnaces, the monotonous throbbing beat of the engines.[6]

The scene, and the core image that follows of the stokers and the coal, is framed by the preceding scene which takes place on a sun-drenched deck and, immediately following the stokers, the arrival of Mildred in the stokehole. While this dialectic of light and shade is the expressionistic dynamic of the play, the juxtaposition of conflicting atmospheres giving rise to a politics which rapidly moves on and out to new concerns, my interest here remains in the everyday, pervasive image of the stokers and the coal. It is in the particularity of that image that the dialectic of the text of performance and its context, as distinct from the literary text, begins to operate. It is a provocative gap and one into which this observer is able to pour a plenitude of half-remembered scenes, words, memories and feelings. It is indicative that this is one fleeting moment of many, and salient to remember how few such experiences are often accumulated or expected in much that is thought to be most radical, innovative and physical in theatre today. For me the strength of the image is its ability to refer me back to childhood and then its power to oscillate from that historical perception to the present day. Quite how this riot of psychological, historical and geographical resonances can be contained by a systematic reading of imagery is difficult to perceive, particularly where the language of that method is unable to deal with incommensurable objects. So what follows is not systematic or sophisticated but perhaps it gives some sense of the relations between an accretion of experience and a theatre deriving its force from the combination of incommensurable things. It is not a 'history of the image', for that as Bachelard shows would be a foolhardy endeavour, but neither is it an acceptance that a sudden salience within the imagination is displaced from historical and political perceptions.

An audience in Britain witnesses this scene with a certain historic and emotional interest. Not only does the image occur in the immediate context of a boat, with a certain resonance for an island nation, but in a subterranean world where there is no sunlight. The only light is that of the furnace and the few watts from a single bulb. And the coal, as the directions imply and Stein demands, is being dug in front of that audience, in real time as well as in theatre time, the effort taking the spectators into the relations between the body and the mineral that has provided a country with an industrial past and marks the twilight of a declining future. Here distinctions between performance art and theatre are practically dissolved as boundaries are superseded by the overall presence of the image between

183

audience and performer. This dialectic, between the human and the earth, the stoker and coal, one of extraction, is the essence of technology. The ability to extract energy from nature is here mediated by the stoker, the middle man, with little control over either end of his labour. The inter-relation of the human and the physical alters the natural order but also makes society as we now know it. It is a labour which drives something else, in this case a 'drunken boat', the pleasure cruiser. On deck, literally high above in Fanti's design, we have heard the elegant Mildred and her Aunt speak of this effort. Mildred says: 'How the black smoke swirls back against the sky! Is it not beautiful?' and her aunt replies: 'I dislike smoke of any kind . . .'.

As the boat steams on, the reality remains that what produced this metaphysical trace is the heart of a country – the coal that has in more ways than any other substance characterised the industrial growth of Britain and its subsequent decline. The trace is temporal and spatial. The image takes me as spectator back through time while simultaneously fan-ning out in space, to places from where the coal comes. There would be few material elements which could achieve such an effect – and these would of course differ in different cultures. That is why this book proposes that theatre resides in culturally specific forms. This is not an argument against the kinds of biological continuities that Timpanaro contests shape our material lives, but it is to have reservations about drawing from that a theory of psychological archetypes or universal images of coherence. A material analysis of the conditions necessary for a 'metaphysics' of theatre, the 'something more' which is spoken of with regard to the effects of the image, is built upon a genealogy of the erratic and obstinate dimensions of the image while retaining the need for an analysis of its spatial impli-cations. This procedure has little of the totalising imperative of a semiotic approach nor does it claim to say everything about what the image con-veys. It merely throws a strong and partial light on the way that one image quite literally works across a stratification of intensities generating lateral thoughts of identity and pleasure. It also importantly connects that image to others, that theatre to others and therefore could be said to be a complementary criticism.

First, why does coal have historical meaning? The division of nature into unrelated parts, for instance the distinction between earth that bears coal and other 'products' such as tin or potatoes and their commercial separation for the purposes of production, consolidates the split in humanity between those who see themselves as producers or consumers. Each product is also seen to carry political and spiritual meaning for cultures and provides a constellation around which issues of identity clus-ter. It is clear from Matthew Arnold's writing of 1869 that it is this substance, coal, that is said to have given character and value to the nation. Arnold has to contest this misapprehension in the name of 'higher' ideals:

Everyone must have observed the strange language current during the late discussions as to the possible failure of our supplies of coal. Our coal, thousands of people were saying, is the real basis of our national greatness; if our coal runs short, there is an end of the greatness of England.[7]

In contrast Arnold believes greatness is a spiritual condition that excites 'love, interest and admiration'. He looks back to the spiritual strength of the Elizabethan period when there was little development of the coal industries, and comfortingly reminds us that culture will see to it that the delusions of placing value on coal and iron will be superseded by standards of 'perfection that are real!'[8] But coal and its mining has persisted to the contemporary time as a material which generates profound mental associations and allegiances within British society, and these are ignored at the cost of understanding how communities work and their relation to wider identities of nationality and class. It was after all the tax on coal brought from the fields of the north-east to the docks of the south-east that paid for the rebuilding of London after the great fire, and the construction of many of the buildings with which London's power as a capital is identified.

The corporeal nature of the miner, the bio-mechanics of his labour, is not a theatrical gesture but a pressing and pervasive historical reality. Again it is a quality that is deeply embedded in English letters as much as in its worldly and oppressed manifestation. D.H. Lawrence in 'Nottingham and the mining country' written in the year of the great strike of 1926, speaks of the 'intimate community' underground:

the pit did not mechanize men . . . they knew each other practically naked and with curious close intimacy . . . and the continual presence of danger made the physical, instinctive, and intuitional contact between men very highly developed, a contact almost as close as touch, very real and very powerful . . . When the men came up into the light, they blinked. They had, in measure, to change their flow. Nevertheless they brought with them above ground the curious dark intimacy of the mine, the naked sort of contact, and if I think of my childhood, it is as if there was always a lustrous sort of inner darkness, like the gloss of coal, in which we moved and had our real being.[9]

A purpose of that effort, and the loss and injury that Lawrence goes on to speak of as the inevitable corollary to the companionship, was to drive a factory system that had begun to produce and reproduce on the back of this elemental extraction. It was this process that made mechanical reproduction possible in the factory system so celebrated by Andrew Ure in his essay, 'The blessings of the factory system', from his *Philosophy of Manufactures* of 1835:

> Steam engines . . . create a vast demand for fuel; and while they lend their powerful arms to drain the pits and raise the coals, they call into employment multitudes of miners, engineers, shipbuilders and sailors, and cause the construction of canals and railways: and while they enable these rich fields of industry to be cultivated to the utmost, they leave thousands of fine arable fields free for the pro-duction of food to man, which must have been otherwise allotted to the food of horses.[10]

The question of coal for Britain is not, despite the literary references one might draw upon, an aesthetic one.[11] That allegory would have too many similarities with Walter Benjamin's characterisation of Fascism's means of aestheticising politics. But its enduring meaning for a nation is borne out by the imagery and the mythical and material qualities of the fight for survival of those dependent on it. The 1984–5 miners' strike, a year in length, is generally seen as the key battle of the British Conservative Government against the trade union movement in the modern period. The way in which the action prompted a wide field of performance in support of its aims, from cabaret to country-wide touring productions by some of the country's most established groups, is indicative of new versions of traditional alliances between the arts, the wives of the miners raising feminist and gender issues alongside those of the industrial workforce. This alliance dispelled, for anyone involved, presumptions about appropriate aesthetic forms for specific causes, which were central to the 1930s debates in European criticism. It was further given an ironic edge by Joseph Beuys' request to meet Arthur Scargill, the Union of Mineworkers' president. Beuys at the time was in London for the preparation of 'Plight', an installation of felt, piano, blackboard and thermometer at the Anthony D'Offay Gallery. Interviewed by curators of the exhibition, Scargill spoke of the sculpture, which had given rise to intense hermeneutic speculation, as evocative for anyone who had been in the unique atmosphere of a mine.[12] His engagement with the work is simply another, and well informed, critical voice. It does not speak for 'the people' any more than a critic in *Art Forum* speaks for the people. Yet what is clear from his perceptions of Beuys' installation is the degree to which the everyday world of work, politics and power is informative of a critical speculation of the most abstract as well as the most overtly social forms of work. That this interpretation was seen by millions on nationwide television compounds the gap between the tabloid-generated perception of a union leader and his apparently sincere critical optimism on experiencing the work of a mentor of the avant-garde.

The installation was dominated by rolls of felt, a recurring material in

Beuys' work. Beuys had wanted to exclude all natural light, which prompts Scargill to begin to make associations between the conditions in the mine and in this gallery. He is inquisitive to know what Beuys might have been working towards with the placing of a grand piano to one side of the installation, and conjectures it is a means of conveying sound which remains an unfulfilled potential. These are the first of a number of what Scargill describes as contradictions in the work, the third element of which is the blackboard, a surface designed to allow a message to be conveyed in silence. The fourth element, the thermometer, is not only as the curator begins to suggest a measure of room temperature, but for Scargill: 'It's much more, it's a gauge I think of his analysis of what is taking place in any given set of circumstances, and also a gauge of what is likely to take place.' The interpretation allows for the abstraction of the installation but there is, in the isolation and desolation that Scargill sees in the work, an indication that 'something can happen and will happen' as a consequence of all the influences that provoked Beuys to put the structure into effect. In a reflection on his own background and interest in art Scargill provides a genealogy common to many, from art as museumed, to art as representation and depiction, to art as owned, to the abstractions of art to be interpreted:

> When I was about seventeen years of age I went to Paris and the Louvre and spent six or seven hours just wandering around looking at the great paintings . . . I love art and I've got a number of paintings myself, not necessarily by internationally famed artists, although one picture is by a very well known artist and it depicts, as you might have guessed, a coal mine, but I also like scenes which depict the Yorkshire countryside. I like scenes of desolation, of isolation, those artists who transpose onto canvas, or put into sculpture, the scenes which project aloneness, in my view anyway convey a sympathy I can associate with. Immediately you come into a room like this you see the effect it has. It makes you almost want to be reverent in your approach.[13]

But the question is asked of Scargill: who is likely to 'get into this room', it is after all a gallery, and what would be the response to this work of those involved in the miners' strike whose latent artistic abilities emerged during those events? Scargill believes two reactions are possible. The majority he believes would say: 'Well isn't this a load of carpet rolls, is that really what it is?' and the other reaction would be 'There's a sense of trying to convey something from the artist'. For Scargill it returns to the potential that the strike brought out in multifarious ways, that there is an artist in everyone, which society represses. This potential will directly affect the way an individual comes to an installation of this kind: 'I think once you are able to tap it, however minutely, the reaction you get to an

exhibition would be different to the one you would have had without it.'
Participation and a sense of context are, Scargill believes, in art as in other
matters, inherent in further freedoms of expression and pleasure. This
pleasure will not only come from the socially relevant it will come from
the abstract which gains its social purchase from the ability the artist has
to take into account 'the feelings of other people'.

The image of the stokers and the coal in Peter Stein's production opens
up the space for poetic and political combinations of this kind to be
thought and experienced. The work deftly incorporates the most social
and abstract issues simultaneously. Between the aspirations for theatre of
John McGrath and 7:84, and the modernism of Joseph Beuys and Scargill's
interpretation of 'Plight' a tract opens up where appropriate contents and
expressions are destabilised. The isolation and desolation of Beuys' work
is not a 'good night out' in the strictest sense, but in Scargill's interpretation is not to be ignored for that. It challenges those with any experience
of the inside of the world, as well as its surface features, to think and
feel more deeply about those experiences. This is the relation between
performance and politics being sought in this book. Not only did Beuys
foreground issues of ecology and politics in his public persona, his work
speaks at all times of the curious relations between the human's ability to
extract from the earth with labour and the material reality of the by-
products of that labour.

But how, given the earlier reservations about the identity and location
of 'the people', is anyone to know what 'the people' want? For John
McGrath and 7:84 a place to start was a conference on what kind of
country people wanted, the expressions of what people throughout Scot-
land wanted to say. From this conference derived questions which gave
rise to another performance of the extraction industry, in this case the oil
industry, a significant production of the 'popular' British Theatre and a
production given further prominence on television: The Cheviot, the Stag
and the Black Black Oil. This performance, in the form of a ceilidh, again
places the relations between the nation as people and the country as
geology at the centre of its enquiry. The influence of capitalism on the
Highlands, the clearances and the suppression of local languages were all
set within a ceilidh, a form which brought a temporal and geographic
aspect to bear on the event. The form was resistant to the traditions of
lament and celebrated the reassertion of localities as central to culture. As
John McGrath says, the form and content are inseparable:

> the role of the Ceilidh in the nineteenth century was very much a
> double one – of reinforcing the Gaelic culture ... and of a political
> getting-together. The Ceilidh became a way of people getting
> together about what was going on ... if you do it for an audience of
> people who have worked in industry, who are working in industry,

then the contact is real, and the dynamics of the play work through the relationship between the meaning and the audience.[14]

Ian Jack, the political columnist, has a phrase for this period of British history that has a reminiscent ring to it: 'Before the oil ran out'. For while the finite extraction of the oil industry gives parameters to the activity as a 'boom', before an inevitable 'disappearance', it is the very claims of 'infinitude' made in defence of coal that adds to its poignancy as an image of waste. For it is not only wasteful of lives in colliery disasters and pneumoconiosis, it is not only destructive to the tradition of 'landscape', but it is also wasting of the imagination. For its deep, pervasive and enduring presence is at odds with the finitude of the communities built on its existence. The two time spans seem curiously at odds. Coal's enduring potential outlives those within its geographical circumference whose lives are lived on it and ended by it. The long-term emancipatory aims of Marxism and the shorter-term hopes and fears of its subjects are here confused and contradictory.

This tension perhaps lies behind the resilience of the communities who resisted suggestions, during the mining strike of 1984–5, that relocation would provide work for those displaced by local closure. Claims were rightly made for the generational continuity of mining communities, as opposed to the abstract imperative of a 'better life' that capital and enterprise would offer 'elsewhere'. Michael Rustin has made a close analysis of such claims of time and place in socialist theory and it would be advantageous to address these issues. For with the intention of establishing a 'geography of theatre' it is necessary to establish the claims of place within a 'spatial praxis', and to understand the conceptual underpinnings of such a dynamic for the theatre. This conceptual framework has for many years provided the rationale for theatre work by companies and centres once vaguely described in Britain as 'community arts' groups.[15] Yet it is clear within that plural title that the diversity of work is enormous, that the claims of particularity and place are often taken for granted, and that the links with imagery such as that produced by Joseph Beuys or Peter Stein are not often enough thought in the same space, the kinds of experience that a Peter Stein production might bring, a Beuys installation suggest, being thought to be of a different order to 'community' work on some *a priori* grounds. I would contest there are important connections between the theatre imagery of all these areas of work, and that the value judgements to be made are not ones along sectarian lines: 'community arts' versus the 'mainstream', but on the basis of the radical and therefore artistic potential of each distinct circumstance in which theatre imagery arises. Arthur Scargill walking through and talking to a Joseph Beuys installation here connects with *The Cheviot, the Stag and the Black Black*

Oil as common coordinates of theatre and its aspiration to reach the everyday in order to know what it is to transform the everyday.

Michael Rustin outlines the dilemma in which any study of this kind is situated with regard to the wider political movements it wishes to address:

> the difficulty for [contemporary socialists] ... has been that their core ideal, equality, has become too thin and minimal an idea to anchor an alternative vision of society. Its main referent in experience is a fast-fading memory of working class communality, born of hardship and territorial segregation. Unfortunately, these communities, and the industrial working class which they supported, have been to a considerable extent dispersed and dissolved, by the positive opportunities provided for mobility, as well as more recently by the demoralization of redundancy and industrial collapse. The miners' strike of 1984–5 showed the limits (as well as the remaining strengths) of this declining spirit of rooted class solidarity and endurance.[16]

Here is a more specific description of what so far has been described as the flux and discontinuity of postmodernism and it is a description which bears as much on the environment of the river and its docks as on the mineral and the mine. Michael Rustin notes the way that this process was already well advanced by the Second World War. Further, the period from which I have drawn texts for analysis, the 1930s, is seen by Rustin as the real beginnings of decline for the British industrial fabric. The analysis of the 'damaged object of the nation' leads Rustin to two conclusions as to why there should be a lack of contemporary resonance in the concept of 'equality'. First, the limitation of abstract universalism, the isolated individual subject being accepted as the basis of an alternative social philosophy. And secondly, the 'denial of the particular location of human beings in space and time ... has led to this abstracted individualism'.[17] The background to this abstract universalism lies in the Enlightenment, and was perpetuated by Marx in an effort to overcome the oppressively feudal nature of local ties and commitments. There has been a corrective to this universalism in contemporary Western Marxism, perhaps starting with Gramsci and leading to Raymond Williams' work and E.P. Thompson's *The Making of the English Working Class*.[18] It is not as Rustin points out that Marxism denied the essential limits of life in time and place, but that it ignored them for other pressing concerns in the passage to a higher life for all. Louis Althusser's concepts of differential development in time and space, and Merleau-Ponty's concern for the consequences of a historical transformation that ignored the present lives of its subjects, are further parameters which could be set to the abstract universalism diagnosed as constraining of equality.

The political implications of an unthinking acceptance of the postmodern dissolution of the 'social' in favour of a 'silent majority', the specificity of communities, and the symbolic importance of the expression of their allegiance is laid down by Rustin:

> It is partly the role of place as itself a locus of meaning, through physical care, conscious expression, shared memories, and the elaboration of such meanings in many forms which makes belonging to a common place a significant marker of social identity. The idea that it need not and should not be, in the modern world – that attachment to place has been made obsolete by ease of communication – doesn't seem a very promising one, from a social point of view.[19]

Theatre is one form for 'the elaboration of such meanings', and it is intimately linked with the temporal and spatial questions which Rustin seeks to foreground. Concerned as it is with bodies in place - becoming – space, the question of 'social imaginaries' can through theatre be advanced in critical and accessible ways. The mistake for a practice which seeks accessibility is to predict the potential resonance of the image with a plurality of responses in a culturally diverse audience. There can be no prediction of this kind: it would be impossible to conceive of the chance encounters that I am ascribing to O'Neill's/Stein's image of the coal in the ship's hold. It is however likely that the corporeality of the image allows for the imaginative potential it generates, for the people shovelling coal are both unique and drilled, individual and collective, men, but also importantly social ciphers. In the case of that image it is important to address the question of the subjectivities, and characters who through action bring that image into being.

The coal that takes us into this analysis of the contemporary relations between theatre and politics is being worked in the image by the stoker. The stoker for O'Neill, in the character of Yank, is a Parsifal figure, a naive but powerful force attempting to understand the oppressions that beset him through the course of the play. As a stoker, Yank shares more than a passing resemblance to another central figure of Expressionist literature, the stoker of the first chapters of Kafka's *Amerika*.[20] That Kafka was originally to call his novel 'The Stoker', after a chapter of that name published long before the rest of the novel, indicates the importance of that role to the unfinished novel. Its opening chapter, the meeting between Karl and the Stoker, the ship berthed in New York, the enclosed world of the ship and the New World visible to Karl through the windows, the grievance of the Stoker and the inarticulacy of his efforts to gain justice, all speak in a literary way, with virtual images of the material scene below decks in Peter Stein's production. The seeing of that production and the reading of Kafka's last novel, though apparently segregated by the mental and the material, I would speculate, are more acquainted as activities than the reading of *The Hairy Ape* is to the production of the play of that name. And that is because the text of *The Hairy Ape* is but a blueprint for the trace of its production. Detailed as O'Neill's stage directions are, they are in the end a writing waiting for the palimpsest of production. This is why the thoughts and feelings theatre generates often resonate with other writings – there are elements of the genre of a Kafka novel which are more to do with the 'essence' of theatre, as described earlier, than the play-text alone, in isolated reading, can possibly aspire to. This is less saying theatre is literary than that Kafka's novel opens a space for theatre in the sense that narratives have already been described as founding of space.[21] Stein's production, utilising as it does the technologies and means of the mainstream theatre but to radical ends, is in itself a minority expression within a majority culture and in this sense it shares a paradigmatic relationship to Kafka's work. Working from West Berlin for many years before reunification, Stein's theatre was one which though speaking German was in both its geographical and aesthetic location a minority radical voice speaking with all the spectacular conventions of imagery that the majority theatre could muster.

Kafka's work has been described as a 'minor literature' in a more specific sense than this general use of the term. There is a case to be made for deepening the idea of a lay theatre with an understanding of its minority status. For avoiding facile descriptions of the 'fringe' or 'margin', spatial descriptions which have little flexibility or objective reference, nor wishing to speak of the 'popular' or the 'people', the status of minor is central to these theatres and their effects. In Deleuze and Guattari's analysis of Kafka, with which this chapter started, they emphasise that a minor literature does not come from a minor language, but rather is something which a minority constructs within a major language. In the case of Kafka, a Prague German – a minority writing of Prague Jews, is a writing that subverts the major language that surrounds it through 'strange and minor uses'. Space is central to minor literature as it is an expression which deterritorialises, its 'cramped space forces each individual intrigue to connect immediately to politics' and it is always made collective by the lack of master voices. Here minor status becomes not so much a 'thing' as a 'condition' within the space of established forms. It is a patois within a dominant culture which forces people to travel to speak. The theatre language that is subverted by groups discussed here is one which demands conformity to a certain long established lexicon of representation and architecture, acting styles and speech. This major language is appropriated to tell other stories, lines of flight from the dominant language and culture that any good theatre reproduces within a social space called entertainment.

Theatre is only ever accessible at the 'place where it happens to be', and understanding its aura is therefore central to its theory. That is why any search for it requires a geography, as well as a history, maps as well as archives. Franz Kafka, Paul Klee, Walter Benjamin, Deleuze and Guattari, provide us with those maps, onto which the dramatic text of Eugene O'Neill, the movements of the theatre of Peter Stein and Pina Bausch, John McGrath and Joseph Beuys can be traced within a single social space. The latter part of this chapter has been concerned with reflecting this heterogeneity of the theatre while not accepting that this plural state of performance be unsurveyable or reducible to illusory theoretical constructs. Each of these documented practices forms part of a wider unwritten whole, and relates to other theatres that still seek 'the people', and are destined to search. For as Kafka reminds us, the Nature Theatre of Oklahoma is everywhere to be found, and nowhere to be confined by description.

6

INSPIRATION
Air and breath

Speech and bodies exist and operate in space but only in places take on the meanings associated with being human. They therefore cannot be divorced from the preceding analysis. Brecht's Mother Courage and Charlie Chaplin's tramp are thwarted by, but continue to live within, the everyday. There is an international difference between languages, a national distinction between dialects, and a political separation between vernacular speech and the mandarin tongue. The body is in different ways geographically rooted, and as phenomenology has shown, spatially orientated. The word 'orientation' itself derives from the historic preoccupation with the East as a primary means of ordering space and is therefore permeated with human and cultural dynamics. The body is not only situated in the world but, through labour, forms habitual patterns which root the body to the locality in which it works. In the urban milieu these residues of previous work patterns are concealed by the needs of capital – for the worker to adapt or face unemployment. Those who worked in the docks demonstrated, when they were involved in the lay theatre, a movement memory, a vocabulary of physical expression which derived from the regime of the quayside. The lightermen who in impossible acrobatic manoeuvres navigated the river with their cargoes demonstrated an equilibrist's skill of improvisation and continual adjustment to circumstance. While theatre research and performance anthropology continue to seek out exotica, imported for the purposes of scrutiny, this other 'tact' is ignored. There is no room for a nostalgic return to the dangerous and oppressive labouring patterns that are gradually superseded, but there is an imperative to transform them through theatre. There is the need for an ethics of the body and speech which traces this relationship between saying and doing in the everyday. For without this association the theatre remains in the world of make-believe.

To have written about where theatre occurs before discussing who it is who produces it is a reminder that theatre is a minority act entering the space of another, or inviting the majority, the audience, to itself. The speech and body of theatre therefore cannot simply refer to the voice and movement of the performer but to the physical relationship between the performer and audience through whom theatre occurs. The sounds of performance are not the words of the speaker and the silence of the spoken to. It is appropriate that between thoughts on geography and history there should be a breathing space where a seminal work on theatre and the everyday is given special thought.

Any discussion of speech and the body, theatre and everyday life, occurs in the shadow of Antonin Artaud. The texts which make up *The Theatre and its Double* remain central to a poetics of theatre in the everyday realm, irrespective of the widespread influence of the 'Theatre of Cruelty' as a concept.[1] Often quoted in general, but less often in particular, these texts have become historically inseparable from a twentieth-century theatre resisting forms of representation which remove it from the real it seeks. Yet their influence on the relations between everyday life and theatre has been schematic, perpetuated in general terms, without the kind of close scrutiny on a continuing basis that might be expected, given the longevity of their provocation. Indeed one could identify many of the analyses of theatre that Artaud advocates in the current practice of theatre, while recognising the specific, intense and wholly segregated influence his work has had on Peter Brook or Jerzy Grotowski.[2] The problem with these texts is the difficulty of reading them as anything but an aberration. Replaced within the context of other writers of the period, including Humphrey Jennings in England and Gaston Bachelard in France, there is perhaps cause to reconsider the work as part of a minority writing scrutinising performance and the everyday. Further his work, as we shall see, opens up perspectives on a theatre history that remains to be told, of the undersides of the theatre, that remind us of its everyday origins.

There is an incessant tension between reason and madness, rationality and irrationality at the heart of theatre.[3] The work of Artaud attests to this, and his work has proved elusive to comprehension beyond the limits of its own theory. There is often the apologia that Artaud's theatre practices, as reflected in *The Cenci*, his single textually recorded dramatic work, hardly maintained his theoretical ambitions.[4] But as we have seen with the Surrealist enterprise, as it was with Baudelaire's 'theatre',[5] there is a sense in which it has been Artaud's life, rather than *The Theatre and Its Double*, which presents us with the significant text to be examined for the theatre. It is in itself an extended performance. But it is a life which must first refer us back to those texts which continue to be separated from the lay theatre, considered avant-garde and esoteric, marginalised beyond the everyday realm. The arts of theory with which Artaud was engaged are ones which have proved remarkably influential within Continental philosophy in the twentieth century and in that domain alone are responsible for a fundamental reappraisal of structures of representation which lie at the heart of any theatre analysis. In this sense the arts of the theory of theatre as proposed by Artaud could be said to have infiltrated all fields from the literary to the anthropological – it really has, for the philosopher if no one else, been the age of Artaud. Given the expectation that the interpretive flow might be in the other direction, from the social sciences and their conceptual languages to the theatre, this is a salient reminder. It is one which bears out Clifford Geertz's concern about the widespread and wholly uncritical use of the theatre as a metaphor in the social sciences.

The partition of this work from any kind of useful context is connected to the notoriety of its language. On closer inspection *The Theatre and its Double* yields itself on a number of levels simultaneously while never sacrificing a surface lucidity and poetic possibility. The depth to which these texts can be mined is demonstrated by Jacques Derrida's influential essays of the 1960s in *Writing and Difference*: 'The Theatre of Cruelty' and 'La parole soufflée'.[6] It is on that site that the confrontation between Artaud's theatrology meets post-structuralist philosophy head on. It would be wise to approach that meeting with some circumspection, through Artaud's texts first, to establish the grounds of what is at issue in his consideration of theatre and everyday life.

The theatre and its double

Artaud's work is unusual in its attempt to ascertain a metaphysics of theatre. The nature of images and their qualities is central to this metaphysics. If, as Artaud says, the theatre was never made to describe 'Man and what he does', if its very purpose was to 'break the structure of belonging, the peaceful and impassive immobility of fundamental structures', it is evident that Artaud is speaking, through his writing, and life, of a total revolution. This is a revolution that no existing theatrical form could accommodate, but which is aspired to through the idealised image of an Oriental theatre. Artaud is seeking nothing less than to eliminate the Greek site, the Classical origin, from which the theatre traditions of the West are traced, and the Greek language that permeates our ways of speaking about that theatre, constantly reinforcing its terms. What is at stake in taking issue with this Greek origin, this unitary influence, goes beyond contesting the theatre as we know it derives from the fifth-century BC Athenian *polis*. This challenge to historical linearity is already widespread in histories of the theatre, particularly those of the theatre anthropology school, which value the influence of 'ritual' forms of performance, the 'Ur Drama' that not unproblematically can be identified in Balinese rituals and is still present today in Balinese society. It rather accepts that the influence of Classical Greek life, of Greek forms of thought, of the development of philosophy and the language of philosophy, have determined forms in very specific ways bound to that age. It then seeks to deconstruct these consequences beginning with perhaps the most obvious example, Aristotle's *Poetics*, by determining its influence in the neo-classical period, and its continuing influence today. A 'non-Aristotelian' theatre is a return to this binary opposition and one which simply reinforces the origin which Artaud sought to dispel.

Why am I here concerned with a contemporary reading of Artaud, by a French philosopher, rather than my own? Texts from the 1930s such as Artaud's have maintained significant influence in the contemporary period through the mediation of what is described as post-structuralist, or post-modern theory. It is that mediation which is of interest for the intellectual environment it has created for a contemporary theatre practice. The need from a theatre perspective is to identify the relations between the texts of high modernism and their post-structuralist critique rather than to ignore the specific way such mediations have taken place. It is no more possible to read Artaud innocently of a complex of influences which range from Surrealism to postmodernism, than it is critical to return Artaud to the everyday moorings from which his work arose. The headlong rush to the harbour of intellectual security that 'isms' provide is rocked by figures such as Artaud who would recognise the mystifications of the everyday in postmodernism as he did in Surrealism.

Theatre must engage critically with these philosophical voices of the time or consign itself to a margin of the discourse that it otherwise wishes to influence. What is more, through consideration of Derrida's interpretation of Artaud, it is possible to gain a certain insight into the working of images in the theatre event which move the theorisations of Jennings and Bachelard forward and into the theatre field. Here there is a conjunction between the 'phenomenology' of the image described in the third chapter and the influences of Surrealism. Indeed the coincidence of dates adds simultaneity to the discussion – the texts of *The Theatre and its Double* were completed and named in 1936,[7] Humphrey Jennings' collaboration with André Breton on the International Surrealist Exhibition occurred in that year in London, Walter Benjamin's two essays considered earlier being completed at either end of 1936 and Gaston Bachelard's major work on the philosophy of the scientific mind was also completed at that time. This correlation suggests another moment in which a modernist theatre might locate its roots as distinct from the social innovations of two decades later. Replacing one watershed with another is not the point, but the complex European dynamic represented by this work is surely as engaging for a contemporary theatre as a small group of English writers.

The central problem for Artaud was how theatre in the West had left everything specifically theatrical, that is *not* words, in the background. This theatre was dominated by dialogue, and Artaud made the distinction raised earlier between drama as a subsection of literary history and the distinctive stage language of the theatre: 'the stage is a tangible, physical place that needs to be filled and it ought to be allowed to speak its own concrete language'.[8] Such a language is only theatrical in so far as the thoughts it expresses escape spoken language. Thus it is an ideal form of expression and, in that sense for Artaud, metaphysical. But here, faced with entering into further thought as to what this metaphysics would entail, Artaud returns to the material, the language that distinguishes theatre from word. Artaud is aware that without further explication the language on which the metaphysics rests will be unthought and inexplicable to the theatre he wants to address. This stage language could be composed of all that was materially expressed on stage, all that which responds to and informs the sensual rather than the mind. While initially working to satisfy the senses this language might be intensified, amplified to 'its full mental effect on all levels and along all lines'. Here Artaud adds: 'It would also permit spatial poetry to take the place of language poetry and to be resolved in the exact field of what does not properly apply to words.'[9] Spatial analysis, in Artaud's terms, the mental equivalent of the physical geography I talked about earlier, moves away from the poetic and the linguistic as verbal language and shifts us into the enquiry opened up by Jennings and Bachelard whose interest was in a spatial poetics as distinct from a literary poetics. Artaud seeks here an equivalent of 'word imagery', a 'substantial imagery' carrying forward the notion of the material and the mental and reminding us of the oscillation between the metaphysical and the material that he wished to establish through the stage. The 'stage' that Artaud often referred to was a 'physical temptation', and the expressive means of the stage were to assume 'an ironic poetry' from their juxtaposition with other means. The result was in different places described as a 'combination', an 'interaction' and a 'mutual subversion', all of which contribute to our thinking of the construction of theatre images. The image in this language is not seen as a progressive coalescence of mutually dependent elements but as interaction of a molecular kind, in a state of constant replacement and redefinition.[10]

The associations with physics go further when Artaud describes the play being built on a stage, in a state of constant transformation, encountering 'production and performance obstacles'. This reflects the working process of the scientist described by Bachelard, the constant approach to the obstacles which create the breaking effect of science. For Artaud the imagination was 'under torture', but not as Bachelard would have described from reason being imposed on the irrational to produce the scientific mind, but from the workings of the material towards the metaphysical. For Artaud the obstacles demanded 'the discovery of active language, both active and anarchic, where the usual limits of feelings and words are transcended'.[11] These concerns were not purely aesthetic for Artaud, any more than they were for Jennings or Bachelard. Each writer shares an ethical concern, and Artaud states his quarrel with the dereliction

198

of the purely psychological and character-based theatre when he says: 'rarely does the debate rise to a social level or do we question our social or ethical system'.[12]

In his essay 'Oriental and Western theatre', Artaud went on to insist that there should be a break with 'topicality', that the ethical sense of theatre would not come from 'solving social or psychological conflicts . . . but to bring out in active gestures those elements of truth hidden under forms in their encounter with becoming'.[13] Against this quietude the theatre of the time was characterised as materialistic and destined to miss its 'intended purpose which is higher and even more mysterious'.[14] There is, on approaching this essay, a question as to the extent to which Artaud was influenced by, inscribed within, what Edward Said has termed 'Orientalism', and certainly his equation of Oriental and Balinese theatre as exemplifying such a mysterious spirit compounds the issue. For as Grotowski makes clear in *Towards a Poor Theatre*, Artaud's analysis was often a misreading of cultural difference: 'Artaud's secret, above all, is to have made particularly fruitful mistakes and misunderstandings. His description of Balinese theatre, however suggestive it may be for the imagination, is really one big misreading.'[15] Artaud reiterated that it was through the language of physical and poetic effect, working at all levels of the senses, that thoughts in the theatre would be deepened, and that such a deepening could be described as an 'active metaphysics'.[16] Insisting that the metaphysical would arise from making 'spoken language convey what it does not normally convey', one enters the realm of the 'Theatre of Cruelty', the incantation in which, and through which, Artaud believed a metaphysics would be attainable. By reaching through the discipline, the technique or the gesture, first principles would be discovered that would place the theatre on a different threshold.

The text which follows 'Production and metaphysics', 'On the Balinese theatre', makes explicit the sources of many of Artaud's reservations about the theatre of his day. It is this theatre which 'through a complex expansion of stage artifice brings them to life, imposing on our minds something like the idea of a metaphysics coined from a new usage of gestures and speech'.[17] Quite contrary to the theatre that Artaud criticises, which rests on rather than transforms the 'everyday' and the 'pedestrian', the power of the Balinese theatre reaccentuates its traditions, its use of gesture, inflexion and harmony preserved alive in relation to the senses. In describing the actors as 'Hieroglyphs' and questioning the possibility of describing their meaning in any logical or discursive language, Artaud was opening up the issues in his work that led Derrida to respond to his 'Theatre of Cruelty' in *Writing and Difference*. Many of the difficulties of comprehension associated with these texts are ironically relieved when the most apparently esoteric theatre theory is placed in the same social space as the most down-to-earth theatre. It is often here that the metaphysics of the stage are already present: the theatre of representation has not already confused the issue by containing these realities within formal structures that belong to another site.

Writing and difference

Jacques Derrida speaks of his engagement with Artaud in reassuringly tentative terms. In *Writing and Difference* he describes 'speaking toward Antonin Artaud',[18] and adds the warning: 'If we understand him, we expect no instruction from him.'[19] This engagement in two essays, 'La parole soufflée' and 'The Theatre of Cruelty', is significant for theatre and everyday life in its foregrounding of a peculiar interface between theatre and biology, theatre and elemental nature and theatre and artifice. Between the speech of theatre and the speech of the prompter there is a tract which is the ground for negotiation, where theatre is literally prompted to do what it does. This is a complex set of issues if only because the prompt has always been concealed from us, both physically and imaginatively. The presence of the prompt literally threatens the theatre as artifice. Derrida's approach to Artaud illuminates these relations between theatre and nature in compelling if difficult ways. It is as much the manner in which Derrida approaches Artaud as what he has to say about theatre that is interesting. Indeed the whole project of speaking 'about theatre' as separate from the questions outlined above is examined and helps us to understand the lasting appeal and confusions that surround Artaud's work. He prompts questions which cannot be solved by theatre because they expose theatre to the reality of its contingency on so many boundary conditions. This is not an excuse for ignoring the work and hoping it will go away.

Early in his essay 'La parole soufflée' Derrida describes a dialogue that will engage with the relations between a 'critical' discourse and a 'clinical' discourse. Derrida is here speaking of madness, a theme never far from the writings about, or of, Artaud. It is a conception of 'the work' of Artaud, an 'enigmatic conjunction' between the body and writing, and one which develops Derrida's previous interest in the mentalities of madness in Michel Foucault's *Madness and Civilisation* about which he had written earlier in *Writing and Difference*.[20] Jerzy Grotowski describes that 'Madness' in the following way:

> Artaud teaches us a great lesson which none of us can refuse. This lesson is his sickness. Artaud's misfortune is that his sickness, paranoia, differed from the sickness of the times . . . Artaud defined his sickness remarkably in a letter to Jacques Riviere: 'I am not entirely myself'.[21]

Artaud's disjuncture with his body and his society is reminiscent of the 'lived' theatre of the Surrealists and Alfred Jarry, both of whom influenced his work and life. The question of 'being more than one', this challenge to unity, was always central to Artaud's thought, but it was also more than something which Grotowski describes in the same writing as 'how to be whole, how to be complete.'[22] For such 'completion' would have been quite contrary to the project of his work, the cause of his life, which was to destabilise the binary and the unitary from which it arose, for other multifarious possibilities. To be complete was to signal an 'end' and this was at odds with Artaud's inscription in an ever receding 'closure'.

The opening of Derrida's essay establishes the relation with a Surrealist enterprise. Here the relations between reason and madness, the work and the life being lived, were always contingent. When Derrida says: 'Artaud's entire adventure is purportedly only the index of a transcendental structure', one is reminded that from Surrealism there never emerged a theatre *per se*, but rather the *lives* of the Surrealists, including in this sense Artaud, inscribed within a theatre of everyday actions. As Nadeau said of Jarry: 'Jarry never played a part, any more than he lived his life. He made himself another life, a marginal one which he fulfilled perfectly. He thus set an example difficult to follow . . .'.[23] Although scholarship has established Apollinaire's 'The Breasts of Tiresias' in Paris in 1917 as the inauguration of a Surrealist drama, there has to be the suspicion that the theatre of Surrealism was the very lives of those engaged within its circumference, and for a time that included Artaud.[24] If for the Surrealist enterprise the aesthetic was wedded to revolutionary forms and hopes, for Artaud these aspirations went beyond the work itself and questioned the binary split between theatre and the everyday. Having discussed his proposition that stage language would lead to a metaphysics, Derrida takes this further when he says: 'Artaud attempted to destroy a history, the history of the dualist metaphysics . . . the duality of the body and the soul . . . the duality of speech and existence of the text and the body . . . Non-theatrical works . . . works that are deported "commentaries".'[25]

Taking as his starting point the various senses of 'soufflée', the breath, inspiration, 'spiriting away', Derrida explores Artaud's resistance to his speech being stolen by a commentator, a listener or a receiver, indeed a public. Breath is spirited away but it is also inspired by another voice. The philosophical play which brings Derrida's attention to a cluster of words around 'spirit' – inspiration, spirited away and prompter – is both metaphoric and a keen analysis of practice. For Derrida believes Artaud desired 'the conflagration of the stage upon which the prompter (souffleur) was possible . . . Artaud wanted the machinery of the prompter spirited away'. There is perhaps reason to believe that Derrida and Artaud should be left to get on at the philosophical level of abstraction, and yet the space that is opened up between the prompt's excision from the stage and the retrieval of an 'original' voice for theatre is too provocative to remain in

201

the realm of French theory. The machinery of the prompter will not disappear that quickly unless we understand it to be both the mechanisms of the prompter as abstract institution, and an inventory of concrete effects which constrain the theatre and continue to shape its possibilities in the modern guise of stage management and direction.

Prompt and speech

The prompter would appear to have all but disappeared in the contemporary theatre, leaving uncomfortable traces in the memories of school plays and lost lines. Last seen out in the open in Pirandello's *Six Characters in Search of an Author*, the species has gone into hiding. Yet the spirit of the prompter remains in a theatre which takes its guidance from the text, managers, impresarios and any number of external voices to presentation. The genealogy of the prompter is an interesting one for an analysis of theatre which marks the divide between the given and the created. If the success of a theatre which Artaud despised was predicated on the reinforcement of this division it is the prompter's breath and speech which most clearly exposes a theatre tyrannised by representation and the word. The prompter reminds the performer and when overheard, the audience, that this divide is a slim one and is maintained fitfully.

The speech of the prompt is clear and loud but how did this official protect the text of theatre as written and recorded? From the medieval period to now the prompt is indissociable from the prompt-book, the earliest iconography of the medieval *regisseur*, or prompt, carrying the text with them. An eyewitness account by Richard Carew in his *Survey of Cornwall* gives an early impression of this role in the miracle plays of the Cornish rounds: 'the players conne not their parts without booke, but are prompted by one called the Ordinary, who followeth at their back with the booke in his hand, and telleth them softly what they must pronounce aloud.'[26] Scholarship on the medieval performance of *The Castle of Perseverance* begins by suggesting that the prompt could have been hidden in God's *locus*. But what would have been the outcome if the actor's lapse of memory had occurred north in the Devil's *locus*? The presumption is unwillingly made that there were several prompters located in various points or even more heretically that, as evidence suggests, the prompter was simply a recognised figure in the proceedings. He was the ordinary within the extraordinary. Whichever, and the latter is far more likely given the iconography, 'keeping the book' is a term for prompting which appears in records of the medieval theatre. It was in the Elizabethan period that this equation became formalised with prompters beginning to be referred to as 'book-holders' or 'book keepers'. It is these guardians of tradition and record that Artaud most wishes to dispel – they are the icons of a theatre ruled by logos. The history of prompt-books is itself an archaeology of repetition and gradual evolution, the layers of notes indicating the genealogy of a production over generations.

The only extant description of the Restoration prompter is that of the veteran prompt John Downes prefacing his *Roscius Anglicanus* of 1708:

> The Editor of the ensuing Relation, being long conversant with the plays and Actors of the Original Company, under the Patent of Sir William Davenant, at his Theatre in Lincolns-Inn-Fields, Open'd there 1662. And as Book-keeper and Prompter, continu'd so, till October 1706. He Writing out all the Parts in each Play; and attending every Morning the Actors Rehearsals, and their performances in Afternoons; Emboldens him to affirm, he is not very Erronius in his Relation.[27]

The role of the prompt was at this time to keep the book, copy out actors' parts, and to literally blow the whistle on the performance. In *The Change of Crownes*, a tragi-comedy performed at the Theatre Royal in 1667, the manuscript prompt copy is of special interest, indicating where the prompter's whistle was to be blown as a signal for scene changes. The scene changes would appear to have occurred instantaneously and in front of the audience on this signal, coming twenty or thirty lines before the expected change.[28]

It was in the early eighteenth century that the prompt became in unexpected ways a figure of conscious interest and exposure within the theatre as distinct from an accepted addition to its central characters. It was at this time that the official was a combination of the modern prompter who prompts and a stage manager who runs the show. Aaron Hill, a remarkable fringe figure of the eighteenth-century theatre, along with his partner William Popple launched a twice weekly broadsheet under the title *The Prompter* at a time when the journalistic coverage of theatre was something of a rarity. The paper was unusual in another sense bringing to bear the most caustic attack on the theatre's structures in print, attacks maintained over a two-year period. Having failed to gain control of the Patent of Drury Lane Theatre, where Hill had hoped to 'reform the stage', and subsequently having failed to establish 'an academical theatre for improving the taste of the stage', *The Prompter* was launched in 1734. The paper unusually combined not just caustic attacks on the theatre of the day but excursions into morality and ethics, sociology, economics and politics. It was named *The Prompter* for obvious reasons that Artaud might have subscribed to: to put right those going wrong and confirm the intentions of those doing right. The first issue of the broadsheet had two mastheads: 'All the World's a Stage . . .', and 'When we daily see so many Men ACT amiss, can we entertain any Doubt that a good Prompter is wanting?' Between these two conceptions of theatre and its criticism, the world and theatre's failings in that world, Hill intervened with an intention to 'give the *Word* impartially to every *Performer*'. To Hill the stage had for too long been freely transcribing the world, without the world taking reprisals. Air and inspiration have an obverse in the passions of an actor which Hill saw as detrimental to the stage: 'As there are flatulent Diets in Life, which, naturally blow up the Body with Wind, so there are Professions in Practice, the most natural property whereof is, to swell the Mind into VANITY. Among these, the Vainest beyond all Solomon's vanities is The Player.'[29] In a device as old as journalism and letters pages, Hill published letters from a fictitious correspondent in the country who attacked this vanity and everything theatre stood for, where Common Sense just in town from 'Barking' was driven out by the absurdities of 'Pantomime'.

The theatre for Hill was a moral institution to improve the mind. It propagated a concept of virtue touching both private and public domains and therefore was of broader purpose than religion. Actors and managers were exhorted to make a moral stage and the extravagance of opera was berated in support of a theatre which would, Hill believed, provide more virtuous direction to its audiences. Hill knew something about these audiences, for in another progressive act for his day he had studied and categorised their types of response, from 'the strong, rambling and volatile', to the 'indolent, heavy and slothful'. Audience response was not beyond the morality and educative purpose of the stage: 'I have in my view to compose for Entertainment of my Readers, a short but necessary treatise entitled, The art of CLAPPING and HISSING instructively.'[30] Hill's view of the stage of his day was as apocalyptic as Artaud's, though in the name of a moral order, the spectators, actors and 'undertaker' managers, as he referred to them, all coming in for twice-weekly damnation. Hill was self-confessedly cleaning out the theatre between Cibber and Garrick. Like a latter-day hygienist he was airing, beating, lifting and hunting down with a broom the menace of recesses in the theatre of his day. His solution to what he considered its 'vain, empty and dangerous amusements' was to propose the establishment of a 'national' theatre, thinly veiling his own ambition: the intention to create a new patent house.

The first issue of his periodical included a long description of the nature of the prompter based on observation of the work of William Rufus Chetwood, at the time prompter at Drury Lane. The detail is unique for that period, or after, and provides an insight into the realisation of the power of the prompt, denying their apparently menial station:

> In one of my walks behind the scenes . . . I observed an humble but useful officer standing in a corner and attentively perusing a book which lay before him. He never forsook his post but, like a general in the field, had many aides de camp about him, whom he despatched with his orders, and I could perceive that though he seemed not to

command, yet his instructions were punctually complied with, and that in the modest character of an adviser he had the whole management and direction of that little commonwealth. I enquired into his name and office and was informed that he was THE PROMPTER . . . (H)e, without ever appearing on the stage himself, has some influence over everything that is transacted upon it . . . He stands in a corner, unseen and unobserved by the audience, but diligently attended to by everyone who plays a part; yet tho' he finds them all very observant of him, he presumes nothing upon his own capacity; he has a book before him, from which he delivers his advice and instructions . . .[31]

The description continues with analysis of his means of control, his command over the emotions of actors, their entrances and exits, their speech. He is a 'Director of the Ignorant . . . a Terror to the evil Actor'. The technology of his control is simple but effective. His instruments of government are a bell which hangs from his arm with which is summoned appropriate musical accompaniment, and a whistle around his neck which signals the change of scenes, from Heaven and Earth to Chaos and back to Creation. The language derived from the prompt persists to a contemporary theatre where a front-of-house manager might 'ring in the orchestra' while signalling to musicians with an electronic light, and in the more generally used and long tradition of stage directions being given as 'prompt side' and 'opposite prompt' to indicate a relation to the prompt's station. The problem was that the prompt's position was by no means consistent from theatre to theatre and these directions were confusing in different locations. They became eclipsed in the early nineteenth century by the more common use of seemingly neutral terms 'stage right' and 'left'.

The prompt was by this time not only an institution of the larger theatres but a part of the provincial touring circuits in Britain managed by individuals like Thomas Wilson Manly, who was known as the 'autocrat of the Midlands'. The prompt throughout this period would only have been answerable to the manager. In seeking the speech of theatre it is likely, from the following account, that the manager's control was complete and exercised through the mouthpiece of the prompt. Manly's meticulous records are continually and caustically critical of his actors, who were being paid between 18 and 25 shillings a week. Manly reports he paid his prompter £1, or one guinea and in 1821 notes: 'Mr. Martin (prompter) leaves to exhibit a big pig!!! his wife off too, Sal. £1.1s. pr wk. Tom Parkinson off as helper to the pig.' Later that decade Manly seems to have become ambivalent about the idea of a prompter at all: 'Little Broadfoot was sent on a fool's errand from town, here [Halifax] by fussy Smythson, who dreamed I wanted a Prompter! retained him at 12s. pr wk till something better offered.' And subsequently the records show that Broadfoot was dismissed for not knowing anything about his role or responsibilities.[32]

Contemporaneous with this hapless touring prompt there was beginning in London a career which brought the arts of the prompt book to their peak and marked a transition between the declining power of the prompt and the ascendancy of the assistant manager, stage manager and director. George Cressall Ellis straddled the nineteenth century, playing actor, prompter, stage manager and stage director. The major part of his work in theatre was 'behind the scenes' but for one telling and significant moment he was exposed on the wrong side of the curtain. To that point, which marked the beginning of the end of his career, he had bridged the British theatre's allegiance to Shakespearian productions of the past and the emerging forms of Boucicault's melodrama: 'No prompter or stage manager ever served the stage more conscientiously, and no one ever took more pains than he to record in prompt-books, which are themselves little works of art, the stage art that was passing before him.'[33] Most prompt-books, part-books and callbooks remained anonymous and unsigned but Ellis' are unmistakable for their style and precision.

Ellis was the link between one master-producer and another. His transcriptions of Macready productions were made for the use of Charles Kean between 1845 and 1850, and then in the 1860s from the Macready and Kean production prompt-books for Hermann Vezin. Ellis' prompt-books have become monuments of the form, his life a faint trace behind them. There remains a single portrait photograph of him and, appropriately, his silver prompter's whistle. He had started his theatre career as a 'Walking Gentleman' playing numerous supporting parts at seasons in Edinburgh. In London in 1839–40 he was billed as a Stage Director at the St James Theatre and stayed there as prompter and deputy stage manager under different managements. In the 1840s he moved to William Charles Macready's Drury Lane as under-prompter to John Wilmott and there kept the meticulous prompt-books of Macready Shakespeare productions which he later transcribed for Charles Kean, for whom he worked at the Princess's in the 1850s. At this time he was billed as stage manager with another prompter making up the books. His texts were now stage manager's work books and cue books. One set of his rehearsal notes not only indicates the finishing touches to be made to a show, but points to one of the enduring forces of theatre that always lay outside even the jurisdiction of the management: 'Pails of water & props w firemen – R&L – each Act'.[34] Charles Kean turned over the annual pantomime to Ellis' care as director, and his status changed again with assumption of work with Kean on the annual Court Theatricals at Windsor Castle for the Royal Family at Christmas. It was here that Ellis was exposed as director in the wrong place at the wrong time: 'At Windsor one evening, Mr. Coe, the Haymarket prompter, raised the act drop before Ellis had got off the stage, thereby causing him to be seen by the audience. When Ellis remonstrated with him, Coe's impudent answer was, "You ought to have got out of the way!!!" [35] This marked the beginning of a decade of declining prominence, though his title improved from stage manager to acting manager and at the St James he directed an Italian espionage performance called *Idalia* with young Henry Irving in a main role. The elements were against him again, with the opening performance proving a disaster: 'An unruly water tank, which in certain scenes was to feed a mountain waterfall, could not be stopped from flowing. The stage was inundated, and while suspense should have been heightening the actors splashed about in chilly slops to the vast amusement of the audience.'[36] The synthesis of his art of prompt-books and direction came in 1869 at the Princess's in a revival of *Acis and Galatea*, a studious representation of the 1842 Macready production at the Theatre Royal, Drury Lane, with Ellis recreating Macready's groupings and action. Here Ellis is recognised as the preserver of theatrical tradition, the theatre as history and repetition, the theatre of texts and continuity, jeopardised at one time by fire, at another by water, and increasingly contingent on the prompt remaining behind the scenes. The prompt's speech remains unheard except by those with the power and responsibility to change the world and the heavens.

Writing the unwritten

The genealogy of the prompter is both metaphoric, as used by Derrida in his encounter with Artaud, and material, as traced by this historiographical operation. Without the mental associations of the role and its power the practices of theatre would be left with an uncritical history, one which speaks of the elision of the prompter, but one unable to come to terms with the endemic traces of the prompter's speech in the contemporary theatre. If the epitome of the non-theatrical was for Artaud the 'deported commentary' of the prompter there was a constant defence against his own speech being deported, or spirited away from his body. It was a warranted fear given the 'use' made of Artaud's writings since their publication. Artaud relates his own body to that of the theatre body. The text of his body and the theatre of his gestures are stolen by a classical theatre where the invisibility of the prompter ensures a contract between a text already written elsewhere and a performer interpreting what they receive. This classical origin is an economy of theatre which Artaud seeks to destroy to obviate the ventriloquism of theatre. The prompter's inhalation is the same air that the performer breathes; suffocated, the performers are robbed of all that could be said in their own name. The theatre of cruelty will, Artaud believes, be the reduction of the organ of the classical occidental stage, a theatre of words, interpretation, translation and enforced deviation from His Master's Voice, in which the stolen speech is mouthed by the emissaries of the omnipotent actor-manager, the enslaved actors and directors. Artaud proposes a theatre withdrawn from text, prompter and the omnipotence of the word. Contrary to much popular misinterpretation this is not a mute theatre.

Artaud was primarily concerned with first principles, the relationship between the individual breath and the relations between that breath, life and inspiration:

> The difficult part is to find out exactly where one is, to reestablish communication with one's self. The whole thing lies in a certain flocculation of objects, the gathering of these mental gems about one as yet undiscovered nucleus. / Here, then, is what I think of thought. / Inspiration certainly exists.[37]

Artaud's language here is reminiscent of the discussion of the composition of images – a flocculation is another way of thinking of images – but also reflects the vocabulary of physics which had influenced the Surrealists. In 'inspiration' is carried the diverse senses of the breath, the spirit and the spirited, but also as Derrida points out and makes play of, the 'prompt', the *souffleur* in French, of the theatre, which is for Artaud the 'theft of language'. Artaud would take us to first principles of inspiration, a metaphysics of life, a 'source of good inspiration' to break the grip of the prompt as commentator, and thief, the text as manipulative of the theatre from its margins to the integrated body within theatre, the body restored to the centre of the activity which has been dominated by an absent master, the word. In a complex passage which makes allusions to Artaud's own sense of being 'dead in birth', of his body being simultaneously not his and that of his relations, of being 'not entirely himself', Derrida pursues the image of the breath as inspiration, the restoration of the body and a metaphysics of the flesh:

> If my speech is not my breath, if my letter is not my speech, this is so because my spirit was no longer my body, my body no longer my gestures, my gestures no longer my life. The integrity of the flesh torn by all these differences must be restored in the theater. Thus the metaphysics of flesh which determines Being as life, and the mind as the body itself, as unseparated thought, 'obscure' thinking – this is the continuous and always unperceived trait which links *The Theatre and Its Double* to the early works and the theme of unpower. This metaphysics of the flesh is also governed by the anguish of dispossession, the experience of having lost life, of separation from thought, of the body exiled from the mind.[38]

Derrida describes Artaud as 'soliciting' this metaphysics and 'shaking' it to establish a departure from that which is proper to oneself, a summoning of metaphysics to interrogate it, to draw upon its values, to be faithful to it. The transgression of such a metaphysics through thought, a project which Artaud believed had not yet begun, risks returning to those metaphysics. But for Derrida this is what provokes the necessity for engagement, for 'such is the question in which we are posed'. In this recognition Derrida is critically part of a postmodern project, attempting, but inevitably failing, to position itself beyond the end of the epoch of 'metaphysics'. The transgression of that limit is an inevitable reinscription within its bounds. But perhaps this reinscription occurs here with the relation between foreground and distance reorientated. The return is a continual awareness of the place of departure as though it were the first time seen, literally a scene, without the work of habit disrupting the eye's connection between near and far that deprives the place of its distinctive arrangement beyond its first witness.

This question was not just a theatre question for Artaud. It was a question of the very origins of the theatre and the Western civilisation from which theatre had arisen. We are posed in the 'question' of the Greek and it was to this Artaud turned his attention:

> Artaud undertakes neither a renewal nor a critique or a new interrogation of classical theater; he intends the effective, active and nontheoretical destruction of Western civilisation and its religions, the entirety of the philosophy which provides traditional theater with its groundwork and decor beneath even its most apparently innovative forms.[39]

The groundwork and décor of the theatre are material preoccupations of what follows in the last two chapters of this book but Artaud's thought preserves us on the hither side of the material, in a meta-theatrical domain. Artaud's revolution would be in the theatre and simultaneously outside it, it would expose the contradiction of there being thought any distinction between the two in the first place. Artaud confronted the problem of representation when he clearly stated that 'the theater was never made to describe man and what he does'.[40] It is these limits to representation that Artaud announces. And it is these limits that convince Derrida that what is being posed in the text of the 'Theatre of Cruelty' are *historic* questions. Historic not in the sense that such questions can be inscribed within a construction called the 'history of theatre' but in an 'absolute and radical sense', not a substitute for social praxis but its critique and guide. Here Derrida is identifying in Artaud the central philosophical question of the relations between art and life, and the dualities that these relations have been built upon. These dualities throughout Artaud's writings are turned into multiplicities, into a 'sheaf' of concerns that Derrida calls *différance*.[41] The theme of the limits of the metaphysics of Western theatre is reiterated with the critique of the representation of life, being a representation of man, and thus a humanist limit on difference. As Derrida says: 'The theatre of cruelty is not a representation. It is life itself, in the extent to which life itself is unrepresentable. Life is the non representable origin of representation,' and as Artaud concludes: 'I have therefore said cruelty as I might have said life.'[42]

Artaud challenges the concept of mimesis as a fundamental principle of art, and like Nietzsche to whose thought Artaud's is uncannily close in many respects, there is a call for the end of imitative concepts, an end to Aristotelian aesthetics and Western metaphysics. Theatre was never able to hold a one-way mirror up to nature, for that mirror and the theories of optics it derived from, was always thought to be a process of material emanation and exchange, between the object and its reflection. The fallacy that theatre took nothing from the everyday, and gave back only self-knowledge has been discredited in Artaud's thought. As can be imagined, this ever-expanding field cannot be an internal question for 'theatrology', of its techniques, of its intra-theatrical revolutions, because these will never penetrate the very foundations of Western theatre with which Artaud takes issue. Indeed if the preceding appears to be an attempt to 'grasp' life in all its aspects, beyond theatre, and therefore to be perceived beyond the parameters of a book of this kind, it is indicative of Artaud's project, and Derrida's evocative reading of it, that I now find myself reaching such a limit. The scale of the enquiry is demanded by the texts, and Artaud's shortest texts also happen to provoke the deepest and most enduring questions for the first principles of a theatre activity.

Indeed to resist this dynamic and envelop Artaud within an internal theoretical enquiry would belong to the very history and stage which Artaud wanted to dismantle. These reservations must confront the Royal Shakespeare Company's celebrated 'Theatre of Cruelty Season' of 1963. For there is no question that such internal experimentation has invigorated, sometimes transformed the theatre, within its own conventions and limits, but it was precisely these limits that Artaud was addressing and they are left completely unthought by their own rearrangement.[43] Rather Derrida asks the question posed by Artaud's problematic: 'What does it mean to break this structure of belonging?'[44] The 'structure of belonging' is not solely, nor primarily, an internal question for the theatre. It provides Derrida with the analysis to see theatre as 'theological', in the sense that it remains governed by a 'speech from elsewhere', that is the 'author-creator' who allows 'representation represent him through representatives'.[45] The representatives are actors and directors, the text is in its own right the representative of another 'real', from elsewhere. It is theological inasmuch as Derrida sees it ministering to 'a passive, seated public, a public of spectators, of consumers, of enjoyers'.[46] This basic structure has never been modified: 'all revolutions have maintained it intact, and most often have tended to protect or restore it'.[47] These revolutions occur throughout the history of the Western theatre, over twenty-five centuries, through what Derrida describes as 'an experience of mutations and perturbations which cannot be set aside, despite the peaceful and impassive immobility of the fundamental structures'.[48]

For Artaud this is not just a neutral immobility but a 'mark of cancellation' and a 'seduction', in other words an active elision of theatres that *might be*, including the 'Theatre of Cruelty'. The central immobility is the nature of 'representation' which would not be discounted from the 'Theatre of Cruelty' but would be interrogated for its origins and meanings. Derrida summarises this agenda as: the stage will no longer *represent*, the stage will no longer work as a *repetition* of the present, nor will it be a *representation* if that is a surface spectacle displayed for spectators. In Artaud's conception of representation there would be 'the unfolding of a volume, a multidimensional milieu, an experience which produces its own space'.[49] Thus the closure of a classical representation gives way to the reconstitution of a 'closed space' of original representation. This is a space produced from within itself without recourse to a master narrative, from elsewhere. This is a space in which positions are possible for those displaced by the theatre whose closure is an interminable 'second half' on which the final curtain has yet to drop. What was to happen on the 'undersides' of this space, this volume, would be governed not by improvisation or formless experiment, as some have associated with the 'Theatre of Cruelty', but by an implacable necessity, a rigour, 'irreversible and absolute determination'. If there is anything to be said for the equation of blood, horror and sadism with the 'Theatre of Cruelty' it is for Derrida to be conceived as the murder of the wielder of the text, logos, a parricide. Thus speech as 'dictation' would be erased from the stage and with it would be removed the ruling terms of diction that encloses theatre in the realm of an exercise of reading.

The dualisms at the heart of theatre with which Artaud takes issue – an imitative language, the separation of concept and sound, the difference between soul and body, God and man, author and actor – were to be challenged by a re-emergence of speech and writing as gesture. The logical constraints of this language would be dismantled through the process of what Derrida calls 'Glossopoeia' and what Artaud calls 'Onomatopoeia'.[50] Such a language would take on the connotations of hieroglyphs, the part that speech played in dreams, described by Freud in the following way:

> If we reflect that the means of representation in dreams are principally visual images and not words, we shall see that it is even more appropriate to compare dreams with a system of writing than with a language. In fact the interpretation of dreams is completely analogous to the decipherment of an ancient pictographic script such as Egyptian hieroglyphs.[51]

Contrary to the facile view of Artaud as an extravagant iconoclast is set his clear expression of wishing to conserve such hieroglyphs as a record of performance. He sought 'a new means of recording . . . whether these means belong to musical transcription or to some kind of code'.[52] Here Artaud reflects the concerns of Paul Klee when he spoke of the 'polyphony' of music, and a new language of artistic transcription, a provocation perhaps to a 'science' of semiotics. Indeed throughout the interplay of Derrida and Artaud's texts there emerges the sense of an 'implacable' order in Artaud's work, a wish for rigour, a distaste for improvisation, and contrary to Surrealist theory a specific notion of dream as directed, and opposed to the disorder of spontaneity.

In this theatrical treatment of dreams Artaud believed that poetry and science must henceforth be identical. While Bachelard believed this to be an impossible alliance, a necessary split to be understood as a fundamental division of the imagination, there is a sense in which Artaud's notion of the directed dream coheres with that of Bachelard's distinction between reverie, day dream and night dream. Again, contrary to the Surrealists Artaud wrote: 'I propose to renounce our empiricism of imagery in which the unconscious furnishes images at random, and which the poet arranges at random too.'[53] Thus in distinction to the developing frame of psychoanalysis, which Artaud placed within the same Western processes that he sought to destroy, and to Surrealism from which he had been summarily expelled, the 'Theatre of Cruelty' would not be a theatre of the unconscious, but of the 'exposed lucidity' of 'consciousness'. Indeed Artaud did not wish to consider dreams in their negative state as psychoanalysis did, as a displacement activity, but rather for their 'affirmative' qualities, for their 'profound poetic bearing' – both for themselves and for theatre.[54]

Rather than speak of what a 'Theatre of Cruelty' might be, Derrida seeks to establish, through Artaud, what it is *not*, which theatre is by its presence unfaithful to Artaud, and the themes of this infidelity. Summarising the first of these exclusions, which present as many problems as they elucidate, Derrida lists: all non-sacred theatre, theatre that privileges speech, an abstract theatre or a total theatre for total man, and all theatre of 'alienation'. Within these themes one might seek to equate theatres one is familiar with or wishes to denigrate in Artaud's name, but this would be senseless as they are categories which fundamentally describe everything that has happened of potential interest in the theatre in the last two millenia. It is the constant failure of each to confront the Western world as Artaud understood it, its dualisms and imitations that is at question rather than a 'Beckettian theatre' here a 'Brechtian theatre' there to be derided.[55]

In more detail, regarding the theme of infidelity described as the theatre of alienation, Derrida says: 'Alienation only consecrates with didactic insistence and systematic heaviness, the non participation of spectators in the creative act in the irruptive force fissuring the space of the stage.' As

Artaud said, the 'V effect' remains the prisoner of a Classical paradox which 'attempts to cast the mind into an attitude distinct from force but addicted to exaltation'.[56] For the 'Theatre of Cruelty', with its closure of the space between performer and audience, the inscription of the audience as public within the very act itself, there was no longer a distance of vision for the 'V effect' to gain a purchase on. Neither would the spectator in this theatre constitute their spectacle and provide themselves with an object, they would be taken over by the nature of the theatre itself, as 'festival'. In this festival, the limits of classical theatricality, the polarities of represented/representer, stage/auditorium, actor/audience, the 'ethico-metaphysical' prohibitions of that theatre would be seen to be the 'symptoms of fear before the festival'. Here Derrida makes a clear distinction between what is being discussed by Artaud, and the 'Happening', which he dismissively contrasts as what the Carnival of Nice might be to the mysteries of Eleusis. The Happening replaces the total revolution prescribed by Artaud with a limited political agitation. As Artaud says: 'The festival must be a political act. And the act of political revolution is theatrical.'[57] It is a theatre which does not speak though in the name of a public or people. Indeed the 'Public' is problematic, contradictory, as it perpetuates the dualism that Artaud sought to destroy with the Theatre of Cruelty. When Artaud said: 'The Public. First of all this Theatre must exist,' he announced the impossibility of such a thing, a 'people' as audience, contingent as they would be on the very thing that would mark their disappearance. Derrida expounds on this impossibility: 'The public is not to exist outside, before or after the stage of cruelty, is not to await it, to contemplate it, or to survive it – is not even to exist as a public at all.'[58]

The question of the 'Public' and its disappearance in the theatre act is one which is central to the proposition of a relation between theatre and everyday life. It is an important concept to which Derrida returns in an analysis of Rousseau, in *Of Grammatology*. Derrida here outlines a theatre that is at odds with the Western tradition, as is Artaud's: 'the theater itself is shaped and undermined by the profound evil of representation. It is that corruption itself. For the stage is not threatened by anything but itself.'[59] Derrida summarises that what Rousseau criticises in his 'Letter to M. d'Alembert', is not the content of spectacle, but re-presentation itself. What could take the place of this theatre, where the actor speaks in words other than their own? What will take its place is reminiscent of a theatre of everyday life, a 'nature' theatre, for Derrida: 'The innocence of the public spectacle, the good festival, the dance around the water hole, would open a theater without representation. Or rather a stage without a show: without *theater*, with nothing to see.'[60] Here oppositions and polarities of theatre, audience and performer, seer and seen, will dissolve, will deconstruct. And what will be left for this deconstructed theatre? What are the objects that are left for it? For Rousseau:

> Nothing if you please. With liberty, wherever abundance reigns, well being also reigns. Plant a stake crowned with flowers in the middle of a square; gather the people together there, and you will have a festival. Do better yet; let the spectators become an entertainment to themselves; make them actors themselves; do it so that each sees and loves himself in the others so that all will be better united.[61]

The Artaudian inflections are clear but as Derrida warns: 'these reconciliations must be affected with the greatest caution. The context sometimes places an infinite distance between two identical propositions.'[62] The open air for Rousseau is 'Nature' and the elemental voice here is clear and free. It is this preoccupation to which Derrida returns in 'La parole soufflée' where the voice of the actor is the unnatural representation of another speech.

Derrida concludes his themes of 'infidelity to Artaud' with that of: all ideological theatre. By this he means all theatre that would make a discourse intelligible for its listeners, an act that could be repeated without a stage. And it is here that Derrida believes we touch on Artaud's historico-metaphysical project, for Artaud wanted to 'erase repetition in general' as repetition separates 'force, presence and life from themselves'. These are central themes to this study, as they recur and reappear throughout the theatre of the contemporary period. The power of repetition though, for Derrida, goes under several names, God, Being and Dialectics, which suggest the philosophical ambitions in his interpretation of Artaud's work and the characteristic return of the question of metaphysics. For it is the 'holds' of these metaphysics which demand the rethinking of old enquiries, the replacing of previous answers with further questions.

Artaud's 'active metaphysics' and the engagement between Derrida's philosophy and Artaud's writing question the relations of theatre to nature and culture. The image is dialectical in its formation and works between the two. There is the sense in which, as Derrida says, the dialectical takes into account our rejection of it, we see on its receding horizon the tragedy not of the impossibility of repetition but its very necessity. Here Artaud presents the contemporary theatre with an inaccessible limit, a theatre where the tension between continual repetition confronts the essence of theatre, which Artaud describes as 'the only place in the world where a gesture, once made, can never be made the same way twice'.[63] This is the 'original' of theatre and is responsible for its aura. But having asserted that potential of theatre, it proceeds within the dialectical limit to 'do the same again'. Derrida concludes his examination of the 'Theatre of Cruelty' with a recognition of this problematic: 'Closure is the circular limit within which the repetition of difference infinitely repeats itself. That is to say closure is its playing space. This movement is the movement of the world as play.'[64] Theatre is inscribed within that closure. It is unable to transgress its limit by the very terms in which it thinks itself: 'the sociality of writing as drama requires a totally other discipline'.[65] Where theatre operates in the logic of the contemporary period, in pastiche and parody, internal reflection and quotation, it attempts to deny the original nature of the audience's difference, its otherness making each assembly for theatre a new event. And within that event no movement is repeatable the same way twice, removing the image from the possibility of its postmodern progeny in other media. The project which Artaud articulates has entered the contents of the theatre of the period, the plays for example of Peter Handke and the performances of Pina Bausch, without deconstructing the ordained relations with audiences beyond 'internal rearrangement'.[66] It is necessary to examine examples of such rearrangement, from Bertolt Brecht through Augusto Boal to the 'community play' movement, to understand why the project of a political theatre is not adequate without the beginnings of an understanding of the 'metaphysics' proposed by Artaud and the revolution of forms that implies.

The enduring quality of Artaud's work is that this mental sphere of metaphysical speculation is derived from the concrete, material problems that theatre poses any practitioner unwilling to 'pretend'. Artaud draws on this material and metaphoric level when he introduces us to the fourth element of the theatre between nature and culture and reinforces his disdain for a theatre of representation: 'And if there is still one hellish, truly accursed thing in our time, it is our artistic dallying with forms, instead of being like victims burnt at the stake, signalling through the flames.'[67] Between the 'improvement' of the theatre of the nineteenth century and the 'safety' of the theatre of the twentieth, is a loss which Artaud stands against. It is a loss of 'agitated crowds hurled against one another' for the politeness of entrances and exits, a theatre of cruelty that will be illuminated by 'sheet lightning like a flight of fire-arrows'. Both, ironically, describe a theatre common to another time, the disappearance of which determines the theatre today.

7

CIRCULATION
Water and hygiene

Where there are cities there is water and there are theatres. The way these interrelate is a historical and political question. From the Egyptian ceremonial spectacles on the Nile, the *Heb-Sed* with floating barges, through Venetian Carnival to the Victorian water spectacles where water was tanked and trivialised there is a movement of cultural enclosure and containment. The theatrical transfer of water to the interior in the nineteenth-century British theatre was a reflection of its containment and control in other spheres of public life where increasingly water was treated as an object of moral authority and hygiene. In the recent past the water-centred urban regeneration of dockland environments is predicated on complex associations which spring from this conversion of the natural to the cultural. Water, like space, is seen here to have a history shaped by the human imagination as well as by urban engineers. It is a history which reveals what it was that submerged the words of Artaud. The 'plague' which Artaud spoke of in *The Theatre and its Double*, like the prompt's theft of speech, is both a metaphor for the ultimate infection of the theatre, and a historic, everyday reality which denies theatre's access to life.

Water and its circulation were elemental to the European hygienist movement of the nineteenth century. By the end of that century the vocabulary of hygiene had given rise to a reformed theatre – one which was to be 'safe', 'healthy' and 'isolated'. A discussion of theatre's removal from the everyday must engage with this moment of circulation and isolation. It was here that a personal realm of desire and risk gave way to legislation and jurisdiction which reaches down to the contemporary theatre and everything it wants to do in public. In the next two chapters these constraints are examined not to propose a return to discomfort or danger, nor to endorse safety at all costs, but to rethink this binary pair within a historical context.

Hygiene was a phenomenon of the city, but one which linked the rural and the urban in intriguing and grandiose ways. As Michel Foucault has shown, hygiene became a privileged discipline of the body in the eighteenth century and conjoined with a preventive medicine to institute a

216

regime of health built on authoritarian interventions and controls. It was a phenomenon indubitably linked with the urban space, which provided simultaneously the most dangerous though potentially controllable context for populations. Where geology and geography speak of regions where climate was literally beyond the control of inhabitants, the city presented simultaneously the panic of epidemics and hope of control from pestilence and death. Foucault's interest is in the privileged breeding grounds of disease, in prisons, hospitals and asylums where medical intervention became a priority in isolated centres of resistance and control. But the hygienist movement reached into all spheres and institutions and the purpose here is to track its entry to the theatre of the nineteenth century. The broad dynamics of the movement will occupy me first as they provide a set of metaphors, images and concepts which are helpful in understanding the relations between nature and theatre. The specific figures of the movement are also worthy of some consideration as they propose a series of reforms which transform the aspects of theatre which are given and those which are created.

The nineteenth century witnessed a proliferation of reports detailing the health of the city. From these reports between 1850 and 1900 can be traced a veritable movement whose purpose was to identify and enact the principles of hygiene as it had developed through the previous century. Central to this enactment was the removal of congestion from the city, in the enduring phrase of F.O. Ward, a key figure in the movement and the progenitor of many of its most radical reforms: what was stagnant had to be put into circulation. The vocabulary arose from the sense of a city where traffic could not travel and movement was endangered by rogue objects, and people. I will show how this vocabulary was to impinge on the theatre by the end of the century, in the name not only of safety but more importantly of hygiene. The principles of health that hygiene was to define, for an art of healthy living, were ones not dissociated from questions of power, desire and sexuality, as Foucault has made clear in his writings. And these, being central to a theatre that is talked about, by Artaud, that once was but is no more, provokes me to ask where theatre became isolated from its neighbourhood, its street and its moral relevance. The relations between these issues and power are complex ones but important to understand for how theatre is removed from critical debate.

Hygienist writings were to parallel and intersect with municipal, public works regulations and these depended for their efficacy on the authority of judgments in law. It was this discourse which permeated the writings of the hygienists and was adopted by those whose justifiable concern was with the state of the theatre. The simple state of accumulation of people in confined spaces was thought to foul the air by 'the miasma of overcrowding, a complex product that is probably vaporous in nature'.[1] A name was given to this state by the hygienists, *malaria urbana*, and its

217

symptoms once identified were to be countered by the principles of circulation and differentiation. Both are concepts which reappear in the hygiene of the theatre though it is important to stress here first their urban, material and political roots.

The new city of the nineteenth century would benefit from preventive medicine, as Foucault shows, but simultaneously from an innovative concept of preventive policing. A paradigm shift was under way in the city from apprehension to prevention, from action on the street to the mentality of surveillance. The eminent Victorian Sir Edwin Chadwick feared that with the development of the metropolis came the disintegration of neighbourhood knowledge and the invisibility and anonymity of the felon. It is significant that the one area of policing he admired was that designed to prevent crime on the river: 'The best organised body of officers is that of the Thames police . . . It has put an end to all the immense extent of systematic depredation which was formerly committed on the property in the River Thames.'[2] Apprehension was to take a subsidiary place in this code to the removal of 'temptation'. Chadwick was dedicated to promoting hygienist principles of purification of the Thames, as though the law of the hygienist and the public works officer met in an area of prevention and purification. For F.O. Ward, one of these prominent hygienists, the purification of rivers and the utilisation of sewage were connected aspects of sanitary organisation and indispensable to the 'perfect working of the whole'. There had long been schemes in Paris and London to occupy the poor, convicted and old with the labour of removing waste from the city, but Ward's vocabulary is one of economic, rather than human, utilitarianism. The requirement to keep sewage and river water separate was traced by Ward to the junction in pipes from the household where the boundary of foul and the fragrant mixed: 'Not only do [water and sewage] cease to be our property, and pass beyond the control of art, but they revert to the domain of nature, spoiled even for her simple service. For this error we are punished by pestilence.'[3] The battle for their interception was no longer to be fought on the banks of the river but in the basement of the private dwelling place.

All matter of waste, any obstacles to outflow, were to be tracked down. Focus fell on the 'working-class' districts of cities which were perceived as dangerous, ill defined and mingling deleteriously with the city. The principles of reducing overcrowding and blockages to the system justified the removal of such neighbourhoods to the outskirts of towns where their isolation would enhance their 'ventilation'. Not only was the circulation of air and the penetration of light possible, these were also the gains of garden suburbs and other willing movements to the fringes of the city, but the city would be freed from the corrupting influence of these districts, which were to be joined to the centres by specially prepared systems of transport. Didier Gille describes this as a centrifugal movement, along with hospitals and cemeteries, the sick, dead and destitute succumbing to the same revolutions. Though the city was vitiated by the movement of bodies and carriages this was not the case in closed spaces such as hospitals, prisons, barracks, churches and theatres, all of which gave rise to special procedures and operations of purification: 'the crowding together of bodies later governed both urban social perceptions and the tactics that sanitary reformers used haphazardly in public space . . .'.[4]

The hygienists inaugurated and ensured the smoothing of this urban space and presented the conditions for the standardisation of theatre places. Where the streets were formalised, allowing for speed of movement and eliminating interference, the theatre's passageways, its gangways and corridors were contrarily flaunting the lack of conformity that hygienists feared. Where immobility and inertia were equated with stagnation and pestilence, so unruliness and disturbance, the common condition of a theatre where intervention was not uncommon from the auditorium, was not to be tolerated. If the installation of circulation as a principle was fundamental to the modern city, as the understanding of circulation was to physiology, so the theatre can be seen to take a place between the biological and the cultural, a place where both the question of human circulation and its relations to public order and safety came into play. But detailed description of these processes is important before drawing further conclusions from them.

It was the circulation of water to and from the city, as well as the purification of its rivers, which occupied Ward, and this provides the sanitary engineering coordinates for a movement. In a speech made in Brussels to the Sanitary Congress in 1856 and in a letter to a member of parliament in 1858 he laid out the principles which he described in the binomial pair: circulation or stagnation:

> Continuous circulation is the fundamental principle of English sanitary reformers. According to their theory, the conveyance of pure water by mains into towns and its distribution into houses, as well as the removal of foul water by drains from the houses and from the streets into the fields for agricultural production, should go on without cessation and without stagnation either in the houses or the streets.[5]

Ward knew he was challenging many old ideas and would replace them with a new combination which ironically drew on much older principles. William Harvey had proposed in his treatise on 'The motion of the heat and blood' that the blood moved in a ceaseless stream, in a circle, and that the heart was the 'great propelling power' of this operation. Prior to this revolutionary principle in 1628, it had been thought that the true blood was only carried by the veins and that the arteries contained little blood mixed with the 'vital spirits'. The heart in this physiology was the generator of the vital spirits, and heat and blood were propelled by the act of inspiration. Flow to particular parts of the body was through their special 'excitation'. In short there was, prior to Harvey, an imaginary respiration all over the body with the lungs and heart providing the better 'ventilation and refrigeration of the blood'. Thus the word circulation before Harvey pertained to a movement of the blood which was thought to be a slow and irregular back and forth motion. Circulation as a principle demanded a redefinition of the body of profound proportions and this was not able to establish itself for a century. However by the mid-1700s, as Ivan Illich points out, money and wealth are described as being in circulation and beginning to be discussed as though they were liquids. Adam Smith's *Wealth of Nations* (1776) is predicated on the circulatory metaphor, where capital's continual return provides the dynamic for markets to be made. It was only later that 'power' itself began to circulate and Ward's principles championed by Edwin Chadwick provide the most obvious distillation of the theme for the social body in the form of the new city.

But the system was not one which denied the country; it enhanced it in the most fanciful way. The purpose of the removal of fertilising matter from the city was to transform it from a 'source of disease' to 'its application elsewhere', expense was to be turned into one of riches and nourishment, the foul into the pure. Harvey's model is foremost in Ward's perception of this system as a social phenomenon – social structures were derived from the individual body. Fruitful circulation was to be inaugurated by means of 'an immense tubular organisation' consisting of two parts: 'Urban drainage and rural distribution, both of which are subdivided again as the arterial and the venous'. In the midst of this system was to be a 'motive organ', a 'central heart', in fact a steam engine. Here the sanitary and the agricultural were seen by Ward to meet in one great movement, a 'vast tubular organisation'. All of Ward's imagery derived directly from Harvey and enhanced the hygienists' political purposes of linking the individual body to the social body with all the moral engineering this entailed. The medicalisation of the city was underway, where its organs could be directly attributed to human engineering and in need of constant examination.

Cisterns and cesspools were to be done away with and with them the pestilential stagnation that was believed to accrue there. Nature was to be galvanised in its efforts: where gravity prevented circulation steam power would assist, just as the steam locomotive had revolutionised the transport of people. Economy and health were uppermost in this language with Ward constantly drawing on the most detailed figures of how much could be saved through these operations and how little would be spent for their initiation. The relations drawn by Ward between steam locomotion and the movement of excrement are important ones as throughout its discourse the hygienists were promoting the idea of circulation as an agent of movement, a homogenising of the heterogeneity of town and country, but a differentiation between parts of the city. This understanding of the city as an organism, redefined along Harvey's lines of circulation, is not an aesthetic nicety but materially affected the citizens of London, Berlin, Paris and Amsterdam in positive and negative ways. Positive in that the death rates of these cities dropped drastically on inauguration of Ward's system, negatively in ways which Foucault described as the inauguration of authoritarian medical intervention.

As with all such totalising objectives the hygienists were unable to account for delinquencies in the system, a deficiency which questions the analysis at the heart of their principles. The evidence of industry in a city in the later nineteenth century questions whether it wasn't rather the reverse image, stagnation over circulation, that still informed industrial procedures. The city that harboured stagnation would deny the hygienists and their cause, and as Didier Gille points out this was precisely the stuff of water in the industrial city of the nineteenth century. This would certainly be true of the south side of the Thames, where the olfactory has only recently been in the process of abeyance. For the olfactory was itself a recognition of a history of industries of more or less stagnation: leather tanning, vinegar fermentation and wet docks were all characteristic of this part of riverside London, where water did not so much move on, as move in and be captured for use. Tanning was a stagnant, excremental process, a process which literally stained its workers, and brought home to all in the wide circumference of its stench the place of rot and death at the heart of daily city life. These industrial images point to the falsity of a binomial operation between circulation and stagnation, for circulation is after all a return to the same place: like revolution, circulation implies that after all things stay where they are. It is however a concept which was used to effect against the imagery of confusion and panic in the city, and used to very specific effect to this end in the theatre. Throughout this period the concept of the city envisaged by the hygienists was not just an antidote to the very real problems of the city and its poorest inhabitants, but the shaping of a city to come. From the sanitary writings to the Hygienist movement there was a slippage between 'potions, remedies and panaceas' which were to become 'laws, principles and structures'.[6] From the rhetoric of the movement it is not clear how circulation succeeded in divesting the urban space of delinquency or disruption. These are easier to trace in a smaller model where hygienism became the platform for appeals to order in the theatre of moral panics.

Theatre hygiene

When Walter Roth introduced his programme for 'theatre hygiene', he understood it to be a scheme for 'a somewhat neglected Department of the Public Health'.[7] His programme was published in 1888, a year before Ward's treatise was republished in London by Edwin Chadwick and the same year that William Buckley's prototype for a 'safety theatre' was unveiled. It was intended for an Australian audience, being the result of his enquiries into Sydney theatres. Roth was arguing for a new science for a new world where the deleterious state of theatre need not necessarily prevail as it would in the more complex circumstances of old cities. The concept of theatre hygiene was a broad one but reflects certain parallels to the Hygienist movement described above:

> 'Theatre Hygiene' may be described shortly as the study of the best structural and decorative arrangements to be adopted in the construction and fittings of theatres, music halls and kindred establishments, together with a consideration of the sanitary and physical conditions of stage-life generally. The object in view is the health, comfort and safety, not only of the public, but of the players and other people employed.[8]

The first part of the statement was in itself a debating point throughout the century for other reasons, as will be seen in the next chapter, but here I am interested in Roth's conception of a 'healthy, comfortable and safe' theatre. The description of these concerns within the parameters of a 'hygiene' debate lends Roth the authority that the movement was building under the umbrella term hygienism. It was only here that laws, principles and structures could be demanded where previously there had been *ad hoc* arrangements between municipal bodies and theatre managers. Hygienism was here crossing borders between architecture and social reform without the subject in question being asked whether it was fair game for such treatment.

Theatre hygiene was prompted by the disasters at the Ring Theatre in Vienna, the Paris Opera Comique and the Exeter Theatre in England. Roth looks from the new world to the old and speaks of the problem of fires and panics and blames the loss of life on restrictions to circulation. What was at fault were 'outer doors kept locked', 'staircases badly constructed', 'exits not adequate', and he concludes that overall the example set by 'the central city of the whole civilised world' was one to be avoided. Although lighting and ventilation had, Roth believed, come in for some improvement, 'until two years ago the sanitary aspects of theatre-life generally – the true Theatre Hygiene – appear to have been entirely overlooked.'[9] A debate had indeed been underway in *The Stage* of 1886 and *The Sanitary Record* of the following year but Roth's intervention is to draw these disparate voices into an entity with a name, and a capitalised name with jurisdiction to enhance it.

The first focus for Roth was inevitably the theatre building itself. The site was to be free on all sides with egress to the open air for light and ventilation. Proper party walls between workshops and the theatre auditorium and between the theatre itself and other buildings were important. Given the predominance of theatres in hotels in Sydney, Roth might well have ironically insisted on a clearer separation just at the moment when the theatre was moving towards control by the same kind of legislation as had already prevailed over public places to sleep. The reason, according to Roth, that these principles were not generally followed was 'ignorance' and 'mammon'. He is neither impressed with the theatre's defective structures nor, significantly, does he see much hope for it given that many performance venues have arisen in buildings designed for 'bazaars', auctions, markets and 'even billiard rooms'. Circulation was all-important. The description of a common theatre experience was in Roth's prose an invitation to almost climatic intensity: 'the stifling temperature in the gallery, the lethal oppressiveness in the pit, and the disturbing general atmospheric influences in other portions of the building, are often a matter of serious consideration to the playgoer when making choice of an evening's entertainment'.[10] Roth called for the ventilation and circulation of air via a series of nozzles and pipes, a tubular system that could be reversed to exhaust foul vapours. Here the foul was replaced by the fragrant in an operation close to the heart of the hygienists. These pipes would be joined, Roth believed, by a system of pipes and sprinklers which could circulate water to all parts on the notice of an alarm.

Movement of air, like water, was salubrious and resistant to the corruption of the mass. The circulation of air was central to public health tactics and surpassed even the preoccupation with the draining of filth. Michel Foucault might have interpreted the demand for effective ventilation as the authorisation of permanent surveillance. But there is a more individual interpretation which would appear to have more meaning for the atomisation of the theatre experience: 'Techniques of ventilation, insofar as they acknowledged the need for space between bodies and gave protection against other people's odors, brought individuals into a new encounter with their own bodily smells and, as such, contributed decisively to the development of a new narcissism.'[11] The prevalence of hand-held fans in the theatre could be described, in this period, as a personal technology of ventilation which stood at the apex of a developing system of controls to the environment. Aerist theories cultivated the desire to 'move up a storey', the first floors of dwellings were to be superseded by the upper levels, the pit was avoided by retirement to the boxes and the circle. But ironically it was these boxes which were said to poison women of delicate constitutions for 'the breath of two thousand bodies, whose cleanliness and wholesomeness are to a greater or lesser degree suspect, makes you sweat all over'.[12] Worried spectators were often forced to leave the theatre in these circumstances.

The staircases of theatres were to be gradually raked rather than stepped steeply, with no landing stages nor the accumulation of people that these points invited. Not only was circulation promoted over stagnation in this way but blockages to corridors were to be removed at all costs. The circulatory principle was demonstrated in other less ordered ways and bore out the irony that to circulate was to return whence you came. Indeed Roth noticed from the records that in states of panic people were wont to rush to the doors whereby they entered and not to those which, in the case of an emergency, were provided for them. But the boundary between prevention of crushing, and the association of that prevention with regimes of disinfection was a slim one with regard to crowded areas of the auditorium such as the pit.

These were understandable controls to panic and loss of life, but Roth takes his hygienist purposes further by identifying the entrances and exits for particular scrutiny. He entreated that all entrances should be sufficiently protected from 'the inclemencies of the weather', concerned as he was with the deleterious effects of emanations from damp clothes during the performance. Here the miasma was approaching that of the urban hygienists whose concern for vapours and their effects motivated circulation and differentiation. The theatre was already, like the city, in its own stratified way, differentiated through economy, and Roth had particular views as to the congestion that would arise around those exits where most people from the cheapest quarters of the building left. Thus the exits from the expensive seats should be situated in the narrower thoroughfares and from the pit and the gallery to the wider streets. The purpose was to 'lessen the magnitude of the crowd gathering' and here the urban plan, the isolation of the theatre in its own hermetically sealed island, and the theatre population come into proximity. The avowed purpose at ingress and egress was to 'keep the audience on the move' and to this end 'stringent measures' were to be taken to clear obstructions. The idiosyncratic arrangements of different theatres and customs could not be tolerated and these measures were soon to deepen into a legislative and juridical language. Roth knew that none of his recommendations would be carried out without such jurisdiction and he proposed a framework of 'legislation', 'licences for all shows including temporary structures', periodic inspections, and annual certification of premises. The scheme for Theatre Hygiene would be neglected in the absence of compulsion, and the inevitable consequence for Roth was the monopolising of theatres by the state, which he suggested would not only lead to a healthier theatre but intriguingly to better acting.

The public and the theatre as a building were given precedence, but

Roth continued his analysis to the individual needs of the audience member and the performer. If the theatre was to be isolated in a healthy differentiation from the neighbourhood, the seat of the individual no less required redesign. Roth is concerned again about the 'cheaper part' of the theatre and the seating therein, believing it to be too close and cramped, leading to deleterious physical effect on the audience member and 'his hat'. Roth proposes a move from the horizontal arrangement of seating to the proscenium, to a vertical arrangement where circulation will be assisted by regular aisles and short rows of seats. Here the audience was to be further subdivided and fragmented. But Roth's concern for the cheaper seats does not indicate a simple class division between what needs attention and improvement and what is satisfactory. Private boxes were not to be encouraged and Roth's pursuance of the well-being of all is demonstrated in his description of an audience member: 'To the public gaze she probably appears as the charming reality of some delightful dream, ie as much as is seen of her; but fortunately I have been favored with a private view . . .'.[13] Roth presumes that the absence of the woman's opera glasses and fan points to them having been dropped over the edge onto the head of someone below as she leans over the box edge in a state of apparant orthopaedic breakdown.

Walter Roth presumes that theatre is a histrionic delusion, a semblance of life, a representation, an illusion above all else. But the Aristotelian theatre which he espouses is for the ordinary theatre-goer never quite achievable. All aspirations to theatre will be thwarted by the unlikely combination of nature and the limitations of culture:

In the auditorium, scenic illusion is well nigh impossible to a spectator, the martyr of a seat much too small to sit upon, a draught from some ill-fitting door presumably closed, playing the harbinger of a long doctor's bill, and an atmosphere of so stuffy and contaminated a nature as to threaten imminent suffocation. . . . Sometimes the public have but themselves to blame, as when, during the progress of a performance, the inconvenience of a forgotten latch key, a 'last train' . . . is suddenly and too painfully realised.[14]

This I would surmise is one of the common experiences of the theatre today and one which is given little attention for the effects it has on what is experienced as theatre. For Roth anything which breaks the illusory quality of the theatre is to be deplored and he cannot understand the propensity for lighting from the foot of the stage giving prominence to the actor's teeth when 'the natural order of things in every-day life' demands that the actor be lit from side and above. The illusion is finally broken by the 'pitching of flowers onto the stage' and, worse, the actor's retrieval of them. All this occurs with a constant disturbance from late arrivals into the auditorium and early departures from it, such practices in need of being 'most rigorously prevented and suppressed'. At this point one would not be surprised to see Roth proposing a theatre police, but he leaves this to those other hygienists whose writings inevitably finished up in areas of preventive policing and juridical extensions to their brief.

In accepting the illusory qualities of the stage, and in emphasising their importance, logically Roth is left to defend the mental hygiene of the performers as well as their physical being. Roth is concerned to hear of the adoption of stage personae in private and everyday life and makes reference to Garrick's continuation as Richard III, and Mrs Siddons' Lady Macbeth, both of which he intriguingly claims spilled into other dimensions of their private worlds. These dangers are particularly prominent and to be avoided in juveniles who, Roth believes, should not be exposed to histrionic training at all. In the end there is an immorality for Roth in expecting the young to expose themselves to danger on the high-wire to satisfy the 'morbid craving for such sensational displays' which should be checked in the audience. Roth's solution is simple but alarming for the theatre of risks: 'There is exactly the same skill in walking on a tight rope three feet from the ground, as there is when the rope is fixed at thirty, with the addition that in the case of a fall, it would be but trivial in the former case, possibly fatal in the latter.'[15] If there are dangerous effects to performance for the young there are positive benefits to be had from the theatre as a profession for the adult. Roth believes that rehearsal and performance keep physical and mental capacities 'healthily occupied' and from the lives of eminent actors and actresses the practice of their art appears on the whole to have had little or no effect in 'curtailing the normal natural existence'. Although the different phenomena described by the term 'stage fright' worry Roth he believes that the lack of it in the boredom of 'long runs' is more deleterious. There had been, for some time, a debate about the mentally injurious nature of such extensions to the life of performances but Roth believes the old adage: ' . . . long runs are bad for art but good for actors.' While the health of the actor is enhanced by regular changes of costume there is concern expressed that costume can contribute to respiratory problems through tight lacing or high collars. Here clothes, cleanliness, stage practice, mental and physical attributes of performers are put into conjunction in theatres that will be cleaned up for the hygienic results. New cities will get the new theatres they deserve. Old theatres in old cities will be isolated where possible from the traffic of the everyday. These were the conditions for the inauguration of the safety theatre that Henry Irving proposed at the end of the nineteenth century, the apotheosis of the planner's intention, the conjunction of the first knight of the theatre and the architect in an operation of containment and control.

In the wake of Theatre Hygiene there is increased and legitimised argument for municipal and state control of theatres, strict conformity to rules and regulations based on the principles of circulation and isolation. Safety for Irving meant instant and direct escape from the theatre and this principle rested on the concept of isolation of the theatre from other buildings. If open sites could not be found they would have to be made, if necessary by the creation of adjacent roads and the narrowing of theatre buildings. Further, the great principle of isolation was to be carried through to the interior where there was demanded the 'instant isolation of the stage from the auditorium'. Neglect of these principles was to be made into a 'criminal offence' and here theatre's laws began to incorporate the hygienic and the sanitary as well as the safety of its personnel.

It is apparent from this short history that the 'cleaning up' of the theatre in the nineteenth century, and the subsequent move of an audience from the theatre to the music hall, was a process which incorporated all levels of public order. The principles of circulation and ventilation were not enough alone for they required the changing of individual behaviour patterns. After all, the hygienists were not often listened to, as the history of Ward's theories attests. What was lacking was the involvement of those within the theatre, and their architects and planners, and it was this alliance under Henry Irving which pointed to a health and safety theatre.

8

COMBUSTION
Fire and safety

In the second part of this book I have considered how some of the conventions and jurisdictions which determine what I can and cannot do under the sign of theatre, came to be. The most intriguing of these determinations are of course the silent ones, those about which least is said but on which most is predicated. These are theatre taboos, a complex of shadowy restraints and controls, from prompting to possession, that transgress the theatre's limit, inform us politely what theatre is not and in so doing inadvertently tell us something about what theatre is. These taboos operate around the boundaries of everyday life and theatre, are culturally contingent and change from one place and time to the next. When derived from the elemental and natural they pose the most elusive problems of interpretation and enforce all the more harshly their control over how theatre and everyday life can be associated.[1]

I will by way of conclusion speak about one of these taboos exemplified by two small boxes and their contents: 'strike anywhere' matches and 'safety' matches. The one you can strike at risk to you, others and furniture; the other only on the box provided, and therefore at little risk to anyone. I accept that in the case of fire, pluralism of choice, the table, the wall, a shoe sole, might reasonably give way to the limit imposed by safety, the box. In the case of theatre, we might be more divided about such a polarity, the choice between a safe theatre and an unsafe theatre, but as these chapters have aimed to show, this is a spectrum within which theatre operates. There is in most places, but importantly not yet in all, no need for us to make a choice, it has already been made for us. The nature of that choice derives from a 'line that separates the inflammable from the fireproof' and that line for cultures 'divides reality in a different way'.[2]

If safety is the governing force circumscribing the configurations of public involvement in theatre, where in the margins is this questioned? The freedom from danger has only in the last century superseded a freedom *for* danger. The contracts of Carnival have always been different, often inverted, and to be in Barcelona at the Festival of Mercè is to recognise

228

and accept the possibility of burning, of being burnt. But that is the point, and for some there would be no point in being there without that risk. It is between the vitality of such theatrical manifestations and the conventions of Western auditoria that theatre has in its myriad alternative forms been conducting a repressed dialogue. Catalan companies such as Els Comediants and La Fura dels Baus make this their axis of operation, often leading to the enactment of containment and control by the host authorities of capitals they visit whose sensibilities of safety are challenged on their arrival. It is in the space between this safety and danger that theatre took its place and continues to articulate its demand on our attention. It is a contract which in the West is no longer debatable, it has become taboo. It has of course not always been so, theatres if not theatre itself, were once simply dangerous. But the way of reading that past is dependent on a writing of history, which in the case of fire is to be treated seriously, but equally sceptically, if we are not to miss the real it hopes to capture in its script. I am not arguing for a dangerous or a safe theatre – I have no right to jeopardise life, nor to take away the other's right to death – but to recognise that, in the absence of critical thought, dangers arise from unforeseen corners and jeopardise both life and theatre. Historiography is one defence against forgetting, and is to be valued by the practitioner whose work is undertaken in its folds.

If the meaning of fire has been forgotten, what kind of history writing will adequately recall its features? Appropriately a writing of the unwritten fostered by Michel de Certeau. Historiography articulates the event and the fact.[3] The event, according to de Certeau, is that which delimits, the fact, that which fills. The event provides the historian with the conditions for intelligibility, the fact creates the possibility of a meaningful statement being made. Thus the event defines, the fact spells out. The event provides the means through which disorder is turned into order, it permits an understanding.

To test this hypothesis and to mark a final boundary between theatre and everyday life I have chosen to examine three events. They all occurred in London and I acknowledge here a necessary geographical limit. The litany could be extended to Chicago or San Francisco, though the consequent analysis might be quite different. The events: the Globe Theatre burns down. The Royal Opera Covent Garden burns down. The Savoy Theatre burns down. The facts: the Globe was destroyed on 29 June 1613 during a performance of Henry VIII, by the firing of a cannon and the igniting of the thatch. Fact gives way to conjecture. Covent Garden was burnt down on 5 March 1856, during a *bal masque* organised by 'The Wizard of the North' as the band struck up God Save the Queen, by the 'spontaneous combustion' of wood shavings in the carpenter's store. Fact gives way to conjecture later under cross-examination. The Savoy Theatre burns down on the night of 12 February 1990. The theatre was dark at the time, the origins of the fire are not thought to be suspicious, though decorators had been completing a programme of regilding over the previous weekend. Conjecture, arriving late but triumphant, is that an electrical fault was responsible, a neat journalistic irony given that the theatre was the first building to be lit solely by its own electric light, thus for the first time, back in 1881, diminishing the historic chance of fire from gas lighting.

Historiography tells us least of a reliable nature about the Globe, and in the space of this absence most is built. Historiography tells us more about the Royal Opera Covent Garden, erecting its foundations in the space between the old and the new, a place in the sequence of Covent Gardens being significant for how it contributes to the tradition, the genealogy of Covent Gardens past and present. Progress nevertheless erases the previous theatres for the sake of the new. The contemporary period is categorically different from this momentum. The Savoy Theatre is rebuilt as an exact copy of Basil Ionides' art deco original. The procedures of history once derived from speculation, in the case of the Globe, and derivation in the case of Covent Garden, now justify conservation. Historiography informs us that the Savoy is a unique art deco theatre; this categorisation is transformed by the authorities into the legislation that it is a Grade One Listed building, and by law has to be replicated. Fire has been harnessed by fakery. The historiographer has begun to supersede the architect. It is worth dwelling therefore on what this new power in the theatre is, before dwelling on the challenges it faces from fire.

In theatre, what has been theoretically elusive is the contextual understanding of places of performance, as Marvin Carlson puts it in the book of that name: how theatres generate social and cultural meanings of their own which in turn help to structure the meaning of the entire theatre experience.[4] If the theatre is a 'normative' type in the urban fabric, from the Classical period, through the Renaissance, to modern times, it is only relatively recently that the burnt-down theatre has been superseded by the theatre of longevity and durability, the theatre which Henry Irving demanded, designed and directed, the Safety Theatre.

In the margins of the history of the theatre on fire, where guilt and recrimination flare in equal measure, the work of the historiographer is muted. For already this site is a place where the 'other' is responsible. The gesture which attaches ideas to places is, de Certeau explains, precisely the historian's gesture.[5] If history is the relations between a place, analytical procedures and the construction of a text, the historiographical process becomes one of delimiting place, the practices therein and their conversion into writing. But fire so fundamentally affects us as to drive all reason from that place, for often the writing of the history of fire is the writing of the dead, literally. And witnesses become in this world, accomplices, their speaking is prejudice.

Let us see how this prejudice operates. In the case of the Covent Garden conflagration the official coroner's enquiry hears from the following parties: three of the four firemen of the theatre, along with Mr Palmer the gas fitter, and Mr Sloman the carpenter. As the periodical the *Builder* of 1856 reports:

> The evidence is, as might be expected, in some points conflicting; and without making any imputation on that score evidences the desire of each department of the establishment to throw blame off its own particular shoulders. The firemen considered that the fire must have been the work of an incendiary; though it did not appear that they had sufficient ground for saying so ... Mr. Palmer's evidence testified to the management of his own concerns, and the general arrangement of the gas fittings; whilst Mr. Sloman contradicted the other witnesses as to the fact of dangerous escape of gas, saying that he had been continually drawing the attention of the proprietors to it ...[6]

Such historical prejudices are, Michel de Certeau believes, precisely the stuff of the writing of history. This writing activates a move from historical prejudices to the situations they reveal, the transformation of prejudices into objects of study, removed to another place where the situation referred to is modified.[7] The living organisation of society, the relations between the gas fitter, the firemen and the carpenter, are changed by the writer of history into a past that can be placed under observation. Here history is not a substitute for their social praxis, but in de Certeau's words: 'its fragile witness and necessary critique'.[8] For de Certeau, this act of interpretation is to reinforce that which binds historical saying to social doing. De Certeau's concern here is one which links the work of the historiographer to that of the theatre practitioner and critic.

There are three stages to this historiographical operation. First the most obvious, but least thought of techniques: the beginning of history being the differentiation between the present and the past. The Globe, Covent Garden and the Savoy all burnt down *then*. This rupture for de Certeau organises the content of history within the relations between labour and nature. It is the agency of those involved that is of issue in all the reports, mostly literally, for under scrutiny are the labouring forces rather than the management and certainly not the fire in its own natural right. Second, historiography takes for granted a rift between discourse and the body, forcing that silent body to speak. Hence, as in the case of Covent Garden, the dual role of the coroner, for though nobody was killed, in the event of fire the coroner maintained jurisdiction over forcing words from potential accomplices to the act. Third, intelligibility is established through a relation with the other, one in which the alterity of the foreigner is 'understood', made to 'mean'.[9] History writing, de Certeau says, calms the dead who still haunt the present by offering them 'scriptural tombs'.

The consequences of this operation are clear. Breakage promotes a selection between what can be understood and what must be forgotten, the new place of each discourse built upon the existence of the dead, the necessity that what preceded has died and will remain buried. For it is this immense dormant knowledge that menaces what we think we know. Thus what is perishable is history's data, progress has become its motto. For de Certeau, the one is the experience which the other must both compensate for and struggle against.[10]

This final return to de Certeau's work, a shadow of his study *The Writing of History*, affords the theatre practitioner a way into the labyrinth that is the historical representation of the more or less familiar. Such historiographical operations have, in the case of fire, had meaning for the theatre as we now conceive it, and they, like the concerns of space, determine what can happen in theatre now as distinct from then. Historiography refers at once to a practice, and hence a reality but also and importantly to a closed discourse, a text that organises its own mode of intelligibility. There is clearly a tension between practitioner as writer, and history writer, the one furnishing the other with a discourse built upon their necessary death. Like a laminated disc the historian grips the practitioner in a giddy piggy-back and both spin back and forth on a cord strung between two clapping hands. That which is applauded must be recorded, that greeted with indifference or incomprehension, elided.

Theatre history concerns itself with that which is dead and gone. It is embarrassed by what continues in all its certitude: tentative and approximate readings are dwarfed by the real they fail to mimic. Even if that real is merely the trace of a structure, the absence of wood, where there was once 'Shakespeare'. The Globe Theatre in Southwark is much more interesting in theory than in rotten reality. Its discovery sent shivers down many an unreconstructed speculator. Therefore, and appropriately for the Globe given its mode of expiry, there should be no surprise that fire provides the motor of a theatre historiography. Fire separates the past from the present so efficiently as to have been the invention of historiography itself. If Prometheus hadn't already been chained to the rock, the historiographer might have been a candidate to satisfy the vulture. Fire is, after the event, an invisible form of erasure. It is not left, its facts are left. It has therefore presented the historiographer of theatre with a unique problem – how to interpret that which is elemental, natural and yet so utilitarian, once so generative of a new theatre, whether through speculation or derivation and today it would appear generative of the same theatre through conservation.

Historiography deals with natural elements in order to change them into a cultural environment. For de Certeau, historical work participates in the movement through which a society transforms its relation to nature by changing the 'natural' into the utilitarian, or into the aesthetic.[11] Historians in their writing metamorphose the environment through a series of transformations which change the boundaries and the internal topography of culture. They 'civilise' nature which has always meant that they colonise and change it. Like the 'stage reform' of the nineteenth century nature is tamed, or ignored in a *mise en scène* which has given up on reality. Is this precisely not the process underway here with regard to ineffable fire?

No, because the relation between labour and nature, a relation that is the rationale of the existence of historiography, is in the realm of fire, disturbed. Contemporary reports from the significant theatre fires of the last century are often unable to comprehend the relations between structure and event: the facts are scarce, the hearsay proliferates as fast as the flames. The event is all. This is peculiar to the event of fire, as building journals from the middle to the end of the nineteenth century, the period of regular conflagration, suggest. It is here, in building journals, that the implications of facts are valued, not in the artistic domain, and it is here that the lobby for stricter regulatory measures, safety theatres, ensues, until adopted belatedly by alliances from within theatre itself.

This line of errant thought can only take us to a dangerous conclusion: that it was not the movement from the street to the interior that compromised a modern theatre, but the advent of the safety-curtain. The intention, artistic principles apart, was to separate performer from audience in the interests of safety. This is hardly an innovative conception given that Artaud sought a theatre of 'a single and undivided locale' which would effectively dismantle the iron curtain and its protection of the audience from performer. As Richard Leacroft says in his comprehensive reconstruction of the development of the English Playhouse:

> It is only just a century and a half since the actor was pushed protesting – through the frame to accord with a particular theory based on the importance of the stage picture, a move, however, which conformed to the need to subdivide the fire-risk of theatres into smaller and more compact compartments.[12]

Leacroft's conclusion is that regardless of the need for theatrical experiment, fire and panic provide the twin constraints on theatre design. But this surely was a relation between competing forces, not an overnight occurrence, nor necessarily, for some, a welcome development. Half a century after the first installation of a safety-curtain at Drury Lane there was still confusion as to its purpose: it was a case of we have the technology but not the psychology. By 1896 the London County Council could demand the installation of fire curtains in new theatres but were without powers to enforce their use.

There was a proliferation of entertainments in London theatre in the late nineteenth century that involved fireworks in conditions of non-ventilation and stifling gas emissions; conditions well known to management and audiences alike if the last chapter's evidence is accepted. But both seem impervious to the obvious conclusions that the contract of attendance at theatre was one which accepted a significant risk to life. Such implications are only obvious if the spectrum of choice between safety and danger is derived from our 'progressive' attitudes rather than what was deemed necessary for theatre to be theatrical in the nineteenth century.

What would the legend of Robin Hood have been at the Pavilion Theatre in Whitechapel if it had not, as was customary, climaxed with his burning hut? The fact that the Pavilion was to burn down the following night, does not in itself seem to have inaugurated calls for the curtailment of such combustible climaxes in the reports of 1856.[13] In the genealogy of theatre fires there is no respect for cultural distinctions of a high art/low art kind. These distinctions are simply marked by the presence or absence of the Royal Party viewing the ruins. Very present at Covent Garden, very absent at Whitechapel.

The contract of attendance and participation in the theatre was however changing, and as Leacroft acknowledges, a decisive shift in this contract occurred around the jurisdictions and legalities of safety. Comfort had always been in doubt, but the ultimate in discomfort, premature death was no longer to be tolerated by the Lord Chamberlain, who as well as censoring the contents of theatre censored its spaces. Goethe might have summed up the situation: when asked what was the nature of a theatre building, he replied: 'I really know it precisely: the most inflammable substances are crammed together and at the soonest instance it goes up in flames.'[14] But the 'impossibility' of staging *Faust* now is well known, and it continues to tease contemporary directors into believing they can create the conditions for performance that have long been replaced by constraint and control. No, inhibitions as well as lives were lost at a time when fire was encouraged to take its toll, and it is relatively recent legislation and planning that has protected the theatre and its patrons, while jeopardising its reasons for assembly.

Hotel fires cut to the quick because of the expectation that a place to sleep is a safe place to sleep. But what of theatre? We have come to expect theatre to be a safe place to sleep – but should we? Do we have a right to expect safety where there was once danger? And what price do we pay for that safety – has theatre not disappeared in direct proportion to the restrictions that govern its performance? To raise this question is also to ask who is in a position to hear it? Where we might ask lies the power in the theatre, what is the arrangement of power that governs performance? On the axis some would say between artistic director and actor, others would say on the axis between executive director and administrator, and another from playwright to audience. But each and all are finally answerable to someone else far closer to the everyday and its tribulations. Søren Kierkegaard, as a regular theatre-goer, albeit for only ten minutes a night and apparently strictly on promotional grounds, knows where the power lies. He asks in his *Attack upon Christendom*: What says the fire chief?

> Hardly is the cry of Fire! heard before a crowd of people rush to the spot, nice, cordial, sympathetic, helpful people, one has a pitcher the other a basin, the third a squirt etc, all of them nice, cordial, sympathetic, helpful people, so eager to help put out the fire. But what says the Fire Chief? The Fire Chief he says – yes generally the Fire Chief is a very pleasant and polite man; but at a fire he is what one calls coarse mouthed – he says or rather he bawls 'Oh go to hell with all your pitchers and squirts.' . . . and to the policeman: 'Rid me of these damn people with their pitchers and squirts, and if they won't yield to fair words, smear them a few over the back, so that we may be free of them and get down to work.' So then at a fire that whole way of looking at things is not the same as in everyday life. Good natured, honest, well meaning, by which in everyday life one attains the reputation of being a good fellow, is at a fire honoured with coarse words and a few over the back. And this is quite natural. For a fire is a serious thing, and whenever things are really serious, this honest good intention by no means suffices. No, seriousness applies an entirely different law: either/or . . . If by thyself thou wilt not understand this, then let the Fire Chief thrash it into thee . . .[15]

As Kierkegaard goes on to point out: 'as it is at a fire, so also it is in matters of the mind'. Where there is the person of ideas of seriousness they will inevitably come upon a company of twaddlers: indeed the person recognises they are right by their very relation to this company of twaddlers, as the fire chief insists, they must be told to get out, for their very presence and effect is the most dangerous assistance the fire could have. Here the mental and the material are uniquely focused, for fire operates on levels that are simultaneously psychological, sociological, philosophical and of course physical and rarely will the historian grasp this complexity in anything but its effects. Its meaning for the theatre is therefore lost under a charred ruin, as though progress towards what we now consider worthy were the utilitarian purpose of the fire spirit.

Theatre is not alone in this. It was Gaston Bachelard who had to take the extraordinary step of writing a book called *The Psychoanalysis of Fire* to elucidate the blind spot of science and thought to the generative power of the experimental process.[16] Fire, Bachelard demonstrated, was not an invisible element, but a veritable force field of opinion and belief, metaphor and meaning, a deep psychological complex. Fire is no longer a reality for science, flame and fire both having disappeared from serious consideration long ago. Bachelard shows this is consequent upon the fact that knowledge of fire itself is unlikely to increase knowledge in general, but rather introduces us to the way that fascination with an object distorts inductions. Fire thus initiates a negative epistemology where knowledge is shrouded by the smoke of ideologies. Underlying fire is a system of heterogeneous values and convictions which, familiar and unquestioned, jeopardise with extreme prejudice the philosophy of science, the writing of history and the practice of theatre.

The theatre's relation to fire is a more complex one than the incendiary permits. It is more conspiracy theory than the lone pyromaniac allows. The theatre practitioner knows that to raise the question of fire and its meaning is to bring into doubt the seriousness of much of what it purports to do, as entertainment, frivolity, as the history of a company of twaddlers in fact. For in rousing this spectre the relations between the theatre I have been writing about in this book, and another theatre are illuminated. In one, nothing can be taken for granted; in the other everything has to be. The meaning of fire for the theatre is not just that there is so little but the terms on which it has been driven away. Theatres can now be expected to survive longer than twenty-two years, the average life span of a theatre in the nineteenth century. It is the absence of fire from the contemporary theatre which marks it off from the past, a present that is out of bounds for the historiographer and therefore insulated from the conclusions that might be drawn as to quite what progress has come from the theatre's propensity to perish in its previous incarnations, its contemporary propensity to remain, its specious immortality. Now the fire chief is on hand to rectify matters, the omniscient fire chief who is trained to treat the theatre like a hotel. But are the contracts of attendance the same? And if they are not, a question for practitioners, historians and critics alike might be: how are they to be distinguished before theatre is extinguished? This might appear a philosophy of the dangerous and ethically a curious place to conclude. But these problems provide a rendezvous for questions which if they are not posed will be even more hazardous to theatre and everyday life. It is after all never too late to ask them. Instinct says: 'When the house burns down one forgets even one's dinner', and Nietzsche's answer is 'Yes: but one retrieves it from the ashes.' Theatre might be forgotten, like the everyday, but like the everyday it is worth retrieving.

NOTES AND REFERENCES

INTRODUCTION

1 See Terry Eagleton, in 'Aesthetics and Politics': 'historically positioned as we are, we cannot possibly identify a "modernist" text without automatically thinking up the "realist" canon from which it deviates'. *New Left Review*, 107, Jan./Feb. 1978, p. 24.

2 'The sociologist who chooses to study his own world . . . should not, as the ethnologist would, domesticate the exotic, but, if I may venture the expression, exoticize the domestic.' Pierre Bourdieu, Preface to *Homo Academicus*, trans. Peter Collier, London, Polity Press, 1988; quoted by David Lodge, 'Review,' *The Guardian*, London, 9 Dec. 1988. Also John Blacking: 'An anthropology of Theatre is not concerned specifically with the exotic, but rather with the biology, archaeology and cultural variety of theatrical performance. If different life styles seem attractive and exotic to us, we should also find out how attractive and exotic our own life style may seem to those who participate in different cultural systems.' Paper circulated and read at: Points of Contact, International Theatre Symposium, Theatre, Anthropology and Theatre Anthropology, at Leicester Polytechnic, 1 Oct. 1988.

3 Henri Lefebvre, *Critique of Everyday Life*, London, Verso, 1991, p. 7.

4 A. Schopenhauer, 'Parerga und Paralipomena,' Part II, 'Gleichnisse und Parabeln', quoted by Félix Guattari in *Molecular Revolution*, Harmondsworth, Penguin, 1984, p. 18.

5 Lefebvre, op. cit., p. 95.

6 James Clifford, *Writing Culture*, London, University of California Press, 1986.

7 Martin Heidegger in *The Question Concerning Technology* makes this point: '*Thea* (cf. Theatre) is the outward look, the aspect, in which something shows itself' while *horao* means 'to look at something attentively, to look it over, to view it closely'. Quoted by Gregory Ulmer in *Applied Grammatology*, Baltimore, Johns Hopkins University Press, 1985, p. 32.

8 Brian Massumi in the foreword to Gilles Deleuze and Félix Guattari's, *A Thousand Plateaus*: 'Deleuze's own image for a concept is not a brick, but a "tool box". He calls this kind of philosophy "pragmatics" because its goal is the invention of concepts that do not add up to a system of belief or an architecture of propositions that you either enter or you don't, but instead pack a potential in the way a crowbar in a willing hand envelops an energy of prying.' London, Athlone Press, 1988, p. xv.

9 Marco de Marinis, 'A Faithful Betrayal of Performance: Notes on the use of Video in Theatre,' *New Theatre Quarterly*, 1 (4), 1985, p. 383.

10 Peter Brook, *The Empty Space*, Harmondsworth, Penguin, 1972.

11 Peter Brook, in interview with Margaret Croydon, May 1972, in *Lunatics, Lovers and Poets*, New York, Delta, 1974, p. 278.

12 Walter Benjamin, *Illuminations*, ed. Hannah Arendt, trans. Harry Zohn, New York, Schocken Books, 1969, p. 220.

13 Michel de Certeau, *The Practice of Everyday Life*, trans. Steven Rendall, Berkeley, University of California Press, 1988, p. 5.

14 Friedrich Nietzsche, *The Genealogy of Morals*, New York, Doubleday Anchor, 1956, p. 255.

1 LAY THEATRE

1 The Theatre Department at Dartington College of Arts, Devon, England, instigated the project, students from Dartington worked on placement within the project and many people from the college and the neighbourhood supported its continuation. Between 1978 and 1983 David Slater was the project coordinator. I am grateful to colleagues David Slater, Teresa Watkins, Fiona Graham and Ann Cleary, and to Colette King, Peter Hulton, Peter Kiddle, Will Fitzgerald, Rawdon Corbett, Roger Bourke, Roger Sell, Joe Richards, Keith Yon, Graham Green, Ric Allsopp, Jane Fitzgerald, Katy Duck, Claire MacDonald, Mary Fulkerson, Sue Lyons, Stephen Lowe, Gordon Jones, Anne Kilcoyne, Jane Bishop, Graham Fitkin, Ronnie Goodman, Dot and Alan Pedel, Jo Brundish, Mara de Wit and Jo Scanlan. Above all it is the students and neighbours of Rotherhithe Theatre Workshop who inform these stories if not my interpretation of them.

2 See Jean Duvignard, *Spectacle et société*, Paris, Denoël, 1970; Clifford Geertz, *Local Knowledge: Further Essays in Interpretive Anthropology*, New York, Basic Books, 1983; Erving Goffmann, *The Presentation of Self in Everyday Life*, London, Allen Lane, 1969.

3 I am indebted to David Slater for introducing me to this work. See David Slater, 'Beyond Reminiscence,' *Theatre Papers* 5 (7), Devon, Dartington College of Arts, 1985.

4 See Raymond Williams, 'Problems of Materialism,' in *Problems in Materialism and Culture*, London, Verso, 1980, p. 117.

5 Dartington College of Arts supported the project financially from its inception with additional support from Southwark Council, Greater London Arts and the London Docklands Development Corporation.

6 See Guy Debord, 'Introduction to a Critique of Urban Geography,' in *Situationist International Anthology*, ed. Ken Knabb, Berkeley, Bureau of Public Secrets, 1981, pp. 5–8.

7 See Anthony P. Cohen, *The Symbolic Construction of Community*, London, Routledge, 1989.

8 See Paul Feyerabend, 'Putnam on Incommensurability,' in *Farewell to Reason*, London, Verso, 1987, pp. 265–72.

9 Stephen Greenblatt, *Shakespearian Negotiations*, Berkeley, University of California Press, 1988, p.17.

10 This analysis draws on Pierre Bourdieu, 'The Uses of the People,' in *In Other Words*, London, Polity Press, 1990.

11 Friedrich Nietzsche, 'Maxims and Interludes', no.126, from *Beyond Good and Evil* : 'A people is a detour of nature to get to six or seven great men. – Yes:

and then to get round them.' trans. R.J. Hollingdale, Harmondsworth, Penguin, 1973, p. 81.

2 REGARDING THEATRE

1 See Meaghan Morris, 'Banality in Cultural Studies,' *Block*, 14, 1988, p. 25: 'Banality is one of a group of words – including "trivial" and "mundane" – whose modern history inscribes the disintegration of old ideals about the common people, the common place, the common culture. In medieval French, the "banal" fields, mills and ovens were those used communally. It's only in the late eighteenth century that these words began to accumulate their modern sense of the trite, the platitudinous, and the unoriginal . . . if banality, like triviality is an irritant that returns again and again to trouble cultural theory, it is because the very concept is part of the modern history of taste, value, and critique of judgement, that constitutes the polemical field within which cultural studies takes issue with classical aesthetics.'

2 The rhizomatic, from 'Rhizome', is differentiated by Deleuze and Guattari from the binary form of the root: 'A rhizome ceaselessly establishes connections between semiotic chains, organisations of power, and circumstances relative to the arts, sciences and social struggles.' Gilles Deleuze and Félix Guattari, *A Thousand Plateaus*, London, Athlone Press, 1988, p. 7.

3 See Herbert Blau, *Blooded Thought*, New York, Performing Arts Journal Publications, 1982.

4 Francis Fergusson, *The Idea of a Theater*, Princeton, Princeton University Press, 1949.

5 Martin Heidegger, *The Question Concerning Technology*, New York, Harper and Row, 1977, p. 4.

6 Terry Eagleton, *Critcism and Ideology*, London, Verso, 1978, p. 64.

7 Antonin Artaud from *The Theatre and Its Double*: 'The theater, an independent and autonomous art, must, in order to *revive or simply to live*, realize what differentiates it from text, pure speech, literature, and all other fixed and written means.' Quoted by Jacques Derrida, in *Writing and Difference*, trans. Alan Bass, Chicago, University of Chicago Press, 1978, p. 237.

8 John Arden, *To Present the Pretence*, London, Eyre Methuen, 1977, p. 210.

9 Keir Elam, in *The Semiotics of Theatre and Drama*, London, Methuen, 1980, p. 2: ' "Theatre" is taken to refer here to the complex of phenomena associated with the performer–audience transaction: that is, with the production and communication of meaning in the performance itself and with the systems underlying it. By "drama" on the other hand, is meant that mode of fiction designed for stage representation and constructed according to particular ("dramatic") conventions.'

10 See W.J.T. Mitchell, *Iconology*, Chicago, University of Chicago Press, 1986, p. 10, for a diagrammatic breakdown of the categories of images discussed here, also, Robert Morris, 'Words and Images in Modernism and Postmodernism,' *Critical Inquiry*, 15, Winter, 1989, p. 337.

11 See Eugenio Barba and Nicola Savarese, *A Dictionary of Theatre Anthropology*, English language edition ed. Richard Gough, London, Routledge, 1991.

12 Antonio Gramsci, quoted in *Formations of Pleasure*, ed. Tony Bennett *et al.* London, Routledge, 1983, p. iii.

13 Morris, op. cit., p. 338.

14 See Tom Harrisson and Charles Madge, *Britain by Mass Observation*, London, The Cresset Library, 1986.

15 Alan Wall, 'Modernism, Revaluation and Commitment,' in *1936: The Sociology of Literature Volume One: The Politics of Modernism*, ed. Francis Barker *et al.*, Essex University, 1979, p. 179.

16 Humphrey Jennings, *Pandaemonium, The Coming of the Machine as Seen by Contemporary Observers*, London, André Deutsch, 1985.

17 Michael Faraday, quoted ibid., p. 249.

18 Joseph Beuys, 'Joseph Beuys in conversation with Friedhelm Mennekes', in *Memorium Joseph Beuys*, InterNationes, Bonn, 1986, p. 31.

19 See Charles Madge, 'A Note on Images,' in *Humphrey Jennings: Film-maker, Painter, Poet*, ed. Mary Lou Jennings, London, British Film Institute, 1982, p. 48.

20 See Madge, in Jennings (ed.), *Humphrey Jennings*, p. 49.

21 ibid., p. 14.

22 ibid., p. 14.

23 Maurice Nadeau, *The History of Surrealism*, trans. Richard Howard, London, Jonathan Cape, 1968, p. 20.

24 Henri Lefebvre, *Critique of Everyday Life*, London, Verso, 1991, p. 123.

25 Nadeau, op. cit., p. 80.

26 Walter Benjamin, 'Surrealism, The Last Snapshot of the European Intelligentsia,' in *One Way Street and Other Writings*, trans. Edmund Jephcott and Kingsley Shorter, London, New Left Books, 1979, p. 232.

27 See Paul Feyerabend, *Against Method*, Revised Edition, London, Verso, 1988.

28 See George Steiner, 'Life-lines', in *Extraterratorial*, Harmondsworth, Penguin, 1975, pp. 180–204.

29 See Thomas Kuhn, *The Structure of Scientific Revolutions*, Chicago, University of Chicago Press, 1962; and Steiner, op. cit., for different perspectives on this process.

30 Charles Madge in *Humphrey Jennings*, op. cit., p. 48.

31 Gaston Bachelard, *The Poetics of Space*, trans. Maria Jolas, Boston, Beacon Press, 1969, p. xv.

32 Gaston Bachelard, *The New Scientific Spirit*, trans. Arthur Goldhammer, Boston, Beacon Press, 1984; *The Psychoanalysis of Fire*, trans. Alan C.M. Ross, Boston, Beacon Press, 1968; *The Poetics of Reverie*, trans. Daniel Russell, Boston, Beacon Press, 1971.

33 For a detailed discussion of the connections between Bachelard's poetics and philosophy of science from which I have drawn for the following discussion, see Dominic Lecourte, *Marxism and Epistemology*, London, New Left Books, 1975.

34 Quoted in Lecourte, ibid., p. 142.

35 ibid., p. 143.

36 ibid., p. 153.

37 E.P. Thompson, Review of *Pandaemonium*, *New Society*, 25 Oct. 1985, p. 105.

38 ibid.

39 Bachelard, *The Poetics of Space*, pp. xii–xiii.

40 This summarises points made by Bachelard in his 'Introduction,' to *The Poetics of Space*, pp. xi–xxx.

41 Sue-Ellen Case, *Feminism and Theatre*, London, Methuen, 1988, p. 132.

42 See Jennings (ed.), *Humphrey Jennings*, p. 21.

43 Thompson, op. cit., p. 105.

44 Richard Kearney, *The Wake of Imagination*, London, Hutchinson, 1988, p. 13.

45 See Richard Kearney, 'After Imagination,' in *The Wake of Imagination*, p.

359–97, for a discussion of the ethical, poetic, and political dimension of this 'poetics of the possible'.

46 Karl Kautsky, 'Marxism and Ethics,' in *Selected Political Writings*, ed. and trans. Patrick Goode, London, Macmillan, 1983, pp. 49–50.

47 For a full discussion of this theme see Edith Wyschogrod, *Saints and Postmodernism*, Chicago, University of Chicago Press, 1990.

48 Michel de Certeau quoted in Wyschogrod, *Saints and Postmodernism*, p. 53.

49 Kearney, *The Wake of Imagination*, p. 451, fn. 3.

50 ibid.

51 See E.P. Thompson, *The Poverty of Theory and Other Essays*, New York, Monthly Review Press, 1978.

52 Kearney, *The Wake of Imagination*, p. 368.

53 See Michel Foucault, *The Foucault Reader*, ed. Paul Rabinow, Harmondsworth, Penguin, 1986, p. 377.

54 Michel Foucault, 'On the Genealogy of Ethics: An Overview of Work in Progress', in *The Foucault Reader*, p. 349.

55 *The Foucault Reader*, p. 348.

56 Martin Esslin, *The Theatre of the Absurd*, Harmondsworth, Penguin, 1980.

57 *The Foucault Reader*, p. 374.

58 ibid.

59 See Richard Kearney, *Dialogues with Contemporary Continental Thinkers: the Phenomenological Heritage*, Manchester, Manchester University Press, 1984, pp. 1–8.

60 See RoseLee Goldberg, *Performance, Live Art 1909 to the Present*, London, Thames and Hudson, 1979, and Michael Kirby's 'Introduction' to *Happenings*, New York, E.P. Dutton, 1966, to pursue these necessary distinctions. As Goldberg says of Performance: 'No other artistic form of expression can be said to have such a boundless manifesto. Each performer makes his or her own definition in the very process and manner of execution' (p. 6).

61 Emmanuel Levinas, 'Reality and Its Shadow', in *The Levinas Reader*, ed. Seán Hand, Oxford, Basil Blackwell, 1989, pp. 130–43.

62 Kearney, *Dialogues*, pp. 57–8.

63 ibid., p. 59.

64 Emmanuel Levinas in a dialogue with Richard Kearney, quoted ibid., p. 63.

65 Antonin Artaud, *The Theatre and Its Double*, trans. Victor Corti, London, Calder and Boyars, 1974, pp. 30–1.

66 See Kearney, *The Wake of Imagination*, pp. 457–61, for an overview of this tendency and its relation to the postmodern imagination.

67 In Britain no one has contributed more to an understanding of this construction, in the contemporary period, than Raymond Williams. Throughout his theoretical and fictional work the concept of Nation and its relationship to community is prominent. His analysis of the concept in *Towards 2000* summarises arguments presented at greater length throughout his work. Raymond Williams, *Towards 2000*, Harmondsworth, Penguin, 1985.

68 ibid., p. 180.

69 The 'debate' which occurred between John McGrath and David Edgar in *Theatre Quarterly* is indicative of different perceptions of this problematic and a challenge which continues today to 'official' perceptions of human geography. See John McGrath, 'The Theory and Practice of Political Theatre', *Theatre Quarterly*, 9 (35), 1979, pp. 43–54, especially 'Afterword', p. 54; and David Edgar, 'Towards a Theatre of Dynamic Ambiguities', *Theatre Quarterly*, 9 (33), 1979, pp. 3–23. Also see David Edgar, 'Ten Years of Political Theatre,

1968–1978', in *The Second Time As Farce*, London, Lawrence and Wishart, 1988, pp. 24–65.
70 Williams, op. cit., p. 185.
71 Oscar Wilde, 'The Soul of Man Under Socialism', in *De Profundis and Other Writings*, Harmondsworth, Penguin, 1973, p. 37.
72 Benedict Anderson, *Imagined Communities*, London, Verso, 1985.
73 ibid., p. 15.
74 Ernst Gellner, *Thought and Change*, quoted in Anderson, op. cit., p. 15.
75 ibid.
76 Luce Irigaray, *Speculum of the Other Woman*, trans. Gillian C. Gill, New York, Cornell University Press, 1985, p. 362.

3 EVERYDAY LIFE

1 Maurice Blanchot, 'La parole quotidienne,' in *L'entretien infini*, Paris, Gallimard, 1959, pp. 355–66, and reprinted in Alice Kaplan and Kristin Ross (eds), 'Everyday Life', *Yale French Studies*, 73, 1987, p. 12.
2 Patrick Wright, *On Living in an Old Country*, London, Verso, 1985; and *A Journey through Ruins*, London, Radius, 1991.
3 It also sits more parochially in Britain between the cultural studies of Dick Hebdige and Robert Hewison, and the poetics of an author like Iain Sinclair whose novel *Downriver* touches on many similar themes in different form. See Iain Sinclair, *Downriver*, London, Paladin, 1991.
4 Charles Madge in response to Geoffrey Pike on 'The Constitutional Crisis and Domestic Anthropology'. *The New Statesman and Nation*, 2 Jan. 1937, p. 12.
5 I am grateful to the staff and the Trustees of the Mass Observation Archive, University of Sussex, for access to, and assistance with, the Archive.
6 Madge, *New Statesman and Nation*, p. 12.
7 Humphrey Jennings, Review of *Surrealism* by Herbert Read, in *Contemporary Prose and Poetry*, ed. Roger Roughton, Dec. 1936, p. 168.
8 See P.C. Ray, *The Surrealist Movement in England*, Ithaca, 1971, pp. 177–8, quoted by Kevin Robins and Frank Webster in 'Science, Poetry and Utopia', *Science as Culture*, pilot issue, London, Free Association Books, 1987, p. 55.
9 *The Yorkshire Post*, 30 July 1938.
10 See Charles Madge and Tom Harrisson, 'The Lambeth Walk', in *Britain by Mass Observation*, London, Century Hutchinson, p. 140.
11 ibid., p. 183.
12 See Jean Baudrillard, 'Simulacra and Simulations', in *Selected Writings*, ed. Mark Poster, trans. Paul Foss *et al.*, Stanford, CA, Stanford University Press, 1988, p. 166.
13 Fernand Braudel, *The Structures of Everyday Life, Vol. 1*, trans. Siân Reynolds, New York, Harper and Row, 1981, p. 24.
14 Notable exceptions to this generalisation would be the Centre for Contemporary Cultural Studies, Birmingham University; Tish School of the Arts, New York; Centre for Twentieth Century Studies, Milwaukee.
15 For an exception see Mark Poster, *Existential Marxism in Post War France: from Sartre to Althusser*, Princeton, Princeton University Press, 1975.
16 Kaplan and Ross, op. cit., p. 1.
17 See Raymond Williams, 'Crisis in English studies', in *Problems in Materialism and Culture*, London, Verso, 1986.
18 Kaplan and Ross, op. cit., p. 2.
19 ibid.

NOTES AND REFERENCES

20 Braudel, op. cit., p. 28.
21 See Patrick Suskind, *Perfume*, Harmondsworth, Penguin Books, 1988.
22 Alain Corbin, *The Foul and the Fragrant*, trans. Miriam L. Kochan, Leamington Spa, Berg Publishers, 1986, p. 60.
23 ibid., p. 232.
24 David Edgar, *The Second Time as Farce*, London, Lawrence and Wishart, 1988.
25 Henri Lefebvre, 'The Everyday and Everydayness', trans. Christine Levich of 'Quotidien et quotidiennéte', from *Encyclopaedia Universalis* and quoted in Kaplan and Ross, op cit., pp. 7–11. If this project sounds optimistic it formed the rationale behind inviting architects, planners, and social theorists to the Council of Europe Workshop on Theatre and Communities which occurred at Dartington College of Arts in 1983. Lefebvre's aspirations were clearly shared by participants at this event. See particularly the work of Erik Agergaard, Ricardo Basualdo and Neighbourhood Open Workshops, in 'Theatre and Communities: A Council of Europe Workshop', *Theatre Papers* 5 (16), ed. Peter Hulton, Devon, Dartington College of Arts, 1985.
26 Kaplan and Ross, op. cit., p. 3.
27 Lefebvre, ibid., p. 7.
28 ibid., p. 9.
29 ibid.
30 ibid.
31 ibid., pp. 10–11.
32 Meaghan Morris, *The Pirate's Fiancée*, London, Verso, 1988, p. 223.
33 See Wlad Godzich, 'The Further Possibility of Knowledge', for a detailed and perceptive analysis of the background to de Certeau's work in: Michel de Certeau, *Heterologies*, Minneapolis, University of Minnesota Press, 1988, p. viii. The following analysis draws upon this essay.
34 Godzich, op. cit., p. vii.
35 Félix Guattari, *The Three Ecologies*, p. 2, paper presented and distributed at the Institute of Contemporary Arts, London, 1989.
36 Godzich, op. cit., p. xxi.
37 Clifford Geertz, *Local Knowledge*, New York, Basic Books, 1983, p. 27.
38 Godzich, op. cit., p. xiii.
39 ibid., p. xiv.
40 Michel de Certeau, *The Practice of Everyday Life*, trans. Steven F. Rendall, Berkeley, University of California Press, 1984, p. xi.
41 See Edward Said, 'Opponents, Audiences, Constituencies, and Community', in *Postmodern Culture*, ed. Hal Foster, London, Pluto Press, 1985, p.135.
42 Recent studies by Herbert Blau and Susan Bennett in very different ways begin to trace out this remainder to the productivist theatre. See Susan Bennett, *Theatre Audiences*, London, Routledge, 1990; Herbert Blau, *Audience*, University of Michigan Press, 1990.
43 Edward Said, *The World, The Text and the Critic*, Cambridge, Mass., Harvard University Press, 1983, p. 291.
44 George Steiner, *Real Presences*, London, Faber and Faber, 1989, and also see the reviews of Wendy Steiner, *Silence*, in *London Review of Books*, 1 June 1989, pp. 10–11, cols 1–4, and Geoff Dyer, 'So God Made Jazz', *The Guardian* 'Review', 19 May 1989, p. 25, cols 1–8.
45 de Certeau, op. cit., p. ix.
46 ibid., p. xii.
47 Kaplan and Ross, op. cit.
48 de Certeau, op. cit., p. xiii.

49 See Michel de Certeau, 'The Historiographical Operation', p. 103, fn. 5: 'However suspect it may be within the ensemble of the "human sciences", the term "scientific" (where it is replaced by the term "analytical"), is no less so in the field of the so-called exact sciences, at least insofar as it would refer to "laws". With this term we can nonetheless define the possibility of conceiving an ensemble of *rules* allowing control of operations adapted to the production of specific objects or ends' in *The Writing of History*, trans. Tom Conley, New York, Columbia University Press, 1988.

50 de Certeau, *The Practice of Everyday Life*, p. xix.

51 ibid., p. xxiv.

52 ibid., p. 25.

53 ibid.

54 The examples describe small parts of longer-term theatre processes described as a lay theatre – the 'dray' being a part of a neighbourhood project in 1983, the police launch part of a street/river event in 1983, the factory the site of 'Multiple Angel', an olfactory event in 1988. See Graham Green and Alan Read, 'An Educational Theatre Project', in *Theatre Papers* 5 (12), Devon, Dartington College of Arts, 1985, and David Slater, 'Beyond Reminiscence,' *Theatre Papers*, 5 (7), Devon, Dartington College of Arts, 1985.

55 Michel de Certeau, *The Practice of Everyday Life*, p. 38.

56 ibid., pp. 38–9.

57 ibid., p. 78.

58 Quoted by de Certeau, ibid., p. 90.

59 ibid., p. 108.

60 ibid., p. 118.

61 ibid., p. 122.

62 This is the radical departure de Certeau puts forward, ibid., p. 166.

63 ibid., p. 167.

64 ibid., p. 173.

65 ibid., p. 175

66 See Patrice Pavis, *Languages of the Stage, Essays in the Semiology of Theatre*, New York, PAJ, 1982, p. 70: 'the modalities of reception and the work of interpreting the performance are very poorly understood.' Pavis goes on to identify the necessity for a strategy, which everyday life analysis takes as its starting point, quoting movements such as that of German Reception Theory as an example of an enquiry to be developed. Pavis points out that the 'idealism' of reception theory, placed as it is in the perceiving subject, has retarded its introduction to a structuralist discourse that fails to open out into the outside world. See 'The Aesthetics of Theatrical Reception: Variations on a Few Relationships', ibid., pp. 67–94.

67 de Certeau, *The Practice of Everyday Life*, p. 188.

68 Quoted in Yvette Biró, *Profane Mythology*, trans. Imre Goldstein, Bloomington, Indiana University Press, 1982, p. 54.

69 ibid., p. 3.

70 Although 'kitchen sink drama' was used to describe plays produced at the Royal Court Theatre and elsewhere, which gave central prominence to the detail of 'working-class life', the term was a derivation from the visual arts field where the socialist realism of John Bratby in the early 1950s was termed 'The kitchen sink school'. See *Fontana Dictionary of Modern Thought*, 1978, pp. 333–4.

71 Biró, op. cit., p. 56.

72 ibid.

73 ibid., p. 57.
74 For a detailed analysis of this period of theatre history see Raphael Samuel, *et al.*, *Theatres of the Left 1880–1935*, London, Routledge and Kegan Paul, 1985, pp. 3–76, and on the metaphysical aspect of theatre: 'Theatre seems to exercise a "metaphysical" influence on politics or at any rate an influence out of all proportion to its size, or the number of its audience. Quite often it seems to prefigure or anticipate major political themes, as though a live performance on stage constituted a kind of symbolic recognition of the entry of some new issue into the arena of public debate' (p. xv).
75 There are numerous examples of such animation from the historical to the contemporary: eg. Eisenstein's production of Tretiakov's *Gas Masks* (1923–4): 'the real interiors of the factory had nothing to do with our theatrical fiction. At the same time the plastic charm of reality in the factory became so strong that the element of actuality rose with fresh strength – took things into its own hands – and finally had to leave an art where it could not command . . .'. Sergei Eisenstein, 'Through Theatre to Cinema', *Theatre Arts Monthly*, 20 (9), September 1936, p. 739. And Armand Gatti: 'it's mostly the place, the architecture that does the writing. The theatre was located not in some kind of Utopian place, but in a historic place, a place with history . . . These rooms that had known the labour of human beings day after day had their own language, and you either used that language or you didn't say anything.' 'Armand Gatti on Time, Place and the Theatrical Event', ed. Jean-Paul Lenin, trans. Nancy Oakes, *Modern Drama*, 25 March 1982.
76 Biró, op. cit., p. 69.
77 ibid.
78 ibid., p. 63.
79 ibid., p. 73.
80 ibid.
81 See Yvette Biró's summary of Roland Barthes' position in *Profane Mythology*, p. 76, and for the original, Roland Barthes, 'Myth Today', in *Mythologies*, trans. Annette Lavers, New York, Hill and Wang, 1972.
82 Biró, op. cit., p. 76.
83 ibid., p. 55.
84 ibid., p. 77.
85 Sigmund Freud, *Totem and Taboo*, quoted ibid., p. 78.
86 ibid., p. 64.
87 See Gilles Deleuze and Félix Guattari, 'Rhizome', in *On The Line*, trans. John Johnston, New York, Semiotext(e), 1983.
88 Biró, op. cit., p. 65.
89 ibid., p. 80.
90 Olivier Perrier, working with Les Fédéres, has over a long period been involved in making theatre in his home village of Herisson, southern France. The work as described to the European Workshop on Theatre and Communities (Dartington 1983), has consisted of a series of performances involving his own farm animals: 'My first show was in 1976, *The Memoires of a Good Man*. I used the courtyard throughout for rehearsals, rehearsing with a horse and a cow Tutune. I used a cattle van as my touring vehicle . . . It was a totally tragic sort of show . . .' See 'Theatre and Communities, A Council of Europe Workshop', ed. Peter Hulton, *Theatre Papers*, 5 (16), Devon, Dartington, 1985.
91 For scripts of these productions see: Howard Brenton, *Magnificence*, London, Methuen, 1981, p. 63: 'WILL: All night. Walked about London. Hours and hours of talk. And so tired. And Jed going on and on. Re-lentless. Burning it

all up . . . And mid-morning train from Euston station. Lovely day. Into Hertfordshire. Got off at a little station. And 'ouses and gardens . . . In the Indian Summer lovely weather. And we walked for miles, over the fields, in the lanes. Jed like he was on a laser beam. Through the English Countryside. Burning on and on.' Also see *Weapons of Happiness*, London, Methuen, 1981, p. 76: 'SCENE FIVE: *Wales. Snow. Brilliant Light. A Winter Orchard. An envelope is nailed to a tree.'*

92 Biró, op. cit., p. 83.

4 ORIENTATION: Space and place

1 See Edward W. Soja, 'The Reassertion of Space in Critical Social Theory', in *Postmodern Geographies*, London, Verso, 1989.

2 Edward W. Soja and Costis Hadjimichalis, 'Between Geographical Materialism and Spatial Fetishism: Some Observations on the Development of Marxist Spatial Analysis', *Antipode* (2) 3, p. 4. I am grateful to Chris Shore for bringing *Antipode* to my attention.

3 See summary of Lefebvre's position in Soja and Hadjimichalis, op. cit., p. 5.

4 See David Harvey, *The Condition of Postmodernity*, Oxford, Basil Blackwell, 1989.

5 From the perspective of theatre it is here of secondary interest that his work was one of critical equality to that of Brecht and this emphasis on other aspects of his writing should not preclude the need to digest all that he said about understanding that particular playwright, and that playwright's regard for the everyday.

6 Walter Benjamin, *Illuminations*, ed. Hannah Arendt, trans. Harry Zohn, New York, Schocken Books, 1969, fn. 3, p. 243.

7 ibid., p. 221.

8 See *Cinema in Revolution*, eds Luda and Jean Schnitzer, trans. David Robinson, New York, Hill and Wang, 1973, pp. 7–10.

9 Benjamin, op. cit., fn. 5, p. 243.

10 Walter Benjamin, 'The Storyteller', op. cit., pp. 83–109.

11 See Terry Eagleton, *Walter Benjamin or Towards a Revolutionary Criticism*, London, Verso, 1981, p. 60.

12 Benjamin, 'The Storyteller', op. cit., p. 84.

13 ibid., p. 90.

14 ibid., p. 101.

15 ibid., p. 108.

16 For a detailed discussion of this tension see Michael Lowy in *New Left Review* 152, Jul./Aug. 1985, pp. 42–59.

17 Francesco Beccari quoted in *History of Cartography*, Vol. I, ed. J.B. Harley and D. Woodward, Chicago, University of Chicago Press, 1987, p. 428.

18 Michel de Certeau, *The Practice of Everyday Life*, trans. Steven Rendall, Berkeley, University of California Press, 1988, p. 107.

19 See Paul Klee, *Pedagogical Sketchbook*, intro. and trans. Sibyl Moholy-Nagy, London, Faber and Faber, 1984, and *On Modern Art*, trans. Paul Findlay, London, Faber and Faber, 1987.

20 Klee, *On Modern Art*, p. 11.

21 Klee, *Pedagogical Sketchbook*, p. 7.

22 ibid., p. 23 (I.6).

23 ibid., p. 43 (II.23).

24 ibid., p. 10.

25 Theodor Adorno quoted in Ernst Bloch *et al.*, *Aesthetics and Politics*, trans. and ed. Ronald Taylor, London, New Left Books, 1977, p. 109.
26 Klee, *Pedagogical Sketchbook*, p. 10.
27 The 'New Dance' movement as its name implies was/is wide and varied, resisting generalities, as is the Contact Improvisation contribution to that movement. But the presence of figures as diverse as Laurie Booth and Gaby Agis in its early development in Britain (1981–83) was to highlight some of the tensions that would inevitably arise between gender issues, forms and contents, a challenge to the 'discipline' of ballet, and the relations between flow and flux. For full documentation of this influential movement see the periodicals *New Dance* and *Contact Quarterly*.
28 Klee, *Pedagogical Sketchbook*, p. 12.
29 ibid.
30 Klee, *On Modern Art*, p. 13.
31 ibid., p. 15.
32 Franz Kafka, quoted by Walter H. Sokel, 'Kafka's Poetics of the Inner Self', *From Kafka and Dada to Brecht and Beyond*, ed. Reinhold Grimm *et al.*, Wisconsin, University of Wisconsin Press, 1982, p. 7.
33 Klee, *Pedagogical Sketchbook*, p. 54 (IIII, 37).
34 See editor's note in Bloch *et al. Aesthetics and Politics*, p. 102: 'Culturally the two men shared certain dominant axes of reference, both temporal and spatial – Proust, Valéry and Kafka, among others.'
35 Walter Benjamin, 'Franz Kafka', in *Illuminations*, p. 134.
36 ibid., p. 129.
37 ibid., p. 120.
38 ibid.
39 ibid.
40 Antonin Artaud, *The Theatre and its Double*, trans. Victor Corti, London, Calder and Boyars, 1970.
41 Walter Benjamin, op. cit., p. 124.
42 See Max Brod, 'Postscript' to *America*, Harmondsworth, Penguin, 1970, p. 269: 'He never actually travelled farther than France and Upper Italy, so that the innocence of his fantasy gives this book of adventure its peculiar colour.'
43 Walter Benjamin, 'Some Reflections on Kafka', in *Illuminations*, p. 143.
44 John Ashbery, 'Three Poems', quoted in Walter Abish, 'The English Garden', in *In The Future Perfect*, London, Faber and Faber, 1984, p. 1.
45 John Berger, *The Look of Things*, quoted by Edward W. Soja in *Antipode*, op. cit., p. 3.
46 Edward W. Soja, ibid.
47 de Certeau, op. cit., p. 129.
48 Walter Benjamin, 'Edward Fuchs, Collector and Historian,' in *One Way Street*, trans Edmund Jephcott and Kingsley Shorter, London, New Left Books, 1979, pp. 302–3.

5 ACCRETION: Earth and depth

1 See Gilles Deleuze and Félix Guattari, '10,000 BC: The Geology of Morals,' in *A Thousand Plateaus*, trans. Brian Massumi, London, Athlone Press, 1988, p. 44.
2 ibid., p. 57.
3 See Roland Barthes, 'The Third Meaning', in *Barthes*, ed. Susan Sontag, London, Fontana, 1983, p. 318.

4 See David Bradby and David Williams, *Directors' Theatre*, London, Macmillan, 1988.
5 The theatre was built for Stein and his company at a cost of 81.5 million Deutschmarks. See Ned Chaillet, *Inter National*, London, National Theatre, 1987.
6 Eugene O'Neill, *The Hairy Ape*, London, Jonathan Cape, 1968, p. 28.
7 Matthew Arnold, *Culture and Anarchy*, quoted in Humphrey Jennings, *Pandaemonium*, London, André Deutsch, 1985, p. 319.
8 ibid.
9 D.H. Lawrence, from 'Nottingham and The Mining Country', quoted in *Nature and Industrialization*, ed. Alasdaire Claire, Oxford, Oxford University Press, 1977, p. 388.
10 Andrew Ure, 'The Philosophy of Manufactures', quoted ibid., p. 71.
11 For a development of this theme in relation to fine art and painting see Peter Fuller, 'Black Arts: Coal and Aesthetics', in *Images of God*, London, Chatto and Windus, 1985, p. 200.
12 I am grateful to the Anthony D'Offay Gallery for providing me with an unedited video recording of this encounter.
13 Arthur Scargill, ibid.
14 John McGrath, 'Better a Bad Night in Bootle', *Theatre Quarterly*, 5 (19), 1975, p. 51.
15 For documentation on the relations between theatre and communities throughout Europe see: 'Theatre and Communities: A Council of Europe Workshop', in *Theatre Papers*, 5 (16), ed. Peter Hulton, Devon, Dartington College of Arts, 1985.
16 Michael Rustin, 'Place and Time in Socialist Theory', *Radical Philosophy* 47, Autumn 1987, pp. 30–6. This article provides the background for the following analysis.
17 ibid., p. 30.
18 E.P. Thompson, *The Making of the English Working Class*, Harmondsworth, Penguin, 1979.
19 Rustin, op. cit., p. 33.
20 Franz Kafka, *Amerika*, Harmondsworth, Penguin, 1970.
21 Given the influence of Kafka's *Amerika* for Tim Rollins and KOS (Kids of Survival) it would appear that it also opens a space for art.

6 INSPIRATION: Air and breath

1 Antonin Artaud, *The Theatre and its Double*, trans. Victor Corti, London, Calder and Boyars, 1974, pp. 23–54.
2 Jerzy Grotowski: 'We are entering the age of Artaud. The "theatre of cruelty" has been canonised, i.e. made trivial, swapped for trinkets, tortured in various ways.' In *Towards a Poor Theatre*, ed. Eugenio Barba, London: Methuen, 1975, p. 85.
3 Peter Stein: '[theater] is an event in which completely irrational things are being reproduced according to definite rules ... This capacity for regulated paradox, for regulated, performed and controlled irrationality is part of theater'. In 'Utopia as the Past Conserved', Jack Zipes in interview with Peter Stein and Dieter Sturm, Berlin: Schaubühne am Halleschen Ufer, 6–7 June 1977.
4 Antonin Artaud, *The Cenci*, trans. Simon Watson Taylor, New York, Grove Press 1970: 'The difference between the Theater of Cruelty and The Cenci will be the difference which exists between the din of a waterfall or the unleashing

by nature of a hurricane on the one hand and, on the other hand, whatever degree of their violence may remain in a recorded impression' (p. viii).

5 Roland Barthes: 'What is interesting about Baudelaire's plays, is not their dramatic content but their embryonic state: the critic's role is therefore not to dissect these sketches for the image of an achieved theater but, on the contrary, to determine in them the vocation of their failure . . . It would seem that Baudelaire put his theater everywhere except, precisely, in his projects for plays.' 'Baudelaire's Theater', in *Barthes, Selected Writings* ed. Susan Sontag, Glasgow, Collins, 1983, pp. 74 and 77.

6 Jacques Derrida, *Writing and Difference*, trans. Alan Bass, Chicago, University of Chicago Press, 1978, pp. 232–50 and pp. 169–95.

7 The texts which make up what Artaud wanted to be called *Le Théâtre et son double/The Theatre and its Double*, were composed over the first half of the 1930s, the last, 'Seraphim's Theatre', being completed in Mexico City in April 1936.

8 Artaud, *The Theatre and its Double*, p. 27.

9 ibid., p. 28.

10 ibid.

11 ibid., p. 30.

12 ibid., p. 31.

13 Artaud, 'Oriental and Western Theatre', in *The Theatre and its Double*, p. 51.

14 Artaud, 'Production and Metaphysics', ibid., p. 31.

15 Jerzy Grotowski, 'He Wasn't Entirely Himself', in *Towards a Poor Theatre*, London, Methuen, 1975, pp. 88–9. As Grotowski says ironically: 'We shout with triumph when we discover silly misunderstandings in Artaud' (p. 90).

16 Artaud, *The Theatre and its Double*, p. 33.

17 Antonin Artaud, 'On the Balinese Theatre', in *The Theatre and its Double*, pp. 36–7.

18 Jacques Derrida , 'La Parole soufflée', in *Writing and Difference*, p. 169.

19 ibid., p. 174.

20 See Jacques Derrida, 'Cogito and the History of Madness', in *Writing and Difference*, pp. 31–63.

21 Grotowski, *Towards a Poor Theatre*, p. 91.

22 ibid.

23 Maurice Nadeau: 'Jarry, confusing in a perpetual hallucination his own existence with that of Pere Ubu, identifying himself with his creation in every detail to the point of forgetting his civil status . . .' in *The History of Surrealism*, trans. Richard Howard, London, Jonathan Cape, 1965, p. 72.

24 See Annabelle Henkin Melzer, 'The Première of Apollinaire's *The Breasts of Tiresias* in Paris', *Theatre Quarterly* 7 (27), 1977, pp. 3–14. In the prologue to this play, Melzer comments, it has been little noticed that Apollinaire proposed a new kind of theatre: 'a theatre in the round with two stages, one at the centre, the other surrounding the spectators' (p. 6). Artaud had moved beyond this conception of stage space when he wrote in the 'Theatre of Cruelty First Manifesto': 'We intend to do away with stage and auditorium, replacing them by a kind of single, undivided locale without any partitions of any kind . . . Direct contact will be established between the audience and the show, between actors and audience, from the very fact that the audience is seated in the centre of the action, is encircled and furrowed by it. This encirclement comes from the shape of the house itself.' Artaud continues: 'Abandoning the architecture of present-day theatres, we will rent some kind of barn or hangar' (*The Theatre and its Double*, p. 74).

25 Derrida, *Writing and Difference*, p. 175.
26 Quoted by A.M. Nagler, *Sources of Theatrical History*, New York, Theatre Annual, 1952, p. 53.
27 See Edward A. Langhans, *Restoration Prompt-books*, Carbondale, Southern Illinois University Press, 1981, p. xix.
28 See Richard Southern, *Theatre Notebook*, Vol. 3, 1948–9, pp. 66–7.
29 Aaron Hill, *The Prompter* 66, Friday, 27 June 1735.
30 Aaron Hill, *The Prompter* 25 November 1735.
31 Quoted in Edward A. Langhans, *Eighteenth Century British and Irish Promptbooks*, New York, Greenwood Press, 1987, pp. xvi–xvii.
32 See Sybil Rosenfeld, 'The Theatrical Notebooks of T.H. Wilson Manly', *Theatre Notebook* 7, 1952–3, pp. 43–5.
33 For details of his career see Charles H. Shattuck, 'A Victorian Stage Manager: George Cressall Ellis', *Theatre Notebook* 22, 1967–8, pp. 102–12.
34 ibid., p. 107.
35 ibid., p. 109.
36 ibid., p. 111.
37 Antonin Artaud, *Collected Works*, trans. Victor Corti, London, Calder and Boyars, 1971, p. 72, quoted by Jacques Derrida, in *Writing and Difference*, p. 179.
38 ibid., pp. 179–80.
39 Jacques Derrida, *Writing and Difference*, p. 188.
40 Antonin Artaud, 'Le Theatre et l'anatomie', *La Rue*, July 1941, quoted ibid., p. 233.
41 Jacques Derrida, 'Interview with Jean-Louis Houdebine, Guy Scarpetta', in *Positions*, trans. Alan Bass, Chicago, University of Chicago Press, 1981, p. 40: 'The "sheaf" which you recall is a historic and systematic crossroads; and it is above all their structural impossibility of limiting this network, of putting an edge on its weave, of tracing a margin that would not be a new mark.' Derrida goes on to point out that *différance* cannot be a 'master concept', and is found rather enmeshed within other concepts and vocabularies.
42 Quoted in Derrida, *Writing and Difference*, p. 234.
43 See Charles Marowitz, *Confessions of a Counterfeit Critic*, London, Eyre Methuen, 1973, pp. 101–6.
44 Derrida, *Writing and Difference*, p. 234.
45 ibid., p. 235.
46 ibid.
47 ibid.
48 ibid., p. 236.
49 See Antonin Artaud, 'The Theatre of Cruelty Second Manifesto', in *The Theatre and its Double*, pp. 82–4.
50 See Derrida, *Writing and Difference*, p. 240, for these distinctions.
51 Sigmund Freud, *The Standard Edition of the Complete Psychological Works of Sigmund Freud*, London, Hogarth Press, 13, pp. 176–7, quoted by Jacques Derrida in *Writing and Difference*, p. 241.
52 Quoted ibid., p. 242.
53 Quoted ibid.
54 For Artaud on Psychology, Poetry and Theatre see 'Theatre and Cruelty', in *The Theatre and its Double*, pp. 64–7.
55 See Derrida, 'Theatre and Cruelty', in *Writing and Difference*, pp. 243–6.
56 The 'V effect', or *Verfremdungseffekt*, whose best-known practitioner was Brecht. See Derrida, *Writing and Difference*, p. 244.

57 Quoted ibid., p. 245.
58 ibid., p. 325, fn. 14.
59 Jacques Derrida, 'The Theorem and the Theater', in *Of Grammatology*, trans. Gayatri Chakravorty Spivak, Baltimore, Johns Hopkins University Press, 1984, p. 304.
60 Derrida, *Writing and Difference*, p. 306.
61 J.J. Rousseau, 'Letter to M. d'Alembert', quoted ibid., p. 307.
62 ibid., p. 353.
63 Quoted ibid., p. 247.
64 ibid., p. 250.
65 See Derrida 'Interview with Jean-Louis Houdebine, Guy Scarpetta', in *Positions*, p. 89.
66 See Donna L. Hoffmeister, 'Post-Modern Theater: A Contradiction in Terms? Handke, Strauss, Bernhard and the Contemporary Scene', *Monatschefte* 79 (4), 1987, pp. 424–38. Hoffmeister begins by calling theatre a 'literary form', p. 424. From then on, although making use of Benjamin's term aura, and the unique 'original' nature of the theatre among the arts, the prognosis is gloomy for a theatre deconstructed by 'post-modern' playwrights. I would take the different view that the postmodern project precisely offers the theatre opportunities to resist and emerge from the literary antecedents which claim it for the word over speech.
67 Antonin Artaud, *The Theatre and its Double*, quoted in Derrida, *Writing and Difference*, p. 179.

7 CIRCULATION: Water and hygiene

1 J.B. Fonssagrives, quoted in Didier Gille, 'Maceration and Purification', trans. Bruce Benderson, *Zone* 1/2, ed. Jonathan Crary *et al.*, New York, Urzone, n.d., p. 228.
2 Edwin Chadwick, 'Preventive Police', an article extracted from the *London Review*, 1829, and collected in *Tracts 1815–1843*, n.d., n.p., pp. 252–308 (British Library catalogue: C.T. 246).
3 A published letter from F.O. Ward to William Conningham, MP. London, Henry Kershaw, 1858, p. 12.
4 Alain Corbin, *The Foul and the Fragrant*, trans. Miriam I. Kochan, Leamington Spa, Berg Publishers, 1986, p. 48.
5 F.O. Ward, 'Circulation or Stagnation', translation of paper given by F.O. Ward at the Sanitary Congress Brussels, 1856, ed. Edwin Chadwick, London, Cassell, 1889.
6 See Gille, op. cit., p. 235.
7 Walter Roth, *Theatre Hygiene*, London, Ballière, Tindall and Cox, 1888.
8 ibid., p. 9.
9 ibid., p. 10.
10 ibid., pp. 26–7.
11 Corbin, op. cit., p. 95.
12 'Obermann at the Opera', quoted ibid., p. 52.
13 Roth, op. cit., p. 24.
14 ibid., p. 45.
15 ibid., p. 48.

8 COMBUSTION: Fire and safety

1 A version of this chapter was first presented at the Association of Theater in Higher Education conference, Chicago, August 1990 under the title: 'What Says The Fire Chief?' and is published in *Theatre Survey*, May 1992. I am grateful to the editors for permission to include it here.
2 Ivan Illich, H_2O and the Waters of Forgetfulness, London, Marion Boyars, 1986, p. 6.
3 Michel de Certeau, *The Writing of History*, trans. Tom Conley, New York, Columbia University Press, 1988. p. 96. For a full discussion of these themes see de Certeau's two methodological essays: 'Making History' and 'The Historiographical Operation' in *The Writing of History*, pp. 19–113.
4 Marvin Carlson, *Places of Performance*, Ithaca, Cornell University Press, 1989, p. 2.
5 de Certeau, op. cit., pp. 56–7.
6 The *Builder*, 15 March 1856, pp. 137–9.
7 de Certeau, op. cit., pp. 33–4.
8 ibid., p. 48.
9 ibid., pp. 2–3.
10 ibid., p. 5.
11 ibid., pp. 70–1.
12 Richard Leacroft, *The Development of the English Playhouse*, London, Methuen, 1986, p. 167.
13 See the *Builder*, 16 Feb. 1856, pp. 191–3.
14 J.W. v Goethe. 'Zahme Xenien, V', quoted by Manfred Rehbinder in *Theatre Space*, ed. J.F. Arnott *et al.* Munich, International Federation for Theatre Research, 1977, p. 202.
15 Søren Kierkegaard, 'What Says The Fire Chief?', in *A Kierkegaard Anthology*. ed. Robert Bretall, Princeton, Princeton University Press, 1973, pp. 448–9.
16 Gaston Bachelard, *The Psychoanalysis of Fire*, trans. Alan Ross, Boston, Beacon Press, 1968.

INDEX